GENDER, JOURNALISM, AND EQUITY

Canadian, U.S., and European Experiences

THE HAMPTON PRESS COMMUNICATION SERIES
Mass Communication and Journalism
Lee B. Becker, supervisory editor

Magazine-Made America: The Cultural Transformation of the
Postwar Periodical
David Abrahamson

China's Window on the World: TV News, Social Knowledge,
and International Spectacles
Tsan-Kuo Chang with *Jian Wang* and *Yanru Chen*

It's Not Only Rock and Roll: Popular Music in the Lives of Adolescents
Peter G. Christenson and *Donald F. Roberts*

Global Media: Menace or Messiah? Revised Edition
David Demers

American Heroes in the Media Age
Susan J. Drucker and *Robert S. Cathcart (eds.)*

The Evolution of Key Mass Communication Concepts:
Honoring Jack M. McLeod
Sharon Dunwoody, Lee B. Becker, Douglas M. McLeod
and *Gerald M. Kosicki* (eds.)

The Ultimate Assist: The Relationship and Broadcast Strategies of the
NBA and Television Networks
John A. Fortunato

Journalism Education in Europe and North America: An International
Comparison
Romy Fröhlich and *Christina Holtz-Bacha (eds.)*

Communication and Terrorism: Public and Media Responses to 9/11
Bradley S. Greenberg (ed.)

Media, Sex and the Adolescent
Bradley S. Greenberg, Jane D. Brown, and *Nancy L. Buerkel-Rothfuss*

Community Media in the Information Age
Nicholas W. Jankowski with *Ole Prehn (eds.)*

Gender, Journalism, and Equity: Canadian, U.S., and European
Experiences
Gertrude J. Robinson

forthcoming

Critical Conversations: A Theory of Press Accountability
Wendy Wyatt Barger

Women Journalists in the Western World: What Surveys Tell Us
Romy Fröhlich and *Sue A. Lafky*

Tilted Mirrors: Media Alignment with Political and Social Change—
A Community Structure Approach
John C. Pollack

GENDER, JOURNALISM, AND EQUITY

Canadian, U.S., and European Experiences

GERTRUDE J. ROBINSON
McGill University

HAMPTON PRESS, INC.
CRESSKILL, NEW JERSEY

Printed in the United States of America

Robinson, Gertrude Joch.
    Gender, journalism, and equity : Canadian, U.S., and European experiences / Gertrude J. Robinson.
        p. cm. -- (Hampton Press communication series. Mass communication and journalism)
    Includes bibliographical references and indexes.
    ISBN 1-57273-612-7 -- ISBN 1-57273-613-5
    1. Women in journalism--Canada. 2. Women in journalism--United States. 3. Women in journalism--Europe. I. Title. II. Hampton Press communication series. Mass communications and journalism.

PN4914.W58R63 2005
070.4'082--dc22
                                                      2005050334

Hampton Press, Inc.
23 Broadway
Cresskill, NJ 07626

CONTENTS

LIST OF TABLES

ACKNOWLEDGMENTS

This book has been a number of years in the making. It started with a 1993 Social Science Research Council Grant no. 81693-0026, which permitted Dr. Armande Saint-Jean of the University of Sherbrooke and myself at McGill University, to undertake a multiyear project. Its purpose was to conduct the first Canada-wide survey on the position of women in the Canadian daily newspaper and broadcasting professions. In the initial data gathering years we were ably supported by three graduate students: Daniel Downs, Joseph Jackson, and Marie-Anne Poussart, whose computational skills and resourcefulness contributed to the success of the project.

David Pritchard and Florian Sauvageau's (1999) publication of *Les Journalistes Canadiens: Une Portrait de Fin de Siècle,* spurred me on to enlarge the project after retirement from active teaching. This book, like so many studies of the profession of journalism, totally ignores the importance of describing the interlinkage between gender and power, which not only affects the status, but also the progress of women and minorities in the profession. Moreover, the claim that the study provides "a portrait of the Canadian profession at the end of the century" raised three additional unaddressed questions. They concern first the comparison of Canadian with U.S. findings. This is an important issue because the United States has the longest tradition of research into the media professions, which goes back to the 1960s and is thus able to chart progress over time.

Beyond that, my own European background and visiting professorships abroad have piqued an interest in the situation of female journalists in various European countries and their status in relation to ours. The introduction of equity legislation on both sides of the Atlantic in the 1980s, furthermore, lent itself to assessing the efficacy of these different types of legislation on females and ethnic minorities in the professions. Throughout this second stage of writing and analysis, I relied on two assistants for table construction and advice. They are Annmarie Larose and Kaisa McCandless. Last but by no means least, I have to mention the sustained help of my son Markus F. Robinson, a computer engineer and entrepreneur, for putting the manuscript into its present electronic form. Any flaws that remain are my sole responsibility.

I dedicate this book to two colleagues and journalists from whom I have learned a great deal about the profession and whose interest in my work has sustained me throughout the project.

They are Dr. Alain Pericard, scholar and consultant in international communications and Dr. Armande Saint-Jean, head of the Department of Language and Communications, Sherbrooke University.

chapter *1*

INTRODUCTION: TACKLING GENDERED JOURNALISM

Theorizing the impact of gender on journalism is a timely task for both personal and scholarly reasons. On the personal level, I can today look back on 30 years of thinking about how gender has impacted my work as a university professor and my existence as a social being. Throughout this period I learned through personal experience that *gender matters* in my teaching, my research, and my everyday life. Although I was initially mystified as to why my lectures seemed to lack "believability" among certain male undergraduates and why my views on academic committees lacked "carrying power," I now know that both of these experiences had something to do with being a female academic in a largely male institution. My observations sensitized me not only to the crucial role of gender in everyday life, but also to the ways in which culture and language affect professional behavior. Throughout my career, I therefore developed and taught courses on women and the media and in the mid-1990s this culminated in a Social Science Research Council grant to survey the progress of Canadian media professionals.

A second reason why it is important to tackle gendered journalism issues is because recent communicator scholarship has continued to perpetuate the orthodoxy that women's minority status in the media professions results from lesser *numbers*, rather than from *systemic* biases inherent in the social reproduction of the profession. These biases, it turns out, are gender-based and lead to classificatory and evaluative procedures, which have negative outcomes for female professionals. Yet, even within the last decade, important communication surveys in North America and Europe have failed to view gender as a *constituting* variable in explaining the differing experiences of women and men in journalism. David Pritchard and Florian Sauvageau's (1999) *Les Journalists Canadiens*, David Weaver and Wei Wu's (1998) *The Global Journalist*, Weaver and Wilhoit's (1986/1999) *The American Journalist*, as well as Weischenberg, Löffelholz, and Scholl's (1993) *Journalisten in Deutschland* (Journalists in Germany) have interpreted gender as an unproblematic *biological* variable like education, class, and ethnicity. Gender is, however, not the fixed attribute of an individual, but is "socially constructed" through cultural norms that codify women's "proper role" in society differently in different epochs and in different countries. Since World War II these role conceptions have been liberalized and greater numbers of women have entered professions like journalism, which used to be closed to them. Another purpose of this study is therefore to compare the participation rates of British, German, and Scandinavian media professionals and to explore their varied work experiences in their editorial offices. Are there European countries where female journalists face fewer barriers than in North America and if so, what explains these differences?

A third reason for using a gender focus arises from the fact that it helps me to elucidate how journalism functions as an integrated social system, which is itself defined by gendered preconceptions. Cynthia Fuchs Epstein (1992) demonstrates how gender provides a system of social stratification, which is more rigid than class because it is grounded in hereditary status conceptions. In all social systems, status defines a person's legal personality and is rigidly enforced by custom, law, or religion. In journalism, gendered preconceptions construct females and ethnic news producers as "different" and turn them into "marginal minorities" in the heterosexual workplace, with lesser rights, remunerations, and conflictual role expectations. It is therefore the *systemic reasons* for the ubiquitous minority status of female practitioners in Berlin, Oslo, Quebec City, or Washington that need explaining. We need to unravel how these inequalities are created and sustained in the profession and how these practices differ from country to country.

The final reason for undertaking a gendered analysis of journalism is to show that these types of analyses provide a more *holistic* and complex theoretical explanation of how journalistic roles relate to professional values. The gender-based scholarship of Lana Rakow (1986), Ruth Bleier (1986), and Kathryn Cirksena and Lisa Cuklanz (1992) have made two important discoveries. The first documents that class, gender, ethnicity, and power are complexly interlinked and that they function interactively in the heterosexual newsroom. Another group of scholars among them Liesbet van Zoonen (1994), Elisabeth Klaus (1998), and Ian Ang (1991), have clarified why news presentation styles and narrative discourses cannot be "read off" from the gender of the reporter. Although both Europe and North America have witnessed a switch from a more "rationalistic" to a more "intimate" mode of news presentation, this development cannot be solely attributed to the use of more female anchor personnel. A newspaper or television station's narrative styles are complexly related to institutional structures and to power networks, which continue to be headed by males. Such a set-up predisposes reporters of either gender to produce the same narrative styles, except in very specific circumstances. This study explores in great detail, when and under what circumstances it is safe for a female reporter to deviate from these reportorial norms. Yet, after 25 years of gender-based communication scholarship, and its acceptance in related disciplines like anthropology and sociology, it has had little impact on communicator, let alone journalism scholarship, where critical analyses using gender as a central category have been virtually absent.

The continuing absence of feminist work from communicator scholarship is graphically illustrated in Michael Schudson's (1992) review article "The Sociology of News Production Revisited." He classifies 30 years of journalism studies as belonging to three different theoretical approaches. Among them are the political economy approach, the sociological investigations, and the "culturological" studies. Schudson evaluates each of these and considers their strengths and weaknesses without acknowledging that gender constitutes a crucial yet invisible determinant of all communicational situations. Political economy studies relate the outcome of news processes to the economic structure of the news organization and focus on the impact of advertisers on media institutions. Although this approach is crucial for understanding the relationship between media industries in a given country, it fails to explore why ideology is not monolithic in contemporary capitalism and how the legal frameworks of different countries affect the relationships between public and private networks and the resulting differences in programming. The sociological inquiries have, from the start, focused on the production moment of the social communication process and used an individualistic point of view to investigate such important issues as reporter–source relationships, occupational routines, and constraints on professional autonomy. They have also provided important insights into the ethnic and gender composition of the reportorial cadres in different countries, the nature of news work and its routinization, as well as the strategic use of professional values to protect reportorial autonomy. Its limitations lie in the symbolic realm, and the failure to elicit what may be called the "para-ideological" values that a journalist develops as a member of her or his profession in a particular society.

Sociological studies, which are frequently based on system theory, are furthermore unable to question how professional producers target audiences and construct social meanings. Such issues are more penetratingly analyzed by a cultural studies approach, that inquires into how a country's symbol system is created and the role of the media as one of the major forms of cultural expression in modernity. Raymond Williams (1981) defined *culture* as a "whole way of life." For media studies, such a definition implies that both media texts and audience-decoding strategies are part of the social communication process, as well as part of everyday life. In the production moment of social meaning-making, one can distinguish between organizational cultures, working cultures, communicative cultures, and professional routines, all of which are useful for the study of journalism as a profession (Lünenborg, 2001). A cultural approach furthermore overcomes the theoretical distinction between the system and the subject, both of which are moments in the process of cultural meaning creation (Klaus, 2000). Symbol systems comprise language, narrative conventions, and underlying cultural values, which are rarely brought to consciousness. Herbert Gans (1979), for instance, discovered that such meta-values as ethnocentrism, altruistic democracy, responsible capitalism, small-town pastoralism, individualism, and the notion of "moderation" guide and frame the reporting of U.S. broadcast journalists. Doubtlessly, news personnel in Germany, France, and Great Britain will manifest different kinds of meta-values arising from their specific historical understandings and professional experiences. Schudson approvingly quotes Tony Bennett (1982) that an important filter through which news is constructed is "the cultural air we breathe," the whole ideological atmosphere of our society, which tells us that some things can be said and that others best not be said (p. 303). Yet, even in this context, he fails to note that gender is an immanent category in meaning-making. What is one to make of such a massive oversight by an author whose historical and comparative studies of news-reporting styles and the advertising industry have been widely acclaimed?

Part of the absence of a gender approach can be explained by the fact that all scholarship has a political dimension. When it challenges orthodoxy, it creates controversy (Creedon, 1993). Feminist scholarship in the academy challenges the ascendancy of Marxist political economy and sociological approaches, as well as the work of postmodern literary and cultural theorists that are entrenched in many departments, universities, and journals (Robinson, 1998). Their predominantly male proponents are not going to cede their theoretical superiority without a fight, to a new group of people, many of whom are furthermore women scholars. Lack of university hiring has exacerbated these contests, especially in Canada, where only 18% of the full-time faculty are women and many of these are not feminists. These scholarly battles involve, among other things, a struggle over the definition of the "orthodox" sources of our interdiscipline, which define the communication curriculum and determine the prestige levels of journals in the field. Since the 1980s, thankfully, feminist publishing sources have proliferated and institutes of women's studies have been established in most universities. These are beginning not only to disseminate feminist scholarship among the younger generation, but also to demonstrate that versions of political economy, organization, and cultural theories are compatible with gender approaches.

Although the lack of visibility of gender-based research is recognized among women scholars, there are other systemic barriers to the advancement of these approaches, which are less well documented. Among these is the role of libraries in the codification of new research domains. Since the early 1990s, the indexing practices of librarians have not kept pace with the explosive variety of gender research that is being produced. Cathryn

Cirksena and Lisa Cuklanz' (1996) "Feminism After Ferment: Ten Years of Gendered Scholarship in Communications" documents that although the annual number of women-related articles quadrupled from about 30 to 120 between 1982 and 1992, these topics still constituted less than 10% of all articles indexed. The lack of timely key words for referencing feminist scholarship and the fact that much of this scholarship is found in book collections, further diminishes the visibility of feminist scholarship. As a result, Cirksena concludes, "communications remains relatively unaffected by the feminist intellectual revolution" (p. 158). This study is designed to rectify this oversight. It demonstrates that feminist approaches provide a more inclusive research perspective that draws attention to the fact that *all* human communication interactions are gendered, not only those of women and minorities, and that the communication styles and values of female and male professionals vary along a continuum, not along strictly bipolar tracks.

A final reason for gender-based research's lack of visibility is theoretical. If it is indeed true that gender cannot be equated with biologically based "sex," how does one make use of this difficult variable in social analysis? In her powerful book *The Double Standard*, Canadian sociologist, Margrit Eichler (1980) argues that explaining matters by "sex" may be both the most useful and the most dangerous manner of explanation imaginable and that it must therefore be applied in what she calls a "dialectical" manner (p. 122). To indicate this dialectic and to signal the socially constructed nature of all human behavior, I do not use the term *sex* but substitute the term *gender*. This does not mean, however, that I do not engage in exploring sex differences in female and male journalistic behaviors nationally and internationally. These gendered analyses follow a two-stage process, as Eichler recommends. As a first step, they chart the presence of gender differences and similarities in all kinds of journalistic situations, where they function in a *descriptive* manner. As is seen here, gender differences are able to "explain" differences in journalistic salary levels. Such an explanation, however, is only of a *probabilistic* nature. It can tell us about the levels of interaction between age, organization size, years of service, supervisory responsibilities, and gender, in determining journalistic salaries. Gender can however never be used as a variable in a *causal* sense, to explain social facts (Eichler, 1980; Gorelik, 1991).

What this means is that one must not confuse descriptions of gender differences with their explanation. In Chapter 5, it is discovered, for instance, that female journalists who are offered promotions into upper management positions are much more reluctant than their male colleagues to accept. This constitutes an observed gender difference in the profession, yet it tells us nothing about the reasons *why* women are less likely to accept the offer of promotion. The explanation may turn out to be a lack of social support for the potential incumbent among top managers, and the woman's resulting "token" status. This is a reason, which under different circumstances, such as the promotion of an ethnic person, would be equally applicable to males. In this case, the observed gender difference has been explained by a nonsexual, nonbiological, social factor.

Karen and Sonja Foss (1989) consider that a proper theory of gendered journalism should accomplish four tasks. It should, first of all, aim for "wholeness" and relate the large number of scattered findings about women in the media professions systematically to each other. The theory should furthermore move us out of what Pamela Creedon (1993) calls the paradigm paralysis, which seems to have afflicted studies of the journalism professions in the past two decades. Most of these studies, as noted previously, fail to make a connection between the profession's social and power structures and the ways in which its practitioners interpret and feel about their work. The theory should furthermore demonstrate how cultural and professional knowledge systems structure the activities of everyday life. A culture-based gender theory, which focuses on the meanings people attach to their behavior, provides such a vantage point. It helps us to decipher how media institutions "engender" different working practices for different types of employees and how these working practices are in turn related to professional knowledge systems and gendered labeling practices. This framework is made up of four components: a theory of gender, a theory of journalism as social group practice, a ritual theory of communication, and a feminist epistemology.

A THEORY OF GENDER

It is very difficult to disentangle gender theory from cultural theories of communication, because these two designations cover such a large variety of different approaches. I am differentiating between the two, however, in order to help pinpoint both theoretical similarities and differences that have caused consternation and debate (Franklin, Lurie, & Stacey, 1992). Although feminist thought is extremely diversified in its theoretical assumptions and its goals, there are certain common elements shared by all types of feminism. Among them are the fact that gender is viewed as a primary category of social organization rather than a secondary add-on to such social categories as class, education, ethnicity, and religion. This entails a focus on women, on men, and on the relationship between them (van Zoonen, 1994). As such, it acknowledges that gender and identity are socially constructed, rather than merely biologically determined. It furthermore makes female experience a central focus of attention and creates new categories for codifying this experience, such as the recognition of emotions and subjectivity, as well as reciprocity between researcher and researched (Melin-Higgins & Djerf-Pierre, 2002). Finally, it is interested in women as social actors in their own right and how their asymmetrical power situations to men have come about. As such, most feminisms have had an activist agenda, namely: promoting social change and encouraging self-actualization for all members of society (Harding, 1986).

Extensive gender research in the past 35 years has shown that gender operates on three levels: the individual, the interpersonal, and group levels, and that it involves three communication processes. In other words, gender informs the social and the symbolic work we do to identify ourselves as women and men in social situations, as well as the meanings we attach to these behaviors. As a classifying system, gender divides people into two mutually exclusive categories: women and men. Because our society does not recognize hermaphrodites as a third possible classification, the biologically based dualism seems to refer to something fundamental and immutable in society. Yet, all people have, within their social make-up, both female and male characteristics like individualism, perseverance, honesty, and emotionalism. The values that are ascribed to these characteristics differ from society to society and over time. Gender also works as a structuring structure in most societies, locating women and minorities into a dominant–subordinate caste system that requires women to constantly announce and act out their subordination. On the all-encompassing ideological level, finally, gender functions as a classifying system that designates women, who constitute 52% of the total population, as a minority, and thus as an "interest group." The effects of each of these classificatory processes are exemplified in the ways in which the journalistic profession is organized and the ways in which it operates as a social system.

Since the 1970s and the rise of the second feminist movement under leaders such as Betty Friedan in the United States, Simone de Beauvoir in France, and Pauline Jewett in Canada, the actions of women and minorities as "social subjects" have been studied from three points of view (Anderson, 1991). Although there is no unanimity on the labeling, they have been variously called the *equity approach*, the *difference approach*, and the *gender approach* (Rakow, 1992). The equity approach focused on the discrimination women encounter in personal and social interactions, including the workplace. The difference approach addressed women's "otherness" and its implications for social experience, whereas the more recent gender approach has focused on the preconditions, contexts, and mechanisms through which cultural and gender differences are constructed and maintained over time. From the point of view of methodology, this means that gender research must reflexively incorporate how gender-specific working situations are created and what they mean to the people involved. Only through a combination of evidence-based and hermeneutic approaches will it be possible to clarify how the gendering mechanisms work in the media professions.

According to the gender approach, an individual's involvement in a profession needs to be analyzed from both a structural (organizational) and a hermeneutic (meaning) perspective that traces how social structure affects interpretation and behavior. The first attempt at the structural analysis of journalism as a profession was provided by the equity approach, which helped to uncover the binary gendering mechanisms, which streamed female journalists into subordinate career paths with differential working conditions and reward structures. In print journalism, these different career paths are initiated through gendered "beat" assignments, such as "lifestyles" and "consumer" reporting for the female professional and "sports" and "national political" reporting assigned to male colleagues. The sex-difference approach extends our understanding by documenting how workplace activities are vertically and horizontally stratified by gender and that female practitioners tend to be slotted into what Pat and Hugh Armonstrong (1986) called a "double ghetto" of sex-stereotyped work areas. This means that females are disproportionally found in the less important beats, as well as the less secure or part-time positions. The beat structure is additionally used to create differential promotion and reward structures for females and males. My 1975 study demonstrated that a female lifestyle reporter had less chance than a male political reporter of becoming desk or managing editor (Robinson, 1981). Consequently, even though social transformations like low birth rates, later marriage, and increased education have propelled 70% of North American women with 4 years of higher education into the labor force, they continue to work in sex-segregated occupations. They are concentrated in the service industries, clerical jobs, government occupations, teaching, and nursing, rather than the so-called prestige professions. In the 1970s journalism, law, and medicine therefore remained predominantly male-gendered with an average of less than 17% of their practitioners being female. These proportions furthermore had remained stable since the turn of the century (Robinson, 1977). Current evidence shows that 30 years later, at the turn of the new millennium, these proportions began to change and that today about one-third of all media professionals on both sides of the Atlantic are female.

The gender approach also permits me, for the first time to explore the hermeneutic or meaning dimensions of the journalistic profession by problematizing the very categories that are at the linguistic base of gender attribution. Because all human interactions and social practices involve a classification into female and male categories, gender is constitutive of all human encounters including professional encounters in the journalistic professions (Rakow, 1986; Robinson, 1998b; Robinson & Saint Jean, 1998). Understanding gender is at once very simple and very complex, as Creedon (1993) observes. It involves the recognition that gender is not only the name of a person, place, or thing, but that it functions like a verb and is integrally involved in the construction and interpretation of everyday events. As such, gender, like the notion of "selfhood," is developed through interaction with significant others who are users of particular language systems. Gender must thus be conceived not as a fixed property of individuals, but as part of an ongoing process of naming by which social actors are constituted and relate to their environment (van Zoonen, 1992). Cynthia Fuchs Epstein (1992) explains how this happens by observing that language itself helps to create "boundaries" by providing the terms by which real and assumed behaviors and things are grouped (1992). These naming practices begin at birth (Bleier, 1987). Gender is consequently "constructed" in relation to a particular place and time and most importantly in relation to the existing power relations of the culture in question, as well as the gendered experiences one has over one's lifetime (Cirksena, 1987).

Feminist communication scholars have benefited from linguistic insights that have demonstrated that language as a signifying system functions both as a mode of description and as a mode of expression. Language philosophers like Jean Bethke Elshtain acknowledge this dualism by making a distinction between "language" and "speech" and by focusing on the creativity of speech. Through speaking we not only influence others, but also more importantly rethink and reinvent our futures and ourselves. In Elshtain's (1982) words, "Speech is the central way we come to know ourselves, reveal ourselves to others and develop and express our identities" (p. 144). Failure to theorize language as an expressive system, results in a faulty class theory of education for political economists and an inadequate theory of the social actor in most system-analytical accounts of the journalistic professions. Although language and understanding are indeed class-influenced through education, David Morley's (1980) *Nationwide* study showed that language is not uniquely class-determined. Sociological analyses of the social actor in turn tend to reduce a journalist's creativity to "role-playing." Such a translation flattens out the moral and emotional dimensions between different types of roles, such as that of being a reporter and that of being a mother. As a result, sociological accounts of social activities become depoliticized and gender differences in consciousness are eradicated.

Gender theory, in contrast, has discovered that there are three types of consciousness that are gender-linked and that these can be used to conceptualize differences in female and male experience of everyday existence (Keohane, Rosaldo, & Gelpi, 1982). "Feminine consciousness" involves the consciousness of oneself as the object of another's attention. Although Marxist feminists like Simone de Beauvoir consider the "feminine" as defined by the male gaze and constructed through male desire as "false consciousness," feminine consciousness provides a ground for explaining differences in human motivation as well as female degradation as a result of asymmetrical power relations. A second source of theorizing is provided by "female consciousness," the deep-rooted and age-old experience in giving and preserving life, in nurturing and sustaining human existence. Although this type of consciousness refers to a profoundly conservative streak in female experience, it is full of radical possibilities if it is combined with a collective drive to extend nurturing obligations into the political realm. In North America and Europe, this consciousness has given rise to maternity and child-care legislation and is now at the forefront of discussions about child poverty in Canada. The third or "feminist consciousness" is developed and refined as women reflect on the asymmetries in power and opportunities that they continue to encounter in their private and their public spheres of existence. These experiences have led to equity initiatives in the workplace and in the professions like journalism. As Shelly Rosaldo (1982) so eloquently argues: "A crucial task for feminist scholars . . . is not only the relatively limited one of documenting pervasive sexism as a social fact . . . but to provide new ways of linking the particulars of women's lives, activities and goals, to inequalities where ever they exist" (p. 417).

How have these in-egalitarian signifying practices themselves evolved? Psychologists Suzanne Kessler and Wendy McKenna (1978) note that the processes of gender attribution are complex and interactive, involving both the person making the attribution and the person about whom he or she is making the attribution. Four different kinds of classificatory operations can be distinguished, through which the deviant/inferior evaluation of women's activities and performances are created and sustained. The first, which they call "gender assignment," is a special case of attribution. It occurs only once, at birth, and is undertaken by a doctor or midwife on the basis of the sex organ a child possesses. The second process is "gender identity" and refers to an individual's own feelings of whether she or he is a woman or a man. In essence, gender identity is a self-attribution that a person acquires both through interactions with parents and later through contacts with playmates and friends (Kessler & McKenna, 1978). Gender identity, as is seen here, should not be confused with "gender-role identity" that refers to how much a person approves of and participates in feelings and behaviors, which are seen as "appropriate" for her or his gender. Distinguishing between gender identity and gender-role identity enables me to explain why women journalists choose different adaptation strategies to the heterosexual newsroom situation. There is now evidence that some choose to become "one of the boys," whereas others decide to become outsiders or feminist professionals. None of these role identities imply that these female professionals are confused about their gender identity, as is shown in Chapter 4, which explores gendered experiences in the newsroom.

Gender roles, according to sociologists, carry with them a set of expectations about appropriate behavior in a social situation. These expectations are in turn gender-defined and vary for female and male role incumbents, such as the notion that females are more appropriate for covering entertainment content and males for sports events. In most societies, gender roles are treated as ascribed because incumbents have no control over receiving the role attribution. In our study of journalism as a social system, the four different types of classificatory procedures that are linked with gender will help explore not only how gender "means," which is different for female and male professionals, but also how the gendered attribution processes are invoked to structure and to justify differential access, promotion, and pay systems for the two groups. Here is a demonstration, then, of the ways in which a gendered classificatory system has social and economic consequences, which are reflected in organizational status and salary (Gerson & Peiss, 1985).

JOURNALISM AS A SOCIAL SYSTEM AND AN INTERPRETIVE COMMUNITY

To view journalism "holistically," it is necessary to have a second theoretical perspective that is able to explain how the profession functions as a social system. Such a theory maps the relationship between journalism's social and power structures and the feelings and understandings that its practitioners have about their roles and tasks. At present, there is no generally accepted designation for such an approach, which Michael Schudson (1992) called "cultorological," whereas Margaret Lünenborg (2001) and Liesbet van Zoonen (1994) call it "cultural." I use the latter designation because the approach links subjectivity, ideology, and culture, which are also of concern to feminist communication scholars involved in national comparisons (Lünenborg, 1997). Such a theory helps to analyze symbolization and representation processes and how they affect journalistic positions, knowledge structures and working practices.

Sociologists and organizational theorists view an occupational group as "professional" when it shows certain combinations of skill, autonomy, training, and education, including testing of competence, codes of conduct, licensing, and a service orientation. The "profession" also provides a body of knowledge that instructs individuals what to do and what to avoid in any given circumstance. Journalists gain status in their work by acting "professionally" and by exhibiting certain predefined traits of their "professional community." These include subscribing to a code of "objectivity" in preparing news stories and in refraining from talking about a story's narrative construction. Beyond that, journalism maintains its communal boundaries by generating a unique ideological orientation, which distinguishes them from other professionals and from the public (Zelizer, 1993). Most sociological descriptions of the professions fail to mention that women's work is systematically structured by gender and that these gender biases are imported into the organizational structure. They also fail to note that this importation is not innocent, but that gender biases negatively affect the ways in which females are able to wield power in the organizational setting. Juliet Webster (1996) comments that the gendering of jobs cannot be reduced to a discussion of women's role in the domestic sphere, or their reserve army status in the labor force, but must also be seen as arising out of the interplay of socially ascribed and therefore shifting roles within organizations themselves. Epstein (1988), who has extensively studied such professions as law, medicine, and engineering, clarifies that the cultural biases against women are imported into the organizational setting through what she calls structural and informal processes. Broadly speaking, cultural biases manifest themselves in interpretative processes that sex-type positions and specialities, and thus in turn affect such structural processes as access, promotion, and remuneration. On the informal level, sex labeling of statuses functions like a filter through which only some can pass (Epstein, 1988). Together, these processes indicate that professions function not only like a social system whose networks of power are structured by gender, but also develop expectations about how females and males should behave in the working situation (Bourdieu, 1991). A country's general "culture" thus sets the stage and when individuals act according to its norms, their behavior reinforces the current gender patterns. All of these processes are explored and demonstrated in Chapters 2 and 3, where the gendered state of the Canadian print and broadcast newsrooms is described (Lamont & Fournier, 1992).

In professions like journalism, law, and medicine, which are prized by males, informal processes for excluding females are often as important as formal processes in maintaining sex segregation. The work of Harold Wilenski (1964) and others has shown that male-dominated professions act as communities, with shared values, common membership, and rituals that reinforce ties among their members. Barbie Zelizer (1993) introduces the concept of *interpretative community* to describe the reinforcing rituals that make journalists' shared past and professional life meaningful. Among these are the fact that practicing reporters rarely admit that they construct reality in news making, which my own inquiry into Quebec news work also documented (Robinson, 1998). The notion of the interpretative community also clarifies why reporters seem to prefer "informal networking," namely a horizontal over a hierarchical authority structure in their editorial offices. This suggests that they function as a loosely organized community rather than a formal membership organization in the professional realm. The notion furthermore explains why reportorial narratives and news presentation conventions can differ from country to country, a discovery I made in studying the stylistic and visual determinants of German television news programming

(Robinson, 1987). Finally, in contrast to law and medicine, journalists seem to reject formal professional trappings such as training in journalism schools (Weaver & Wilhoit, 1986/1991), the use of journalistic textbooks (Becker et al., 1987), and specific codes of journalistic behavior. Training, according to Zelizer (1993), is instead considered a combination of "osmosis and fiat" (p. 222). This notion of training will have implications for the ways in which the professional qualifications of female journalists are assessed in Canada and elsewhere.

Margareta Melin-Higgins and Monika Djerf-Pierre (1998) use Zelizer's notion of journalists as an interpretative community to explore the kind of "culture" that reporters develop on the job in Britain and Sweden. They define this culture as the meanings and values that develop among a distinctive social group and the lived traditions through which these understandings are expressed. The notion of a journalistic culture, therefore, implies that professional definitions are historically grounded, which means that they can be changed and that there is a meaning framework through which professional values are created and recreated. A process theory of meaning-making can explain how and why power structures fluctuate and meaning-making is not hegemonic. Within media industries, other groups such as marketing or editorial personnel, as well as some viewing publics, contest the descriptions of events they are offered (Frye, 1983).

Margaret Lünenborg (1997) notes that the journalistic culture is also gendered in western Europe, but that this gendering takes slightly different forms in different countries, as Chapter 4 demonstrates. Gendering manifests itself on two levels: in the social interactions of its practitioners, and on the meaning-making level through gendered expectations about how female and male colleagues are expected to do their work. Variations in social interactions are mapped on to the organizational level through structural and economic context factors, such as a country's social policy legislation and the marital status and child-care arrangements that are available to its practitioners. Western Europe's maternity and child-care arrangements are more extensive than those in North America. Despite these differences in context factors, however, female media professionals in all countries are placed in a subordinate social situation vis-à-vis their male colleagues because journalism as a social system reifies "maleness" and "information" journalism as the norm. It thus enshrines very specific workplace practices, such as a 10- or 12-hour working day, as "normal," and evaluates "entertainment" programming as somehow "inferior." John Hartley (1996) notes that dichotomous descriptions such as hard news–soft news, word–picture, and so on are gender-based and reinforce a systematic bias against popular, screen and commercial media. How female professionals respond and deal with their deviant status in Germany, Britain, and Scandinavia helps me to specify and compare the similarities and differences in their adaptation strategies and to determine whether these follow individual or more general patterns. Up to the present it has been implied that female professionals make purely individual choices and are therefore personally responsible for the outcomes. Our systemic analysis demonstrates that this is not the case and that women's structured inferiority in the newsroom results in a small number of *patterned* responses to their status inequalities in North America and Europe.

The cultural approach also enables me to identify the networks of power relations mentioned by Zelizer (1993), which are *outside* of the authority structure represented by journalism's formal position hierarchy. This informal power network, which is gendered, defines which people can be influential beyond the boundaries of their positions (Epstein, 1988). It furthermore designates those who will become top managers and explains why the "glass ceiling" remains in place, although it has moved up a few levels for turn-of-the-century Canadian female broadcasters (Agocs, 1989). The notion of a professional culture furthermore clarifies yet another gender outcome, the fact that female professionals do not have the same opportunities to convert what Pierre Bourdieu (1977) calls their "cultural capital" into other forms of "economic" or "political capital" on the job, except in very special situations.

On the interpretive level, the notion of a male-gendered journalistic culture helps to explain two puzzling phenomena. They are the conflictual self-definition of female professionals in the male-gendered newsroom and the prevalent locker room humor, gossip, and unwanted intimacies that women journalists experience in their newsroom work. Our cultural perspective suggests that these are not "normal behaviors," as is usually assumed, but exclusionary strategies. They are related to the female power imbalances in editorial offices that are also expressed symbolically through strategies designed to keep female colleagues "in their place." Among these strategies, my Canadian research has demonstrated there are not only locker room humor and sexual innuendo but also "personality stereotyping." This process classifies female colleagues into a small number of female *types*, such as "mom," "kid sister," "girl next door," or "bitch," which are already familiar from content analyses of entertainment programming. Through these classifications, females are made both nonthreatening, as well as excluded from participating in the group as full members. This explains why it is so difficult for female practitioners to develop alternative journalistic role conceptions, except under very special circumstances. In general, it turns out, the male-gendered newsroom with its gendered practices reinforces conformity with the male norms. This means that female practitioners must "redefine" and "import" alternative or feminist worldviews into their professional setting, which is not easy to do (Lünenborg, 1997). Chapter 4 explores which group of female journalists undertake this arduous task and why they constitute a relatively small minority.

A "RITUAL" THEORY OF SOCIAL COMMUNICATION

The third component of a "holistic" theory of journalism must explain the profession's public sense-making activities. Such a theory of social communication must address the interrelationships between gender, power, and the production of public texts. Different versions of such theories have been variously called "cultural" (Grossberg, Nelson, & Treichler, 1992), "symbolic" (Burke, 1954), "semiotic" (Geertz, 1973), and "ritual" (Carey, 1988). All of these theoretical approaches agree that public sense-making is a reflexive process in which both communicators and viewers/listeners are involved. I adopt the "ritual" designation proposed by James Carey, to acknowledge my indebtedness to the Chicago school of symbolic interactionism. Here, such scholars as John Dewey, George Herbert Mead, and Robert Park laid the foundation for an interactive theory of social communication, which was further elaborated by Kenneth Burke and Ervin Goffman, a Canadian from Manville, Alberta. From their writings, Carey (1988) argues, we learn that communication is a symbolic process in which reality is produced, maintained, repaired, and transformed. Such a definition implies that communication processes are at the center of human existence. They are not only involved in constituting our own gendered identity, but communication processes, at the same time, provide the frameworks through which we, as social beings, comprehend our surroundings. Through the duality of language and other symbolic codes, we both learn to "describe" and to "inhabit" our particular world. A ritualistic view of social communication views human behavior, or more accurately human action, as a text. Our task as scholars is to construct a reading of these texts, or as literary critics would have it, an interpretation.

Herbert Blumer (1969) offers three propositions that explicate the centrality of communication processes in human behavior. The first is that human beings act toward things on the basis of the meanings that the things have for them. This statement implies that we, as humans, continually interpret what we encounter: physical objects, other human beings, categories of things and institutions, as well as the activities of others. The second assertion concerns the source of meaning, which for symbolic interactionists arises out of the interactions one shares with other human beings. Meaning is thus not located in the thing itself, or in the psychological make-up of the perceiver with her attitudes and cognition. Meaning-making is instead discovered to be a labeling process that involves language. As such, it has a social dimension that is reflected in the reactions of other people when the label is used. The third proposition asserts that meanings are handled in and modified through an interpretative process that the person uses to deal with the things she or he encounters. According to Blumer, the activity of interpretation is not just a matching operation, but has two components. It encompasses a selection process involving the object on which attention is lavished, and a second process of checking, suspending, regrouping, and transforming meanings in the light of the situation in which one finds oneself (Blumer, 1969). Human beings, in other words, are symbol-making and symbol-using creatures.

On the interpersonal level, we as symbol-using creatures, are born into a language and symbolic community where George Herbert Mead (1934/1962) points out we learn the difference between "I" and "me" through interaction with our parents and friends. Language and thought are thus not individual, but social achievements through which we learn to negotiate the world in which we grow up. We do this through naming and labeling those features of the world that seem worth attending to. According to symbolic interactionism, reality is brought into existence, is produced by communication, by the construction, comprehension, and utilization of symbolic forms (Berger & Luckmann, 1966; Carey, 1988). In this labeling process, gender is one of the most important categories, as Suzanne Kessler and Wendy McKenna (1978) have argued above, because it involves the four classificatory operations through which the deviant/inferior evaluation of women's worth and performances are created and sustained.

It is well known that in our postindustrial society, the media are not only major public meaning-making institutions, but also the stages on which public opinion is created. In John Hartley's (1996) elegant prose: "as the sense-making practice of modernity, journalism is the most important textual system in the world. . . . Only drama competes with it for the same global extension, social pervasion, formal variety and scope of subject-matter. But unlike drama, journalism purports to be true; its importance lies not only in its gigantism as a physical product, but also in its real and imagined power to affect other systems, actions or events" (p. 36). Two aspects of this influence have been extensively documented: the media's "agenda-setting" and "priming" powers (McCombs & Shaw, 1972). Robert Hackett (1991) elucidates that these two affectivities of the media are part of a broader phenomenon: The media, in effect, provide their viewers/listeners with a "frame" and a map for perceiving the social and political world beyond their immediate experience. He argues that news and other programming helps citizens construct understandings of what is important, what is good and valuable, what is bad and threatening, and what is related to what on a given day in the public domain of citizen interests. The media's frames thus have both a cognitive and an affective dimension, as our discussion of programming for female listeners/viewers in Chapter 7 illustrates. To understand the process of framing happenings and transforming them into news stories, it is necessary to scrutinize the news product itself and to relate it both to its conditions of production and its conditions of reception. Frames, according to Erving Goffman (1974), are constructed by members of a given society out of attitudes toward everyday life. Embedded in this process is the presupposition that objects of the world are as they appear—a presupposition that is shared by others and thus socially sanctioned. This "social realism" is what enables the competent citizen to reduce the complexity of the daily environment by directing her or his attention to only a small range of occurrences. Although relevance frames are socially constructed, they remain relatively constant over time. Gender is used in virtually all societies as a way of classifying the world and determining the worth of people and of their actions.

Symbolic interactionism has revealed the circular nature of all communication processes and documents the interconnectedness of all participants in the social communication loop. Stuart Hall was one of the first to incorporate this theoretical insight and relate it to a society's power structure in his encoding-decoding theory. For Hall, meaning structures are the discursive rules and codes of language that allow the program message first to be produced and later, when received, to have "very complex perceptual, cognitive, emotional, ideological and behavior consequences" (Hall, 1980, pp. 130-131). Hall thus differentiates between the meaning structures of producers and those of audience members, as well as between the respective frameworks of knowledge and relations of production that are involved in this process. He is also responsible for discovering the important "transformative" processes that take place in the communicative circle when events are transposed into and out of message forms, as journalistic producers encode and viewers/readers decode program messages. These processes are clearly not symmetrical because encoding and decoding call on very different types of knowledge on the part of producers and viewers/interpreters in the social communication circle. Nor do message decoders have the same power in public meaning creation, as do the encoding journalists, who determine which stories are selected and how they are to be narrated, as well as where they are going to be placed in the program schedule.

These theoretical insights are useful for clarifying the "gendered points of view," that female and male reporters bring to their reportorial work in Chapter 7. This chapter also investigates how these points of view are modified by the gendered newsroom power structure, as well as rules of "good information journalism" (Freedom Forum Media Studies Center, 1993). These prescribe how different types of narratives are to be applied to different kinds of events. Because news discourses are structured ways of speaking about public issues, print and broadcasting have developed different narrative traditions. In both cases, journalists do not invent; rather they appropriate pre-existing narrative styles as Gaye Tuchman (1978) and Michael Schudson (1992), among others, have demonstrated. Communication studies have, up to the present, insisted that there are no gender differences in narrative styles, yet these findings are more a result of faulty method than of theoretical impossibility. The "ritual" approach offers a venue for exploring these theoretical issues in greater detail and for clarifying the conditions under which narrative similarities and differences can and will be constructed.

FEMINIST EPISTEMOLOGY: STANDPOINT THEORY

Feminist epistemology, or how we come to know, is a fourth domain that has helped feminist thinkers shed light on how knowledge creation is also inflected by power structures. Certain social groups, among them scientists and journalists, have been able to claim that their type of knowledge is superior to that of other groups in society. These claims have been grounded in the assertion that there is only one model for knowledge-seeking, the "scientific." It is supposedly value-neutral, objective, dispassionate. and protected from political interests through its method. Feminist theorists have questioned the absolute foundation of knowledge and thus joined what is called the anti-foundationalist epistemological camp (Hekman, 1987). They argue with Nietzsche that truth is plural and that its foundations lie in the shared historical and cultural meanings of the social world. Consequently, knowledge creation does not have a single epistemological source, reason, but multiple sources, including the emotions and subjectivity. As such it cannot be achieved through a process of abstraction from the social world, as the natural sciences claim, rather knowledge is always situated, perspectival, engaged, and involved. Yet, feminists have gone beyond these anti-foundational themes, by voicing two additional critiques: concerning epistemology itself and the functions of language (Hekman, 1987). Where natural science critics reject the assumption that knowledge can be generated only through a subject-object relationship, feminists note that the rational mode of thought is itself inherently sexist. This sexual bias is grounded in the dichotomous logic on which Enlightenment thinking is based. Such a theory of knowledge has used biological distinctions to reify the male way of thinking, by defining deduction as the "rational" norm, and the female portion of the couplet, induction, as the "irrational" deviation. Dichotomous reasoning as a process, feminists argue, is grounded in an inadequate understanding of the function of language, viewed primarily as a "descriptive" medium. Roland Barthes (1977) corrected this view when he pointed out that language not only describes aspects of social reality, but this reality is itself constituted through language. Language, in other words, also has an "expressive" function in social communication. The invention of the title

"Ms." in the early 1980s, to designate a woman in her own right rather than in relation to a male being, "expresses" egality between gendered human beings and has led to a change in social consciousness.

There is continued debate about what it means to adhere to a feminist epistemology and whether the concept implies a contradiction of terms. I do not accept this view. Instead, the epistemological position that I inhabit proclaims that there is no absolute grounding for knowledge. Consequently, there are also many ways of constructing knowledge by varying methods. These constructions may be based in experience and in logic and they may be arrived at through induction or deduction. No viewpoint can therefore claim to be privileged or complete. Yet, even though viewpoints are incomplete, the explanatory terms they utilize can be classified according to their importance. Gender is clearly one of these fundamental concepts. Beyond that, I reject dualist strategies of thought, because all dualisms are inherently sexist since they are grounded in the basic male-female dualism. In these dualisms, males are always implicitly the knowers, whereas females are there to be known. Such a dichotomy of knowers implicitly involves hierarchies of power and the sexual organization of daily life. Many open questions still exist in what Sandra Harding (1987) calls the "transitional" feminist epistemological project (p. 186). Neither feminists nor anti-foundational critics are agreed about the radical changes that are currently taking place in human society to provide adequate foundations for theorizing female, Black and third-world knowledge contributions. It is also too early to know whether new epistemologies will be based on moral qualities associated with persons, rather than with the sexes as Hekman (1987) suggests. We also don't know whether the new epistemology will require the development of multivaried logics, as I suggested in an article entitled *Monopolies of Knowledge in Canadian Communication Studies* (Robinson, 1998b).

If knowledge is not universal, eternal, and value-free, but produced in a culturally and historically specific time and place, bodies of knowledge arise from and contribute to social interests (Haraway, 1991). The journalism profession, like other symbol creators, has benefited from its ability to classify the world in terms of biological dualisms that pit maleness against femaleness. In each of these classificatory systems, the "female"-designated couplet is evaluated as less worthy (Cirksena & Cuklanz, 1992). Through the ability to name and to define public issues, users of language systems not only constitute categories of thought, but also communicate hierarchies of status. It is consequently not gender that causes women's behavior, but our *gender system* that places women in an inferior social position. The same gender system furthermore makes women's inferior location appear "natural," as though it results from biology and psychology, rather than from culture and power. North American and European cultures in general continue to reproduce and amplify these gender asymmetries, which through habituation become viewed as part of the natural order (Bleier, 1987). Following Roland Barthes (1977), the *meaning* of gender in a professional setting must therefore be studied on three theoretical levels: as a classifying system, as a structuring structure, and as an ideology. The subsequent evidence will demonstrate that as a classifying system, gender is used to assign social status in the media professions and the ways in which work assignments are made. On the structural level, gender has behavioral consequences that manifest themselves in workplace "climate," in the ways in which female reporters are expected to act in the heterosexual workplace and how they are excluded. On the ideological level, finally, gender notions permeate management practices and under special circumstances, as Chapter 7 shows, may also influence the styles of reporting that female and male practitioners employ (Péricard 1995).

In summary, gender theorists agree that social identity and gender are constructed through language and naming practices. These practices are not only complex, but also layered and use differences in consciousness and socialization as their starting points. Gender theorists furthermore agree that naming and labeling involve classification processes in which power and meaning categories are involved. It is well known that gender inflects meaning categories negatively for females, whereas it tends to inflect them positively for males. And finally, when gender functions as an ideology, where "difference" is equated with "lesser rationality," as the Enlightenment philosophers preached, then all kinds of inequalities of treatment become justifiable for women and minorities. In Chapters 2 and 3, the operation of gender in the print and broadcast newsrooms is explored, while the workplace "climate" becomes the focus of Chapter 4. Together, these chapters explore the Canadian journalism profession "in the round."

chapter *2*

CANADIAN PRINT JOURNALISTS: A MILLENNIAL PORTRAIT

Although the professional and working profiles of U.S. journalists have been studied for well over half a century, only fragmented information about Canadian news producers was available until recently. It is all the more remarkable therefore that two national surveys have been carried out since the mid-1990s. The first by David Pritchard and Florian Sauvageau (1999) used a purely demographic approach and investigated the distribution of journalists in the various media sectors, as well as their role conceptions, job satisfactions, and political orientations. Gender, in this study, appeared as a simple biological attribute. My own surveys of 1975 and 1995, in contrast, use gender as one of the important variables for exploring not only women's contemporary position in the profession, but also the changes in women's and men's professional lives and behaviors in the last years of the 20th century. By including gender as one of the explanatory variables of human social and therefore communicative behavior, I am trying to question mainstream cultural biases and explore the *sources* of gender distinctions and their *dynamics*. Pierre Bourdieu (1977) suggests that these dynamics involve political struggles over who has the right to classify social reality, and thus to decide what will become the legitimate vision of the world institutionalized in social structure.

Women have been able to challenge mainstream explanations of their lack of participation in the prestige professions only since the 1970s, when the second feminist movement helped them to penetrate the scientific establishment and develop their own explanatory perspectives. At the time, Epstein (1988) points out, four theories were available to explain women's lack of presence in the prestige professions. The first ascribes the lack of women in journalism to differences in socialization patterns, which discourage young women from entering male-gendered professions. The belief that early socialization results in distinctive and enduring traits and attitudes in girls and boys has been repeatedly challenged on two grounds. First, there is no direct evidence that links sex-role socialization to occupational outcomes (Reskin & Hartmann, 1986). Beyond that, it has been found that socialization is not an episodic, but a lifelong process that permits reorientations in different life stages (Epstein, 1988). My own comparative evidence shows that it was not "attitudes" but concrete barriers to access that made it difficult for female journalists to join the profession in the 1970s (Robinson, 1981). A second explanation, called the human capital theory, ascribes women's occupational segregation into poorer jobs to rational economic choices on the part of employers. Here, it is argued that people invest in training or choose certain occupations with a goal of maximizing their lifetime earnings. Because it is expected that women leave work when they become mothers, it was argued that they would not invest in specialized training to gain entry into the media professions. The evidence shows that this explanation is faulty as well because it predicts that female media professionals make less educational investments than their male counterparts, an outcome that is not corroborated by the current Canadian evidence. Furthermore, the theory fails to account for the ways in which job attributes, rather than family responsibilities, affect both female and male job choices (Epstein, 1988). Long hours and a difficult work environment, as is seen here, encourage proportionally more women than men to become freelancers.

A third explanation for the dearth of women in the prestige professions is called the social-structural theory. This theory ascribes differences in career tracks to available opportunities and documents that barriers to access limit women's entry into occupations like journalism, which are dominated by men. The following sections demonstrate that the barriers in 1975 and in 1995 continue to exist, but that they have lost some of their stringency because of market forces. In Canada, broadcasting jobs increased substantially in the 1980s and 1990s due to the entry of private stations like Global, which have further expanded CTV offerings. In contrast, the print media have remained virtually static and newspapers have been closed through media mergers. These two tendencies are reflected in the growing proportion of broadcast jobs occupied by Canadian women. A fourth explanation, discrimination, is much less frequently advanced and has been documented primarily by feminist scholars. Discrimination in the workplace results from men's wishes to keep women subordinate in their other roles, thus maintaining patriarchy in society. Job segregation by gender is the primary mechanism through which this superiority is maintained in a capitalist economy (Armstrong & Armstrong, 1990). Studies of other prestige professions like law and medicine have indicated that although males in professional associations claim that their main interest is to improve standards, economic self-interest helped fuel female exclusion (Epstein, 1988).

Although all four sociological explanations are able to illuminate different aspects of women's professional situation in the media, they do not clarify the situation as a whole because they ignore both the importance of gender divisions as an underlying principle of social organization and the importance of culture. They fail to mention that social actors are "gendered beings" who are able to raise gendered expectations about their suitability for a particular job or a particular authority position in the organizational hierarchy. These expectations, as previously mentioned, are culturally determined. This means that culture sets broad guidelines for what women and men should do in a given society. These guidelines help shape the education of children, the ways in which we interact with family, friends, and co-workers, and most importantly, how we communicate with others. Culture thus sets the stage and when individuals act according to its norms, their behavior becomes part of the pattern. Because the pattern is widespread, it seems normal and natural and therefore reinforces the values underlying it. As seen in Chapter 1, binary and exclusive notions of gender intricately structure Canadian and North American culture, like that of Europe. This chapter begins to explore how gender distinctions in the media professions are maintained by a variety of *organizational* processes, such as access, promotional patterns, beat structures, and pay, and how these are systematically related to the newsroom power structure.

To begin the analysis, it is important to note that media institutions are embedded in a particular sociopolitical system, which in turn affects their shape and form. Although there are media institutions in China, it cannot be assumed that their organization and operation are the same as those in Western democracies. Even between Western democratic states, Margaret Lünenborg (1997) has demonstrated, media systems vary along public/private as well as regulatory regimes and construct different viewership patterns. Canada's sociopolitical set-up is different from that of the United States in that it contains a mixed public and privately owned broadcasting system like many European states, whereas its press and magazines are in private hands (Dorland, 1996). This broadcasting system is regulated by an independent federal agency, the Canadian Radio-Television and Telecommunications Commission (CRTC), which has control over licensing. There are four additional factors that differentiate Canada from its southern neighbor. They are the country's huge land mass, its small population (one tenth that of the United States), its cultural dualism, and its corporate enterprise culture. Canada's 10 provinces and 3 territories, among them Nunavut, where the native Innuit achieved self-government in April 1999, are home to a population of only about 30 million people. These people are furthermore not evenly distributed across the continent, because almost half of all Canadians live in the triangle bordered by Quebec City, Montreal, and Toronto. Ontario and Quebec, consequently, have the largest concentration

of print and broadcast outlets, 58 of 113 dailies and 59 of Canada's 119 television stations. Historically, Canada is a young nation, about 136 years old.
It was founded in 1867 by two distinct cultural groups, the French and the
English, whose political contract is reflected in the country's parliamentary
institutions, its utilization of both the common law and French legal systems, and its cultural practices. Two parallel media networks in the two official languages signify these political facts and serve two distinct viewer
groups, the 25% Francophone population mostly situated in Quebec, and
the ethnically mixed audiences in English Canada.

Another feature that differentiates Canada from the United States is
what Hershel Hardin (1974) calls its "corporate enterprise" culture. Canada
paid for the high cost of building its national information and political infrastructures through state investment. This, together with private funds, set up
the national telephone, broadcast, and rail/air services, as well as the national health and social services infrastructures. Canada's dual public/private
broadcasting system, which parallels a regionally focused network of stations and newspapers in the Maritimes, Quebec, Ontario, the Prairies, and
British Columbia, is a manifestation of this economic reality. The country's
regionalism is further reflected in the fact that Canada lacks a national newspaper (the *Globe and Mail* and the *National Post* are primarily read by the
urban elites in the country's five metropolitan centers), and that the majority of its newspaper outlets, 84 of 113 dailies are small (less than 50,000 circulation) and regionally focused. Ownership patterns started out by reflecting this regional pattern, but have become much more concentrated in the
past 30 years. By 1995, group-owned papers had grown to 86% of all properties, from 58% in 1985 (Kubas, 1980). Chief among these is the Thompson
chain with 38 papers, followed by Southam (18 papers) and 16 independent
titles, of which the *Globe and Mail* is the best example. Smaller chains are
Sterling (9 papers), the Toronto Sun Corporation (9 papers), Uni-
Media/Hollinger (3 papers), and 8 papers owned by two Quebec conglomerates: Power Corporation (4) and Québecor (4). Assorted individuals own
the remaining 13 small papers. As we shall see in Chapter 8, cross-ownership of print and broadcast outlets, which began in the 1990s, has had further deleterious effects on popular sovereignty and the Canadian public's
right to know. In general, Canada's regional dispersal of its small population
has, from the beginning, privileged the electronic media, which constitute
the only national forum for public debate. Satellite links, cable networks,
and recently the fiber optic backbone for the information highway, make the
country one of the most electronically sophisticated in the Western world.

North American journalism did not emerge as an occupation until the
mid-19th century, when technological innovations like the electric printing
press and the telegraph revolutionized news production and distribution.
The emerging penny press with its daily deadlines required permanent news

staff, and thus laid the foundation for the emergence of the paid reporter (Weaver & Wilhoit, 1986/1991). From the beginning, the professional and social roles of journalists were contested because many of the early practitioners lacked proper education and training. In the United States, the first journalism courses were introduced between 1900 and 1920, but in Canada the founding of journalism programs had to wait until after World War II and English- and French-language professionals followed very different training paths. English Canadian journalists in Canada's parliamentary democracy have, from the beginning, subscribed to what Siebert, Peterson, and Schramm (1956) call the "social responsibility" theory of the press. In such a system, the media not only have the responsibility to inform, entertain, and sell, but also to raise conflict to the plane of discussion, which means to construct a public discussion agenda.

The social responsibility theory assigns a "fourth estate" function to the press and expects journalists to check on government activities while playing a "neutral observer" role. Until the mid-1970s, Quebec journalists were more activist, both individually and as a group, than their English Canadian counterparts. Armande Saint-Jean (1998) notes that two trends developed out of this stance. The first was toward labor union activism that attempted to transform the power structure within media institutions and to give journalists more power in the face of growing media concentration. This trend erupted in a series of labor disputes and strikes in Quebec's major newspapers and the French-language Radio Canada broadcasting services, which reached their crescendo in 1977-78. The second trend drew well-known Francophone journalists into active political engagement on both the national and provincial scenes. Broadcasters Gerald Pelletier, Jeanne Sauvé, and others left for federal politics and played important roles in the first Trudeau government of the 1970s, whereas others like René Lévesque, Pierre Laport, and Claude Ryan entered provincial politics (Saint-Jean, 1998). In 1976, Lévesque was elected head of the secessionist Parti Quebecois government, while Ryan was elected leader of the Quebec Liberal Party after serving as editor of the prestigious *Le Devoir* newspaper.

By the late 1970s these trends had peaked in the aftermath of the Front de Libération du Québec (FLQ) crisis. This crisis arose from the abduction of British Trade Commissioner Marc Cross in front of his Montreal home by a radical Marxist cell, calling itself the Front de Libération du Québec. Five days later on October 10, 1970, another cell kidnapped and subsequently murdered Quebec's minister of labor, Pierre Laport. To stem the crisis, Prime Minister Trudeau imposed the War Measures Act, which brought troops into the city and imposed censorship on the French broadcasting system. The crisis was not resolved until December 3, 1970, when Mr. Cross was released in exchange for free passage to Cuba for the captors and their families (Robinson, 1975). By the time the referendum on sovereignty association

was called in 1980, Quebec journalists had revised their professional ideology and agreed with their English counterparts that good journalistic practice
required them to be a "witness to" or "critics" of the situation, rather than
active agents in the political arena (Raboy, 1983). As such, they had accepted
the classic North American notion of journalistic detachment and as objective witnesses they presented the facts in this and the subsequent referendum
of 1995, without carrying their opinions into the news columns. Such
changes in role definitions, as we shall see in subsequent chapters, affect the
ways in which journalistic work is structured and good practice is defined.

GENDER AND THE JOURNALISTIC WORKFORCE

To provide a snapshot of how the Canadian journalism corps is distributed
by media sector, I utilize the Pritchard and Sauvageau study of 1999, which
for the first time provided a breakdown of five important media sectors: the
daily press, radio, television, weeklies, and the Canadian press (CP) plus the
three important news magazines. This survey uses the methodology of
Weaver and Wilhoit (1986/1991), which is also the basis for my 1975 and
1995 organizational surveys (see the Appendix). Pritchard and Sauvageau
did not, however, differentiate their findings by gender and therefore remain
silent on which media sectors are most open to women. Luckily, my own
surveys, undertaken first in 1975 for the press only and then in 1995 for both
print and broadcasting, can answer some of these questions.
    The findings from the three surveys complement each other if one is
mindful of their differing purposes and methodologies. The Pritchard and
Sauvageau study tries to *estimate* editorial personnel in five different media
sectors and thus provides the broadest snapshot of the Canadian media professions ever attempted. It is based on a representative sample of 127 media
groups whose personnel lists functioned as the base for these estimates.
From these personnel lists, a sample of 741 journalists was selected for telephone interviews, of these journalists, 554 (75%) interviews were completed. My own surveys conducted in 1975 and 1995, respectively, in contrast,
sample *the total universe* of daily newspapers and television stations and
their actual personnel in order to provide a more detailed picture of the
progress women have made in these two sectors in the intervening 20 years
(see the Appendix). My gender breakdowns consequently are both more
complex and more detailed than Pritchard and Sauvageau's aggregate statistical profiles and permit me to investigate the *sources* and *dynamics* that keep
the Canadian journalistic gender structure in place.
    According to Table 2.1 there were approximately 10,516 full-time
employed journalists in Canada in the mid-1990s, who were just about even-

TABLE 2.1 Gender Distributions in Canadian, U.S., and European Media Sectors (in percentages)

Media Sector	Total Canada	Canada Male[a]	Canada Female[a]	Germany Female[b]	Denmark Female[b]	Italy Female[b]	US Female[c]
Daily Press[d]							
No.	3,451	2,489	962				
%	32	72.1	28.9	27	24	18	34
Radio							
No.	3,240	2,462	778				
%	31	76	24	22	28	26	26
Television[d]							
No.	1,305	819	486				
%	13	62.8	37.2	26	32	32	25
Weeklies							
No.	2,160	1,425	735				
%	21	66	34	32	N/I	N/I	50
Canadian Press (CP) news magazines							
No.	360	252	108	108			
%	3	70	30	31	25	N/I	24
Total							
No.	10,516	7,447	3,069	11,127	N/I	N/I	1,410
%	100	71	29	31	32	25	34

[a]Based on Pritchard and Sauvageau (1999)
[b]Based on Lünenborg (1997)
[c]Based on Weaver and Wilhoit (1998)
[d]Robinson Surveys 1995. N/I= no information.

ly divided between the print and electronic sectors. Of these journalists, approximately 32% (3,451) were employed by daily newspapers, 31% (3,240) in radio stations, 13% (1,305) in television, 21% (2,160) in weeklies, and a small 3% (360) in the CP agency and in the three news magazines. Unfortunately, these figures excluded the Canadian magazine market, which has long been the highest employer of female editorialists. The breakdown of the media sectors by gender indicates that there was great variation in women's representation *between* media sectors. Women had the highest representation in television (37%), followed by weeklies, where they represented 34% of the staff and 30% in the less well-paid CP agency and the news magazines, which included *Maclean's* on the English and *L'actualité* on the French side. The two sectors where women were least well represented, according to Table 2.1, were the daily press and radio, with participation rates of 28% and 24%, respectively

Because western European researchers also undertook studies of media women in various media sectors, comparative figures were for the first time, available for Germany, Denmark, and Italy. Interestingly, these figures indicate that the average representation of women in all media sectors was remarkably uniform across Canada (30%), the United States (34%), Germany (31%), and Denmark (32%). This relative homogeneity is all the more surprising in the light of the great sociopolitical and media regulatory differences that existed in the five countries. Sector comparisons furthermore indicate that in all five countries, daily newspapers and radio, the two older media sectors, employed proportionately fewer women, than the broadcast outlets. Daily newspapers in Italy employ a low of 18% women in comparison to Denmark's 24% and Germany and Canada's highs of 27% and 28%, respectively. Only the United States had achieved one third (34%) representation in this sector. The percentages of women in radio were about the same as in dailies, ranging between 22% in Germany, 24% in Canada, 26% in the United States and Italy, and a high of 28% in Denmark. Within-sector comparisons show, furthermore, that the best employment possibilities for women were in the television sector because of the introduction of gender-equity rules in the public-service institutions on both sides of the Atlantic. Interestingly, it was Canada that had the highest proportion of women in the television sector (37%), versus 32% each in Denmark and Italy, and only 26% in Germany as well as in the United States (25%).

The similarities in the gender ranges of the five countries suggest that it is the working conditions *within* the different media sectors that determine what kind of reception women will receive, rather than the larger social and political contexts in which these sectors operate. This indicates that the profession's *social practices* reinforce whatever gender biases exist in the larger society. In Canada, it has been demonstrated that anti-discrimination requirements as well as the growth of private television outlets throughout the 1980s, contributed to improved broadcast access for female professionals (Raboy, 1996). Even in Germany, there was growth in television employment, although not as marked as in Canada. Elisabeth Klaus (1998) explains that the introduction of private television stations in the 1990s gave German female journalists, including those from the former German Democratic Republic (DDR), new employment opportunities. Because the private sector favors entertainment programming to attract new audiences, women were also the preferred hirees. For the first time, they were seen as news presenters, game show hostesses, and discussion animators (Klaus, 1998).

These global figures do not explain, however, *why* these gender discrepancies should continue to exist 30 years after the second feminist revolution led by people such as Pauline Jewett in Canada, Betty Friedan in the United States, and Simone de Beauvoir in France. This revolution encouraged women to seek advanced education and to move into the public sphere by joining the labor forces of North America and Europe. Most journalistic studies, as mentioned earlier, do not occupy themselves with gender discrepancies in the professions and continue to assume that it is "normal" for women to remain a minority in law, medicine, and journalism. After all, historical evidence confirms this situation by indicating that the female representation in the prestige professions has declined from 12% to 10% in the United States since 1900, a reduction that was also part of the Canadian experience (Robinson, 1977). However, as suggested earlier, normalcy is in the eye of the beholder (e.g., in the gender stereotypes that researchers continue to carry in their heads as they set up their studies). Pritchard and Sauvageau's (1999) survey reflects the lack of awareness that gender structures not only social communication patterns, but also professional opportunities. They themselves implicitly subscribe to a sociostructural explanation to justify the existing discrepancies between female and male participation rates in the different media sectors. Citing the supposedly lesser educational backgrounds of female staff, their younger age and finally, their lesser professional experience. Pritchard and Sauvageau conclude: "We do not know whether discrimination exists or not, but it is evident that certain women continue to experience various obstacles in their professional advancement which are connected with their sex" (p. 42). The following discussion demonstrates that these sociostructural explanations might have been relevant in the 1970s, but are no longer relevant in 2005, when female educational achievements are higher than those of their male counterparts and their years on the job have also increased.

In the early 1970s, William Bowman (1974) documented widespread differences in educational background in the U.S. journalism corps. He found that 60% of male journalists had a bachelor's degree, compared with only 50% of females. By 1983, however, the educational gap had been closed for journalists south of the border and about 74% of both women and men held at least a bachelor's degree (Weaver & Wilhoit, 1986/1991). More recent U.S. surveys indicate that by the mid-1990s, women were *more educated* than their male compatriots, which is a trend that also holds for Canada. Here, Pritchard and Sauvageau (1999) found that 62.4% of females, but only 53.2% of males, had a university diploma. My organizational survey of print journalists indicates that 56% of Canadian female but only 55% of the male professionals, held a bachelor's degree in 1995. Furthermore, 11% of female, versus 10% of male journalists had a master's degree. If one adds the rubric "some college" to the above figures, it turns out that fully 77% of female and 72% of males have some university training. The Pritchard and Sauvageau survey corroborates these figures and indicates furthermore that there is a wide variation in scholarity between the different media sectors. The personnel with the highest educational levels are found in daily newspapers and in television newsrooms, where 65% of females and 61% of the male personnel have some form of university diploma, whereas only 41% in weekly newspapers and 49% in radio have the same qualifications.

All together, these figures (see Table 2.2) indicate that journalism is today a highly professionalized occupation, requiring substantial amounts of advanced training. In the general population, only 10% of Canadian women and 11% of Canadian males had a university diploma in 1991, according to Statistics Canada. The figures also show that there is *no longer* an educational deficit among female professionals. They are rather, as a group, educationally superior to their male colleagues in journalism. This finding demonstrates that the "human capital" theory that predicts that women will invest less in professional education because they are likely to drop out of the labor market is quite misleading in the context of 21st-century realities. In fact, exactly the opposite is true. Women who are trying to enter the prestige professions prepare themselves well and have more educational background than their male colleagues. That does not guarantee, however, that they will overcome the gender- and ethnicity-based barriers, which our evidence will show, continue to exist. In the past 20 years, these have, however, become subtler, so as not to contravene Canada's growing social equity values.

The second sociological variable that is usually cited to explain the disproportionately small number of women in the journalism professions is their age differential. For comparison purposes, this differential is measured in terms of *median* age figures, indicating that half of the sample is above and the other half below this value. Age, however, is not used alone to justify gender discrepancies, but is usually connected with *experience*, which is in turn measured in terms of number of years on the job. I have noted elsewhere that this type of interpretation is itself gender-biased because it implicitly values "practical experience gained on the job" higher than "theoretical" experience gained through education (Robinson, 2001). Pritchard

TABLE 2.2 Canadian Print Journalist's Educational Level in 1995 (by gender in percentages) (*N* = 3,451)

Highest Grade Completed	Females %	Males %	Total %
High school	4	14	10
College	21	17	18.5
Undergraduate degree	56	55	55.5
Certificate	8	3	5
Master's	11	10	10
Doctorate	0	1	1

and Sauvageau (1999) found that the median age for female journalists in Canada is 37 years and for male journalists it is nearly 4 years more, namely 40.7 years. They additionally discovered that women had about four years less experience than their male counterparts, 12.3 years versus 16.5 years. Interestingly, this variance is not significant at the 0.001 level according to their own regression analysis and must therefore be assumed to be spurious. Table 2.3, which is based on my proportional gender sample and compares the ages of female and male respondents in the daily print and television sec-

TABLE 2.3 Ages of Canadian Print and Television Journalists (1995) (by gender in percentages) (Proportional Gender Sample *N* = 124)

Years of Age	Females (*N* = 49) %	Males (*N* = 75) %	Total (*N* = 124) %
20–29 years	20	10	14
30–39 years	49	35	40
40–49 years	27	35	32
50–59 years	4	19	13
60 years and over	0	1	1
Mean age	36 years	41 years	39 years
Median age	34 years	40.5 years	38 years

tors, shows that the median age of women was 34 years and that of the males 40.5. These figures indicate that women in dailies as well as in television are indeed 3 years younger than women in the other media sectors, like radio and weeklies, whereas the male median is the same in all media sectors. This finding is reasonable, considering that the males are not only proportionally more prevalent, but have also been able to enter the journalistic profession at a relatively uniform rate throughout the past 30 years, while gender barriers hindered female entry until the 1980s.

Such an interpretation is corroborated by the *age distribution* comparison between the two genders. Table 2.3 documents that 69% of females were between 20 and 40 years old, whereas only 45% of males were in this range. More than half (54%) of all males, instead, were between 40 and 60 years old, indicating that they had much more even access. These age discrepancies, as seen here, are beginning to disappear in broadcasting. Comparative figures from the surveys of Weaver and Wilhoit (1998b) indicate that Canadian professionals are on average slightly older than their American counterparts. More than half (54%) of Canadian journalists were between the ages of 20 to 39, whereas in the United States, nearly two thirds (60%) were in this age group. Slightly less than half (45%) of Canadians were middle aged, between 40 and 59, in comparison to only 35% of the Americans, suggesting that there was proportionally less new recruitment into print and television in Canada, than in the United States.

A third statistical index that is frequently offered to explain the differential professional status of females and males is "experience." Table 2.4 based on my proportional gender sample (see the appendix), provides a snapshot of female and male journalists' professional experience. It demonstrates that with the aging of the journalism corps in both the United States and Canada in the decade between the mid-1980s and the mid-1990s, years of experience also increased, but only for one gender, females. This means that the median years of experience for both genders are today within 1 year of each other: 10 years for male, and 9 years for female professionals. Interestingly, in 1982 not quite half (43%) of U.S. females were clustered in the group with the least amount of experience (1 to 5 years), whereas in the second category of 6 to 10 years of experience, both genders were equally represented at 26%. By the mid-1990s, U.S. women had doubled their experiential averages by 5 years. Fully 87% of all female personnel now had between 5 and 10 years of experience, whereas among their male compatriots there was no change. As Table 2.4 indicates, Canadian figures contrast sharply with this picture. Among the females, 51% had from 1 to 10 years of experience, while 58% of the males were in these two categories. More interesting, however, is the discovery that another 37% of female personnel had between 11 and 20 years of experience, in comparison with only 30% of males, whereas in the top category of 21 years or more, the female to male

TABLE 2.4 Years of Experience of Canadian and U.S. Journalists 1995
(in percentages)

| | United States | | | | Canada | |
| | 1982[a] | | 1992[b] | | 1995[c] | |
Experience	Males	Females	Males	Females	Males	Females
1–5 years	26	43	26	45	26	30
6–10 years	26	26	26	42	32	21
11 to 15 years	15	12	15	6	20	22
16–20 years	10	8	10	5	10	15
21 years and over	23	11	23	2	12	12
Median experience	10	7	10	9	16.5	12

[a]*Based on Weaver and Wilhoit (1986/1991).*
[b]*Weaver (1998b).*
[c]*Proportional gender sample N = 124 (see the appendix).*

ratio was the same (12%). This shows that both genders in the Canadian journalism corps are increasing their experiential levels. This is reflected in the higher experiential medians in Canada, which stand at 12 years for females and 16.5 years for males, as against 9 years for females south of the border and 10 years for males (Pritchard & Sauvageau, 1999). These figures indicate that in the Canadian journalistic workforce, the age as well as experiential differences are being closed 10 years later than in the United States: in the 1990s rather than in the 1980s. Weaver and Wilhoit (1986/1991) ascribe the change in U.S. experiential statistics to the fact that the growth rate in the journalistic profession itself *stalled* in the United States in the 1980s, whereas this was not the case in Canada, as my subsequent breakdowns show.

From a gender point of view, the closing of the experiential gap in both Canada and the United States suggests that "years of experience" is also a suspect indicator for justifying gender differences, because it harbors latent stereotypes. In this case, these preconceptions involve mistaken assumptions about the similar shape of "career patterns" for female and male practitioners. This can be demonstrated by comparative evidence that probes the frequency and reasons for career interruptions in my proportionate gender sample (see the Appendix). Overall, 27% of Canadian female journalists, but only 19% of males at all levels of the hierarchy had interrupted their career at least once, a difference that is statistically significant at the 0.001 level. For women, I discovered, these interruptions were overwhelmingly caused by the birth of a child, whereas for men they represented temporary absences for travel or relocation. Career interruptions thus function as career-*building* strategies for most male practitioners, whereas they turn out to function as career *inhibitors* for females in Canadian journalism, because they *reduce* the "years of experience" credited to them. Pregnancies and the responsibility for child-care arrangements after birth are still disproportionately the responsibility of females, even though maternity leave policies are in place. Yet, in Canada, in contrast to Europe, these policies offer only between 15 weeks of maternity—plus 35 weeks of parental benefits after childbirth, even though the federal entitlements under the Employment Insurance Act are 52 weeks. Because provincial employment standards laws govern actual leave provisions, these vary greatly across the country. Only Canada's more progressive provinces like Quebec, Ontario, and British Columbia offer the federal maximum of 52 weeks. Melin-Higgins and Djerf-Pierre correctly deduce from this state of affairs that journalistic "culture," defined as a working community that develops shared understandings about professional life, is not homogeneous or hegemonic. Female subgroups within this working community, by reason of their unique work–family relationships, will have to develop not only different strategies for building their professional careers, but also different understandings of their work roles in the heterosexual newsroom. I discuss these issues under the heading of "workplace climate" in Chapter 4.

WOMEN'S REGIONAL DISTRIBUTION IN THE CANADIAN DAILY PRESS

Because Canada's population is not evenly distributed across our huge continent, it must be assumed that the size of the media sectors that serve these viewers and readers, as well as the distribution of the journalistic staff, reflect regional variations. Regional variations are important because they can serve as indicators of better access opportunities for women to print and television jobs. Because Ontario and Quebec together were home to 63% of the population, they also had the greatest concentration of print and broadcast outlets in 1995: 58 of the 114 dailies and 59 of Canada's 104 television stations. Although these numbers seem to indicate substantial diversity in media voices, both the press and television are highly concentrated, which led to two opposite developments since the 1980s, the decline of the press market and the growth of private broadcasting. Each of these had implications for journalistic employment. In the English-language press, four chains dominated the ownership picture in 1995. Among them were Thompson (18 dailies), Southam (21 dailies), Hollinger group (28 dailies), and the Toronto Sun group (10 dailies). Quebec's 11 newspapers were held by only two groups, Québécor (4 dailies) and Power Corporation (4 dailies) with the remaining three papers owned by English Canadian chains (Dornan, 1996). Although these statistics are depressing from the point of view of information diversity, the ownership picture further deteriorated by the end of the century under the twin economic pressures of globalization and convergence of electronic technologies. Conrad Black has purchased a number of Thompson and Sifton papers in Regina and Saskatoon, as well as Paul Desmarais' 41% share in the Southam chain. This made him one of the largest press owners in Canada before he divested himself of many of his properties in 2000.

How has newspaper reduction affected women's employment in the Canadian press over time and have there been regions in Canada where access for women was easier? These two questions, although intricately related, require separate analysis. Table 2.5, based on the organizational survey (107 outlets), reveals that in 1995 a total of 3,451 Canadians were working as full-time journalists in daily newspapers, compared with 2,450 in 1975. In this group, the gender ratio was 21% female in 1975 and 27.9% female in 1995, 20 years later. Although these figures are disappointing and can be explained by a lack of growth in the print sector overall, there is one consolation, the total *pool* of women journalists has nearly doubled. In other words, of the nearly 1,000 new persons hired since the mid-1970s, the women's proportion has doubled, growing from 504 to 962. These figures indicate that although managements have hired proportionately more

TABLE 2.5 Full-Time Journalistic Staff in Canadian Dailies 1975–1995 (in percentages)

	Journalistic Workforce (1975)[a]		Canadian Workforce (1975)	Journalistic Workforce (1995)[a]		Canadian Workforce (1993)[b]	U.S. Journalistic Workforce (1991)[c]
	No.	%	%	No.	%	%	%
Men	1,946	(79)	66	2,489	(72.1)	56	65.6
Women	504	(21)	34	962	(27.9)	44	34.4
Totals	2,450		100%	3,451		100%	100%

[a]*1975 data Robinson (1981).*
[b]*Based on Human Resources Development Canada (1993).*
[c]*Weaver/Wilhoit (1991).*

women than 20 years earlier, the generally small number of new recruits was
inadequate to ameliorate the historical gender imbalances in Canada's newspaper staffs. The small 7% improvement in newspaper employment over 20
years indicates, furthermore, how ingrained gender biases remain in the
daily print sector, in comparison to the Canadian labor force in general,
where these biases are shifting as more women work outside the home to
supplement the family income. In the two decades between 1975 and 1995,
women's labor force participation grew by 10 percentage points to 44% and
by the millennium it reached an astonishing 56%, double the growth rates
in the prestige professions like journalism, law, and medicine (Human
Resources Development Canada, 2001).

Part of the 6% difference between Canadian and American female participation rates is accounted for by regional variations. Table 2.6 demonstrates that women's chances at employment were greater in certain regions
of Canada than in others. Women, for instance, had much better access possibilities in Ontario dailies (+9) and the Maritimes (+4), than in Quebec and
the Prairies, where the number of women hired dropped by 7 and 4 percentage points, respectively, between 1975 and 1995. The most obvious reasons
for these opportunity differences arise from the fact that new newspapers
were created or that the circulation of existing papers increased. Ontario,
with only 37% of the total population, is an example of the former, increasing its dailies from 44 to 45 in the 20-year period, whereas the Maritimes
continue to publish 16 dailies, but with growing circulations. Only in
Quebec, both the number and the circulation of newspapers dropped from

TABLE 2.6 Changes in Regional Distribution of Canadian Newspaper
Journalists 1975–1995 (by gender in percentages)

Region	Females			Males			Totals
	1975[a] %	1995 %	% Change	1975[a] %	1995 %	% Change	1995 %
Maritimes	9	13	+4	8	10	+2	11
Quebec	21	14	-7	25	21	-4	19
Ontario	41	50	+9	43	41	-2	44
Prairies (Yukon)	19	15	-4	15	18	+3	17
B.C.	9	8	-1	9	10	+1	9
Total staff	504	962	N/A	1,946	2,489	N/A	3,451

[a]1975 data Robinson (1981) (see the appendix).

13 to 11 making its 25% of the population the least well served and offering few opportunities for women to enter the journalistic profession.

The above comparisons indicate that regional staff increases in Ontario and the Maritimes are positively related to women's participation in the profession, yet this direct relationship is further modified by the growth in *proportional representation*, as Table 2.7 indicates. In the past 20 years, Ontario has had the greatest increase in the representation of women in editorial positions, increasing a full 12 percentage points from 20% to 32%. Only one other region, the Maritimes, increased its representation 8 percentage points, while the other 3 regions had growth rates of only 3 to 4 points. This indicates that a final factor affecting female rates of access to newspaper jobs is circulation size. In 1975, most female staff worked in small circulation dailies, whereas in 1995, the opposite was true, with the majority of female print journalists (like their male colleagues) employed in large dailies. These large dailies are disproportionately located in Ontario, Table 2.7 indicates, which employed half, or 1,509 of the total of 3,451 Canadian journalists in such papers as *The Globe and Mail, The Toronto Sun* and the *Ottawa Citizen.*

Quebec, in contrast, was the province with a substantial *decline* in female print employment since the 1970s. The comparisons in Table 2.7 indicate that Quebec had only about half (656) of the total number of journalists found in Ontario (1,509) and that only 57 additional people were hired to editorial positions since the 1970s. Of these, 30 were women. Yet, these women constituted only 21% of the journalistic work force, to Ontario's

TABLE 2.7 Regional Distribution of Canadian Print Journalists 1975–1995 (in percentages)

Region	1975 (N = 2,450*) Female No.	Male No.	Females %	1995 (N = 3,451) Female No.	Male No.	Females %
Maritimes	45	146	24	121	252	32
Québec	108	491	18	138	518	21
Ontario	207	845	20	478	1,031	32
Prairies Yukon	97	297	25	141	448	24
B.C.	47	167	22	84	240	26
Total	504	1,946	21	962	2,489	27.9

1975 data Robinson (1981).

32%. In other words, Quebec had the *lowest* gender percentages in all of Canada. Only one in five persons was a woman, in *Le Journal de Montréal, La Presse, The Gazette,* and *Le Journal de Québec,* whereas in Ontario and the Maritimes, the ratio was one in three. Many factors negatively affected print growth in the province until the 1960s, among them the Catholic Church, which inhibited newspaper growth, through its role in education and the index of forbidden titles. Quebec is unique, furthermore, in that its modernization phase coincided with the introduction of television, a medium that is much more widely respected and used in Quebec than in English Canada. Studies have shown that this medium has spawned its own situation comedy format, the téléroman Québecois. In contrast to other situation comedies, it focuses on the Francophone working-class family and utilizes well-known local pop stars and actors. Overall the figures indicate that the ratio of women to men in each market category did not significantly change between the 1970s and the 1990s, indicating that gender-based recruitment barriers remain strong in daily journalism and are reinforced by Quebec's lack of newspaper growth.

Access and Beats

The task force on Women in the CBC (1975) notes that every job should be open to anyone who has the training or ability to do it. In a gendered profession like journalism, it is therefore important to check the opportunity of women reporters to cover any beat available in their organization. Status in the media is defined in two ways, either professionally through the kind of news one covers, or hierarchically through the position one occupies in the organization. One indicator of professional status in print journalism is the kind of news a journalist will report on a regular basis. Traditionally, reporters are divided into two categories: generalists who are assigned by editors to cover whatever stories are of interest on a particular day and beat reporters or specialists, who are assigned to either a geographic area, a particular topic, or an institution (Fishman, 1980; Gans, 1979). Beat reporters can consequently be classified as either locational (covering a region or agency) or substantive (covering a particular subject area). In print, the prestige of the beats follow roughly from the certainty with which a story will be included on the front page. This means that a reporter of Parliament Hill will be near the top of the list, whereas the gardening or entertainment beats will be near the bottom. Beats, in short, comprise an informal status structure that is not directly related to the position one occupies in the editorial hierarchy. Lubin (1971) has already documented that U.S. female journalists are segregated into the so-called women's or soft news beats, such as fashion, personalities, and culture, although Weaver and Wilhoit (1986/1991) claim that by the 1990s "there is no significant difference . . . in whether men or women print and broadcast journalists . . . covered a specific beat or subject area" (p. 169). The question to be determined is, whether gender-typing of beats is practiced in the Canadian journalistic profession and whether it persists? If so, combined with other professional criteria like "experience" and trustworthiness, "soft news" beat assignments would constitute yet another systemic barrier to equitable promotion and recognition, because it is based on gender and not professional preference or competence.

To assess whether beat assignments have become less gender-stereotyped between 1975 and 1995, William Bowman (1974) used a 30-item beat classification, which derived from U.S. investigations. It assigned each journalist working at a daily newspaper to a number of subject areas that were tallied. I followed Bowman's classification to determine the gender proportions for the different beats assigned to female and male reporters in the Canadian newspapers. If 51% or more of the beat personnel were male, the beat was designated as such. If females predominated, the beat was designated as "female," whereas a beat where assignments were gender-neutral was designated as "balanced." Low percentages indicate that only a few of the larger newspapers covered these areas.

Table 2.8, based on the organizational surveys, shows that in 1975, 16 of the 30 beats were predominantly male-gendered and 6 were female-gendered, with 8 beats were covered by both groups of journalists. The male coverage areas were sports, labor, business, urban affairs, weather, outdoors, federal government, real estate, agriculture, provincial government, travel, organizations, police and the courts, municipal government, education, and science. The female-covered beats were lifestyles, consumer affairs, religion, social welfare, ecology, and health. The eight "balanced" areas, covered by both female and male journalists were other topics, local news, national news, personalities, regional news, human interest, minorities, and entertainment. The exclusion of female reporters from more than half of all beats constitutes a formidable gender-based barrier to gaining experience in important news areas. In addition, the table shows that, following the U.S. example, the six female beats were primarily in the "soft" categories, except for ecology and health, which at the time were new topics and consequently not yet gender-typed. The only redeeming feature, in contrast to the United States, is that in 1975 Canadian female journalists, because they tended to work in smaller circulation newspapers (less than 50,000), had a chance to cover local, regional, and national news, which as "hard" topics, are important in demonstrating professional competence.

By 1995, a number of factors had changed in newsroom work. Chief among these was the attempt by media conglomerates to streamline reporting and to do away with the beat structure. Instead, a general pool of reporters was assigned to a number of subject areas. This initiative, our

TABLE 2.8 Canadian Print Journalists and Their Beats: 1975 & 1995 Compared (by gender, in percentages of staff assigned to beats)

Beats	Newspapers (1975) % 106 Dailies Male Beats (16)	Newspapers (1995) % 113 Dailies Male Beats (8)
Sport	83	66
Labor	77	-
Business	74	-
Urban affairs	67	-
Weather	67	75
Outdoors	65	100
Federal government	63	-
Real Estate	61	-
Agriculture	60	59
Provincial government	58	54
Travel	58	86
Organizations	57	-
Police/Courts	52	-
Municipal government	49	-
Education	44	-
Science	43	-
Personalities	-	75
Religion	-	63
	Female Beats (6)	Female Beats (10)
Lifestyle	86	77
Consumer	61	100
Religion	58	-
Social welfare	50	92
Ecology	43	54
Health	37	68
Minorities	-	90
Organizations	-	83
Labor	-	71
Science	-	62
Education	-	58
	Balanced Beats (8)	Balanced Beats (12)
Other topics	83	79
Local news	69	67
National	65	balanced
Personalities	60	-
Regional government	58	balanced
Human interest	56	balanced

Minorities	55	-
Entertainment	52	67
Business	-	balanced
Municipal government	-	balanced
Provincial government	-	balanced
Police/Courts	-	balanced
Urban affairs	-	balanced
Real estate	-	balanced

respondents noted, was a failure and all papers have since returned to beat specialization, making use of reporters' experience in their chosen fields. The comparative data from 1995 indicate that women's access to subject areas has increased substantially. Not only were the number of male-dominated beats cut in half, from 16 to 8, but the "balanced" beats increased from 8 to 12, offering female reporters access to a much greater variety of topics. Interestingly, six previously "male" beats, among them such high-profile topics as business, municipal government, police and courts, real estate, and urban affairs moved into the "balanced" category and were covered by both female and male reporters. Two beats, religion (female) and personalities ("balanced") moved into the "male" domain. Surprisingly, however, there has also been an increase in the number of "female"-designated beats from 6 to 10, indicating that gender-typing of topics continues to be practiced. Female reporters lost the topic of religion, but gained five new ones in addition to the five they covered 20 years ago. Four of these come from the "male" domain: organizations, labor, science and education and one from the "balanced" domain (e.g., minorities).

All of these switches indicate that the binary beat arrangements are not static, but can be changed over time. Why and under what circumstances these gender changes in topics occur, are not yet well understood. As a matter of fact, I know of no other researcher who has raised this issue. My hunch is that there may be two processes at work. One, interest groups develop new public concerns that then become debated in the public arena, such as environmental and Internet regulatory concerns, which did not exist 20 years ago. Being new, they are usually not gender-typed and are therefore assigned to the most competent reporter. Topic switches may also occur when the boundaries between "public" and "private" are redefined, as in the case of spousal violence. Bourdieu (1977) would argue that both of these processes are examples of male professionals, who set the rules in the heterosexual newsroom, transforming their organizational "capital" into "symbolic" capital as new beats appear. This would imply that over time they would shift into topics, which are perceived as high profile, or as offering added

value. In the move to "infotainment" in the 1990s, the topic of "personalities" previously "female"-typed, is now "hot" because it includes sports and
movie stars, in addition to the usual coverage of politicians. The topic may
also provide added value in the form of first night tickets, invitations to
Genie and Oscar celebrations, and travel opportunities.

In the light of this reasoning, it is important to go back and scrutinize
the increased number of "balanced" beats, to determine which group benefited from the topic increases in this domain. Although there was an overall
increase from 8 to 12 topics in the "balanced" category in 1995, further
analysis shows that only 2 of the 12 were in fact male-dominated. They are
entertainment (67% male), and local news (67% male) and other topics
(79% male). Additional "hard news" topics such as business, municipal government, regional government, provincial government, as well as police and
courts and urban affairs, were covered by both genders. This comparison
suggests that female reporters did indeed benefit from the *increase* in the
"balanced" topics and were thus moving toward greater gender equality in
this domain of newsroom work

POSITION AND PROMOTION

Two important ways in which gender has been shown to structure newspaper work is through assignment to the lowest job category and different
rates of promotion for female and male professionals. In North America,
there are six job categories that are hierarchically organized, whereas in most
of Europe there are only five (Lünenborg, 1997). The causes of these differences are not well understood. Weaver and Wilhoit (1986/1991) describe the
job levels in the following manner: *rank and file reporters*—all journalists
doing reporting or covering a beat; *star reporters*—a broad variety of writers
in the feature, medical, political, and editorial ranks, critics, correspondents
and columnists (most of these positions carry little or no managerial responsibility); *desk heads*—comprising bureau chiefs, chief or editorial writers,
and editors from all but the major departmental divisions (i.e., art, education, lifestyles, entertainment, local and national news, travel, and urban
affairs); *day and night editors*—city and wire desk chiefs, executive (business) and news editorships; *assistant editors*—those second in command in
the organization, such as assistant managing editors, associate editors, contributing editors, editorial page editors, and the like; *chief editors and publishers*—the top category with overall responsibility. Here I counted editors-
in-chief, executive editors, managing editors, senior editors and directors of
editorial boards, plus owner/publisher personnel, who furnish the financial
backing for the media enterprise. The following comparisons based on the

organizational survey, demonstrate that by the end of the millennium, Canadian female reporters not only increased their general participation rate in the newspaper profession, but also moved up the ranks in a more egalitarian manner.

The position distribution of daily journalists in 1995 (Table 2.9) demonstrates that females moved out of the entry-level rank-and-file reporter position, where roughly two thirds (63%) had been located in 1975. The figures show that in 1995, only about half (55%) of all women occupied this entry position. Table 2.9 discloses another important development, the substantial movement of both females and males into middle-management positions. Today, 272 women and 703 men are day/night editors and these positions contain 28% of the total female and male staff. For females, this movement constitutes a substantial position upgrade into middle management, where they can begin to have an impact on the work environment. Table 2.9 also indicates that the professional hierarchy in the Canadian press has been flattened to five levels since 1975 and that the desk head position has been virtually eliminated by the end of the century. Whether this rearrangement of responsibilities was a result of technology and the increased use of computers and databases is as yet unknown. Yet, the relatively small growth in daily newspaper jobs overall, lends some credence to this hypothesis.

Although the last 20 years have witnessed substantial professional promotion for females, a question remains as to whether these promotions have included management-level positions. Our proportional evaluation of women's progress up the professional ladder offers a very encouraging picture. It demonstrates that gender is no longer a primary barrier to all top

TABLE 2.9 Comparison of Positions of Canadian Newspaper Journalists 1975–1995 (by gender in percentages)

| | Females | | | | Males | | | |
| | 1975 | | 1995 | | 1975 | | 1995 | |
Position	No.	%	No.	%	No.	%	No.	%
Reporters	318	63	529	55	973	50	1,234	50
Star reporters	76	15	71	8	234	12	175	7
Desk heads	55	11	35	4	234	12	95	4
Day/Night editors	20	4	272	28	214	11	703	28
Asst. manag. ed	20	4	33	3	155	8	109	4
Editor-in-chief	15	3	22	2	136	7	173	7
Totals	504	100	962	100	1,946	100	2,489	100

management positions. In 1975, most women were found at the bottom three levels of the hierarchy occupying only 3%–4% of the top management positions. By 1995, this picture had drastically changed. Female journalists had not only penetrated the middle management day/night editor positions (28%), but also reached the one-third mark (33 females and 109 males) at the assistant managing editor's level. Only the top or editor-in-chief level was still out of reach. Here, women held only 12% of these positions (22 females and 173 males) not much more than they occupied in 1975 (11%). This indicates that recruitment into the top echelon media positions continues to be monitored by a male network, as it is in Canada's boardrooms generally (Agocs, Burr, & Sommerset, 1992).

Unfortunately, detailed comparisons of the status of female journalists in the United States are not available. The Gannett Foundation's (1989) *Women, Men and Media* study, provides only aggregated figures, noting that U.S. women constitute 25% of middle management and hold 19% of editor and 7% of general manager positions (Berns, 1989). Weaver and Wilhoit (1991) also fail to provide a breakdown of positions by gender in their 1982 and 1991 studies. Yet, even these aggregated figures suggest a less rosy picture south of the border and raise questions about whether U.S. affirmative action laws are less effective in promoting gender-equity than their Canadian variants (Robinson & Saint-Jean, 1998, p. 358). This point is discussed at greater length in Chapter 6.

Additional findings in Table 2.10 illuminate another fact that was not evident in 1975: The majority of females and males in 1995 no longer

TABLE 2.10 Position Distribution of Canadian Newspaper Journalists by Market in 1995 (by gender in percentages) (*N* = 3,451)

Position	Small Circulation (<50 K)		Medium Circulation (50-100K)		Large Circulation (>100K)	
	No.	% F	No.	% F	No.	% F
Reporters	562	35	260	32	939	26
Star reporters	86	31	43	30	117	26
Desk heads	30	37	17	6	83	27
Day/Night editors	299	26	124	19	550	31
Asst. managing editor	50	41	30	21	62	8
Editor-in-chief	124	8	31	10	40	22
Total staff	1,151	30	509	26	1,791	27
	33%		15%		52%	

worked in the 83 small circulation dailies, but were found in the 16 large metropolitan papers (52%). As a result of this switch, small circulation dailies continued to offer women the best promotion opportunities. In these dailies, nearly half (41%) of all assistant managing editors were women, as compared to one fifth (21%) in medium circulation papers, and a tiny 8% in the metropolitan dailies. Such figures reconfirm that the top editor-in-chief position is still reserved for the male elite. Yet, even here female staff began to make inroads. Table 2.10 demonstrates that females held only 8%–10% of the editor-in-chief positions in small and medium circulation dailies, but doubled this percentage, to one fifth (22%) in the metropolitan dailies. This confirms that female progress in the newspaper profession is still uneven and that the old rule that circulation size is *inversely related* to professional mobility, continues to hold. Male incumbents, in contrast, have excellent opportunity structures in all newspaper hierarchies, holding an overwhelming 92% and 90% of the top positions in small and medium-sized dailies, while they are beginning to be challenged in the large circulation papers (78%).

Overall, the discussion indicates that by 1995, Canadian females have made remarkable progress and moved up the corporate ladder in the newspaper profession. The female to male comparisons indicate that in all papers, one sixth of upper level managers (editors-in-chief and assistant managing editors) were women, a doubling of their access and representation since 1975. In addition there were regional and beat changes, which gave women better access to metropolitan papers, especially in Ontario and Quebec. This meant that there was a significant pool of educated women prepared to move into the top management levels of all Canadian newspapers. The beat comparisons additionally confirm that female reporters had access to 22 of the original 30 beats, greatly increasing their capabilities not only to learn, but also to cover important hard news stories. Beyond that, the comparisons show that proportional representation from the desk head level upward had been achieved in two out of the three circulation categories (small and metropolitan) and that future efforts would have to focus on increasing these proportions to the point of equality in all markets, to properly represent the composition of the Canadian population.

SALARIES AND REMUNERATION

For at least 30 years there has been a spirited debate about whether gender affects the salaries of female journalists. These debates continue based on two opposing positions. One group of researchers (the majority) asserts that gender discrimination in salaries does not exist. They argue that existing discrepancies can be explained by differences in experience, educational level, size of organization, and position held. The other group points out that census data demonstrate that the North American and European workforces continue to pay unequal salaries for work of equal value performed by women. Both of these categorical positions provide problems for analysis, the former because it aims to *explain away* statistically demonstrated inequalities and the latter because it is difficult to argue from sectorial salary aggregates to the pay situation in a particular profession. The Canadian evidence permits a judicious evaluation of these issues and comes to a set of conclusions that lie somewhere between the two extremes.

To begin with, it must be observed that journalism has never been a lucrative profession. It offers none of the high salaries that are realized in such professions as law, medicine, or accounting. Interestingly, this situation has not materially changed since the 1970s, even though journalistic salaries have tripled in the past 30 years. In 1975, the mean income of Canadian male print journalists was $12,827, whereas for the full-time female professionals it was $10,958. In the United States, the mean salary for daily newspaper journalists at the time was $11,133 (Bowman, 1974). My 1975 study explained this gender deviation in terms of both differences in position and in experience, arguing that nearly three fourths (74%) of female, but less than two thirds (62%) of male journalists were located in the bottom two rungs of the job hierarchy (Robinson, 1981). Beyond that I found that women had an average of 5 years less work experience in the profession than their male counterparts.

Yet, I had lingering doubts about the supposed nonexistence of the $2,000 salary discrepancy, because Bowman had found a $4,540 discrepancy between U.S. male and female professionals in the same period. In his salary survey, nearly 68% of the females reported incomes of less than $10,000 a year, whereas nearly the same proportion of the males (66%) made more than that figure. Bowman's regression analysis determined that media experience, city sizes, as well as gender were the three most significant predictors of a journalist's salary. Of the more than 40% variance explained by the regression coefficient, experience accounted for half, circulation for about 12%, and gender for fully 7% of the difference. In other words, U.S., as well as Canadian female journalists saved their papers on average between $2,000 and $4,500 and a year in salaries throughout the 1970s, although there was a Female Employees Equal Pay Act in place in the United States since 1956. By 1986, Canada too had passed an Equal Opportunity Employment Act, which mandated both equal pay for work of equal value, but also the employment of visible minorities, aboriginal, and disabled persons (Human Resources Development Canada, 1993). Although these acts are important, salary data for both countries demonstrate that the acts speed up, but do not by themselves, eliminate gendered salary imbalances.

Table 2.11, based on the organizational survey, demonstrates that by 1995 median annual newspaper salaries had tripled to $42,267 and that these proportional increases applied to all six ranks. Salaries ranged from a low of $29,432 for rank-and-file reporters to about $42,235 for middle-level day/night editors and median salaries of $58,487 for editor-in-chiefs. Income increases, however, were not the same in all media sectors. In Canada, the highest *average* salaries in 1995 were earned in television ($59,100), followed by daily newspapers ($57,150). News agency and news magazine personnel, in contrast, received $55,050, whereas radio personnel made averages of $43,900 and weekly newspaper journalists earned only $30,150 (Pritchard & Sauvageau, 1999). In the United States, news agency and news magazine personnel led the income pack, with television in the middle and radio and weekly newspaper staffs the least well paid (Weaver & Wilhoit, 1998b). I know of no studies that try to explain these sectorial differences between the two countries, although the higher television pay in Canada may be the result of superior salary scales at the unionized Canadian Broadcasting Corporation (CBC).

My more detailed breakdown of mean salaries for Canada's six newspaper positions shows that there are substantial differences *within* these rankings. Where the previous table suggests that editor-in-chiefs received nearly double ($58,487) the median salary of a reporter ($29,432), the range was in fact much greater. Table 2.12, which tracks differences *within* positions, indicates that the salary ranges between the bottom reporter ($32,552) and the top editor-in-chief positions ($112,320) were fact closer to four times greater. Even within the six ranks, however, there were enormous variations

TABLE 2.11 Median Canadian Newspaper Salaries 1975–1995 (by position)

Position	1975[a] Cdn $	1995[b] Cdn $
Reporters	10,452	29,432
Star reporters	11,388	32,448
Desk heads	12,584	39,000
Day/Night editors	14,196	42,235
Asst. managing editor	15,288	52,000
Editor-in-chief	16,224	58,487

[a]Robinson (1981)
[b]1995 figures based on organizational survey.

TABLE 2.12 Mean Canadian Newspaper Salaries 1995 (by position) (*N* = 3,451)

Position	Mean Salaries (Cdn $)		Weekly Range (Cdn $)	Females in Position %
	Weekly	Yearly		
Reporters	626	32,552	469 - 828	30
Star reporters	787	40,924	603 - 937	29
Desk heads	822	42,744	687 - 937	26
Day\Night editors	692	35,984	605 - 953	28
Asst. managing editor	1,878	97,656	687 - 2,500	22
Editor-in-chief	2,160	112,320	875 - 3,000	11

in mean weekly salaries. For reporter positions, where women constituted 30% of the staff, they varied from $469 to $828 a week and for star reporters, where women held 29% of all positions, the range was between $603 and $937. A further discovery is that day/night editors had mean weekly salaries of $692, which was less than the mean of $822 a week earned by desk heads. This seeming discrepancy, however, disappears when the weekly ranges for these two positions are compared. The evidence shows that in both positions, salaries ranged from a low of about $605 to a high of about $953. The greatest salary variations, it appears, were found in the top two positions. On the assistant managing editor's level there was a $1,813 difference between the bottom and the top of the range. This increased to a difference of $2,125 for the editor-in-chief position. Doubtlessly, women's very low representation here, 22% of the former and only 11% of the latter, negatively impact average female salaries at the top of the hierarchy. These more detailed salary variations within the six ranks suggest that gender and salary are not linearly, but indirectly interrelated, which means that there are other *intervening* variables that contribute to the gendered salary inequities.

For the past 30 years, research on female and male income differences in journalism have demonstrated that one of the most important intervening variables in determining salary is the size of the media organization in which a journalist works. In newspapers, this is usually measured by circulation. Table 2.13 indicates that in 1995 reporters in small circulation (below 50,000) papers earned a mean weekly salary of $562, whereas medium circulation papers (50–100,000) paid $626, and large circulation metropolitan papers with a circulation of more than 100,000 had weekly salaries of $885. Similar progressions are documented for desk head positions where women consti-

TABLE 2.13 Mean Weekly Salaries of Canadian Newspaper Journalists in 1995 (by gender, circulation, and position in dollars) (*N* = 3,451)

Circulations Thousands (K)	Small Circulation (>50K) Cdn $	Med.Circulation (50–100K) Cdn $	Lg. Circulation (<100K) Cdn $
Reporters	562	626	885
Star reporters	625	787	1,158
Desk heads	687	784	1,135
Day/Night eds.	687	692	1,275
Asst. manag. ed.	812	1,593	2,500
Editor-in-chief	875	1,875	3,000
% Female	30	26	27
No. female/male	342/809	130/379	489/1,302
Personnel totals	(1,151)	(509)	(1,791)
	33%	15%	52%

tuted the largest percentages, between 27% and 37% of the total personnel. Desk heads received mean weekly salaries of $687 in small, $784 in medium, and $1,135 in large circulation papers. Table 2.13 additionally demonstrates that female journalists had the best chances of breaking the "glass ceiling" as assistant managing editors in small circulation dailies, where they constituted 41% of the total personnel. Their salaries of $812 weekly, however, were only 50% of those in medium circulation papers ($1,593), where 21% of the staff were women. This constitutes a full two thirds less than the $2,500 weekly salary which metropolitan dailies paid their staffs, only 8% of whom were females. This evidence suggests not only that circulation impacts on salary, but that on the assistant managing editor's level there seems to be an *inverse* relationship between salary and gender: the higher the proportion of female journalists, the lower the salary. At the top, editor-in-chief's level, where women only held between 8% and 10% of these positions in all markets, the weekly salary discrepancies were four times the base of $875 and the top of $3,000. These salary trends confirm that position and circulation continue to be complexly interrelated with gender.

To summarize, by the mid-1990s, the organizational sample of females and males (see the appendix) indicates that there was still a discrepancy between the mean annual salaries of the two genders. My figures show that almost one third (29%) of all Canadian media women had annual salaries below $40,000, whereas slightly less than one fifth (19%) of males were found in this salary range. Furthermore, nearly two thirds (61%) of all female, versus three quarters (74%) of all male professionals had salaries in the $40,000 to $80,000 range. In the top salary ranges (more than $80,000) in contrast, both genders were virtually equally represented at 10% and 7%, respectively. Pritchard and Sauvageau also find an annual salary discrepancy in their large sectorial samples of media personnel. Their 1995 figures show that female journalists earned average yearly salaries of $45,600, whereas males earned $50,550. To try to assess the significance of these differences and to better understand the complex effects of gender on journalistic salaries it is instructive to scrutinize Weaver and Wilhoit's (1986/1991) statistical tests. They performed two types of regression analyses on their data: the standardized regression coefficients (ß) as well as the Pearson correlation coefficients (simple r). Both of these reveal that six factors affect salaries to varying degrees. They are years of experience, size of organization, unionization, managerial responsibilities, and education as well as gender.

Over the past 30 years, these regression analyses confirm that over time, the salary disparities ascribed to gender have substantially diminished in the United States. Yet, this diminution has not happened across the board, but has occurred in different ranks of the journalistic hierarchy at different times and at different rates, with the younger recruits benefiting the most. Wilhoit and Weaver's ongoing studies confirm that in 1971 the median annual income of males younger than 25, was 36% higher than that of females. In the 1980s, with increased entry of females into journalism as well as into the workforce generally, these discrepancies began to disappear, and both groups earned about $11,017 at the reporter level. Going up the hierarchy, however, in the 25- to 34-year age group, salary disparities still existed, but had dropped from 17% to 13%, while at the top of the hierarchy, which few females at the time had penetrated, substantial salary differences remained. This is captured in the finding that *median* female to male salary disparities still amounted to an amazing 40% in the early 1980 (Wilhoit & Weaver, 1986/1991). Twenty years later, however, the median salaries of $19,000 in 1981 had nearly doubled to $32,297, and both genders were beginning to benefit more equally.

The researchers' regression analyses demonstrate that part of the salary discrepancy is explained by differential experience (females' 3 years less work), as well as fewer years as supervisors (4 years), as well as the 1970s educational gap. Since then, however, this gap has been eliminated and female personnel have more scholarity than their male counterparts. Despite these gains, however, gender remains a restraining variable among the standardized regression coefficients (beta) accounting for -10% of the 54% difference in 1980s salaries. By the 1990s Weaver and Wilhoit's (1998b) continued surveys of U.S. journalists demonstrate that the female staff's median salary had grown to 81% of that for men and that gender was becoming *less important* in salary predictions. By 1991, women were receiving average salaries of $27,000 and males $31,500 leaving a discrepancy of $4,500. Yet, in explaining this discrepancy, the regression analyses demonstrate that gender no longer plays as important a role as before, explaining less than 0.01 of the salary variance. This constitutes a substantial reduction of the -0.10 ß, found 10 years earlier (Lafky, 1993; Weaver & Wilhoit, 1998b).

To determine whether a similar diminution in the gender-related salary differences has occurred in Canada, Table 2.14 compares the strength of the two sets of predictor variables for Canadian and U.S. journalistic salaries. This table reveals a number of surprises that indicate that the social environments in which the two journalism corps work are substantially different. To begin with, it appears that in Canada the size of the work organization is a much more important predictor of salary, than years of experience. It has a ß of 0.41 in Canada and of only 0.27 in the United States. This means that the size of the organization has a greater *direct* influence on salary here than south of the border. The importance of organization size on salary is graphically illustrated in Table 2.12, which documents the substantial weekly salary differences between Canada's small and large circulation newspapers. Nearly three quarters (73%) of Canada's 111 daily newspapers are, after all, small papers with circulations of less than 50,000 (Dornan, 1996). In the United States, these proportions are reversed. Table 2.14 additionally documents the greater predictive value of "unionization" in Canada, than in the United States (ß = 0.19 to ß = 0.14). This variation is a result of the fact that

TABLE 2.14 Predictors of Income Levels of Canadian and U.S. Journalists

	Canada[a] (1995) ß	US[b] (1983) ß
Years of experience	0.38	0.41
Size of organization	0.41	0.27
Unionization	0.19	0.14
Managerial responsibility	0.12	0.14
Years of schooling	0.12	0.13
Sex	0.03	-0.10
Chronological age	0.02	-0.02
	$R^2 = 0.56$	$R^2 = 0.54$

[a]*Pritchard and Sauvageau (1999).*
[b]*Wilhoit and Weaver (1986/1991).*

more Canadian than U.S. journalists are unionized, nearly two thirds (65%) of newspaper personnel, in comparison to less than 17% in the United States (Weaver & Wilhoit, 1986/1991). The variables of "managerial responsibility" as well as "educational background," in contrast, have very similar ßs (between 0.12 and 0.14) in Canada and the United States, indicating that the editorial set-ups and educational accomplishments of the staffs are similar. Finally and most importantly, the strength of the *direct influence* ß associated with gender in Canada has been reduced to the lowest 0.03 significance level, a substantial drop from the proportions 30 years ago.

Whether this implies, as Pritchard and Sauvageau (1999) claim, that gender differences in journalistic salaries have evaporated in Canada, is another matter, because they do not provide the Pearson correlation coefficient (simple r), which measures the *indirect effects* of gender on the five other predictor variables. Wilhoit and Weaver found that the simple r-value for sex was -0.25 for the U.S. data in 1983 and that gender predicted less than 1% of the variation in pay when the six variables listed in Table 2.14 were controlled statistically in 1998 (Weaver & Wilhoit, 1998b). A careful scrutiny of the interrelationship between gender and the predictor variables, based on my representative gender sample, suggests that *most of them* are not in fact neutral predictors as claimed. I have already suggested in the previous section how "years of experience" measure "years on the job," which disadvantages females who take maternity leave. The "years on the job" criterion also does not recognize that more female than male journalists have bachelor degrees in journalism (21% to 17%). "Size of organization" also has an implicit male bias as Table 2.10, which traces female representation in different positions, shows. Large circulation papers with the best salaries have the lowest proportion of females in the entry-level reporter positions (26%), while they constitute 32% in medium and 35% of the staff in small circulation papers. "Unionization," furthermore, is least likely in small and medium circulation papers and therefore once again manifests an implicit male gender bias. Only "managerial responsibility" can be viewed as a gender-neutral variable because, as Table 2.12 shows, women have the same managerial opportunities as desk heads and assistant managing editors in small and large circulation papers. What is one to conclude from all of this? Certainly not that gender biases have evaporated in the 21st century. But rather that gender considerations continue to influence not only the *official criteria* determining a female journalist's compensation package, but also the *informal means* by which her primarily male peers will assess her performance. This topic is discussed at greater length in Chapter 5, where the "glass-ceiling" phenomenon is described and scrutinized.

chapter *3*

WOMEN'S STATUS
IN CANADIAN TELEVISION

Canadian broadcasting is a hybrid system that, according to the 1991 Broadcasting Act, is made up of three sectors: the public broadcasting system (CBC/Radio Canada); the private-sector stations and networks; and the community broadcasting sector with its mandate to provide a community access channel. In the 1950s, after the CBC had become a respected information source during World War II, the corporation was mandated to introduce television as a public service monopoly. This additional service, could not, however, be innovated through existing license fees and advertising revenues, so that in 1961 Canada's first private-sector network, CTV, was licensed. In the following decades, private television networks grew rapidly and soon overtook the public sector, which suffered from under financing by the government (Raboy, 1996). Fewer than 50 stations in the 1970s had grown to 111 by 1980 and further increased to 119 by 1995, providing not only increased employment for broadcast journalists, but also increased private ownership, amounting to 85% of all television stations. Of Canada's 119 stations, only 50 are CBC-owned or affiliated, 18 are independent, and eight groups own the remaining 51 stations. In English Canada they are Baton Broadcasting (15), CHUM (5), Craig Broadcasting (3), and Global (6). French-speaking Quebec also has four private ownership groups: Quebec Télé Métropole (7), Télé Quatre Saisons (8), CFCF (3), and Radio-Québec (4) (Audley, 1983).

A comparison of the regional distribution of television stations in 1995 indicates that the Prairies have the largest number of stations, 33, serving a population of 4.9 million. They are followed by Quebec with 31 and Ontario with 28, serving populations of about 8 million in the former and 11 million in the latter. A comparison with the daily newspaper distribution shows that Quebec is well served with television stations, whereas it has a disproportionately small number of newspapers per population. As mentioned earlier, this discrepancy can be traced back to the impact of the Catholic Church's responsibility for education and social services until 1960. In the following decade of the "Silent Revolution," which modernized Quebec, these were transferred to the provincial government, and thus brought into line with English Canadian practices. Ontario, in contrast, is well served with papers, but underserved by television, with 24% of all stations serving a population share of 37%.

In 1995, these 119 television newsrooms, according to the organizational survey, had 1305 journalists working full time. Of these, 486 (37.2%) were women and 819 men (62.8%). The greater proportion of female journalists in broadcasting (compared with 28% in the daily print media) can be attributed to the fact that 87% of all TV stations, but only 83% of the daily newspapers were unionized. Interestingly, the representation of females in Canadian television newsrooms was four percentage points above that in the U.S. industry, where 33% of the staff at the time were females. According to Weaver and Wilhoit, this discrepancy can be largely explained by the fact that the U.S. television market had stagnated since the 1980s, whereas it expanded in Canada during the same period (Weaver & Wilhoit, 1998b). Surprisingly, my personnel figure, which is based on an organizational survey, is only about half as large as the figure (2,738) estimated by Pritchard and Sauvageau (1999). The discrepancy results from three incorrect assumptions made by these researchers. To begin with, their estimates are based not on individual media sector totals, but on a list of all sectors lumped together, which leads them to an inaccurate figure of 117 TV stations, when in fact there were 119 Canadian stations in 1995. Yet another level of inaccuracy is introduced because their personnel estimates are based on a sample of less than three quarters (73%) of these television stations' personnel files. The final level of inaccuracy occurs when only one third of these stations' personnel names are actually counted and ambiguities about their full- or part-time status are not verified (Prichard & Sauvageau, 1999). In contrast, my organizational survey acquired staff information directly from each station and therefore provides a more accurate picture on television staffing, as well as the industry's promotion patterns and remuneration.

In line with the television medium's more even distribution across the regions, Table 3.1 demonstrates that the 1,305 broadcast staff are also more evenly distributed across Canada, than the print personnel. In 1995, the regions with the highest overall percentage of television journalists were Quebec (29%), followed by Ontario and the Prairies, both of which had 27%, of the total staff. Only the two coastal regions—the Maritimes and British Columbia—had less than 10% each of the total staff (9% and 8%, respectively). Canadians' living patterns explain these differences. They

TABLE 3.1 Regional Distributions of Canadian Television Staff in 1995 (by gender and region) (N = 1,305)

Region	Females		Males		Total		F
	No.	%	No.	%	No.	%	%
Maritimes	51	11	66	8	117	9	44
Quebec	133	27	249	30	382	29	35
Ontario	142	29	207	25	349	27	41
Prairies	126	26	224	28	350	27	36
B.C.	34	7	73	9	107	8	32
Total	486	100	819	100	1,305	100	37

show that 80% of the country's viewers lived in the three regions, which have the majority (54%) of all television stations: Ontario (28), Quebec (31), and the Prairies (33). The Atlantic and Pacific regions had small populations and therefore trailed with 16 stations in the Maritimes and 11 in British Columbia (BC).

Female staff figures mirror this geographical pattern and thus do not give females the same access chances across the country. Table 3.1 shows that in the most populous two regions, the gender proportions differed by only 2 to 4 pencentage points. Twenty-seven percent and 29%, respectively, of the female and 30% and 25% of the male staff were located in the heavily populated regions of Quebec and Ontario. In the Prairie region, there was only a 2-point difference between female (26%) and male staff (28%). In the most easterly (Maritimes) and westerly (BC) regions with 2.3 and 3.5 million inhabitants, however, the staff representation differences also were 3 and 2 percentage points respectively. What this indicates is that both the central regions of the country as well as the peripheries provided equally good access to employment for female professionals. This does not mean, however, that there were the same remuneration opportunities, because as the press information has shown, this depends on the size of the market in which a station operates.

Just like the press, Canada's 119 television stations can be subdivided into three groups. The majority of these television stations (47) are located in small markets (42%) in cities with less than 100,000 people and of these, 15 function merely as transmission points, reducing the number of small stations to 32. Another 41 (35%) of all stations are located in large markets (more than 500,000 people). Only 31 stations, constituting 23% of the total, are located in medium-sized cities of between 100,000 and 499,999 viewers.

This distribution is similar to the one found for daily newspapers. The three regions with the largest number of stations had a different mix of station sizes, which is important to know, because the size of the organization affects television salaries. The Prairies had about an even number of large (12) and small (15) stations, whereas Ontario had a predominance of large (11) and medium (12) stations. Quebec followed the Prairie pattern with 11 large and 14 small stations, as did BC with an equal split of large (5) and small (5) stations. Only the Maritimes had a disproportionate number of small (8) and medium (6) stations, as against two large ones, which suggests that salaries would probably be lowest here.

Although differences in the distribution of female and male television journalists were not found between regions, I did discover notable differences in the placement of female and male journalists in the three groups of stations. Table 3.2 demonstrates the obvious, that women's proportional representation in television jobs was about 10 percentage points higher than those in print, representing 37.2 % of the staff. Social scientists argue that a group, which represents one third of the staff, is large enough to affect organizational change. Beyond that, Table 3.2 shows that females had the best career chances in large markets with more than 500,000 viewers, where over two thirds 63% of all female staff and 58% of all male staff were located. Interestingly, the figures were almost equally good in medium markets up to 499,999 viewers, where females constituted 36% of a much smaller total staff. Even in the small, under-100,000 viewer markets, female television staff still constituted a substantial 32%. This suggests that gendered salary differentials will also not be as pronounced as they are in print. All together, these tables show that from the point of view of access, female television personnel have a better chance of finding work in the Maritimes and in Ontario, and that they will have a better chance at promotional equity than their Canadian print colleagues.

TABLE 3.2 Market Distribution of Canadian Television Staff in 1995 (by gender and city size) ($N = 1,305$)

City size	Females		Males		Total		
Thousands (K)	No.	%	No.	%	No.	%	% F
Large (>500K)	308	63	476	58	784	60	40
Medium (100K–500K)	91	19	159	20	250	19	36
Small (<100K)	87	18	184	22	271	21	32
Totals	486	100	819	100	1,305	100	37

POSITION AND PROMOTION

The progress of women up the television hierarchy was faster than that for newspaper staff, because, since the late 1970s print had stagnated in Canada, whereas the private television industry blossomed. This means that a larger pool of younger women was hired into broadcasting than into print in the past 30 years. Table 3.3 indicates that the job hierarchy in the television newsroom was made up of six positions: news writers, reporters, correspondents, desk heads, producer/directors and executive producers. Interestingly, this hierarchy does not follow a straight pyramidal form because smaller newsrooms combined the news writer position (0.5% of the pool) and that of the correspondent (3% of the pool) with other job categories. Television consequently had a much larger proportion, with almost two-thirds (58%) of its staff in the reporter position. Yet, female staff was also doing very well in the four other positions, where females were proportionally represented (at 32%) among news writers, correspondents, and desk heads. This indicates that the glass ceiling had moved up and manifested itself only at the top (e.g., the executive producer level). Yet even here, females constituted a surprising one fifth (18%) of the top personnel. Most striking however, is the very high proportion of females in the producer and director categories in which they held almost half (41%) of the positions. This shows that there was a large enough pool of qualified female television journalists from which future executive producers could be recruited.

Table 3.4 explores the relationship between job position and market size and shows that in 1995, Canadian female journalists had a better chance of

TABLE 3.3 Position Distribution of Television Journalists in 1995 (by gender) ($N = 1,305$)

Position	Females		Males		Total		
	No.	%	No.	%	No.	%	% F
News writers	24	5	44	5	68	5	34
Reporters	305	63	447	55	752	58	41
Correspondents	12	2	24	3	36	3	33
Desk heads	49	10	110	13	159	12	32
Producers/Directors	79	16	114	14	193	15	41
Executive producers	17	4	80	10	97	7	18
Totals	486	100	819	100	1305	100	37

TABLE 3.4 Positions of Canadian Female Television Journalists by Market 1995 (in percentages) (# 1,305)

Town population thousands (K)	Small TV Stations (<100K)			Medium TV Stations (100–500K)			Large TV Stations (>500K)		
	Staff	F		Staff	F		Staff	F	
Position	No.	No.	%	No.	No.	%	No.	No.	%
News writer	2	2	100	5	4	80	60	18	30
Reporters	192	73	38	162	70	43	399	164	41
Correspondents	2	0	0	10	1	10	24	11	46
Desk heads	20	2	10	32	9	28	107	39	36
Producers/Directors	15	2	13	23	5	22	155	71	46
Executive producers	40	8	20	18	5	11	39	7	46
Staff Totals (No. & average %F)	271	87	32	250	91	36	784	310	40

access in large television stations (more than 500,000 viewers) where 60% of all staff or 786 people were employed. Yet, promotion opportunities were not linearly related to market size. Small market stations had the highest proportion of female executive producers (20%). Medium market stations had the highest proportion of reporters (43%). And large market stations offered the most promising promotion opportunities overall. In these stations, 41% of reporters, 46% of correspondents, and 46% of producers/directors were female. Eleven of these large stations were located in Ontario: 8 in Toronto that constitute 67% of the Ontario TV workforce, 2 in Ottawa, and 1 in Hamilton. In Quebec, the 11 large stations were overwhelmingly located in Montreal (5), which employs 96% of the workforce. Quebec City had 4 stations, whereas Hull and Sherbrooke each had one station at which the final 4% of the personnel worked.

In both Canadian and U.S. television, beat reporting is not as important a criterion for professional status as in print journalism. In the United States, nearly half (42%) of all print reporters covered a designated beat. In television, the figure was substantially lower, with less than one third (28%) of all reporters assigned to beats (Weaver & Wilhoit, 1986/1991). Interestingly, Canadian beat figures are much lower than those in the United States, both in print and in broadcasting. Only one third of all print reporters worked in beats and a minuscule one fifth (18%) of television journalists had a beat assignment. Our figures show that there was no gender preference in the assignment of beats, 9% of females and 11% of males had such assignments. There are two explanations for the lack of beat assignments in television. The first has to do with the fact that the majority of Canadian television newsrooms are small (47) and therefore do not have the requisite personnel to specialize. The second has to do with the different working situations in broadcasting and print, where the assignment of a reporter to a particular story is more often based on availability, than on specialized knowledge (Kaniss, 1991).

Despite these trends, television beat assignments were gender-stereotyped, just as they were in print. Of the 25 topics covered in 1995, 7 were male-designated, 7 were female-designated, and the remaining 10 were covered by both genders. When the actual topics that were covered by males and females in television are compared, it appears that the gendering of beat topics was more persistent in the male domain, than in the female-designated topics. Male television reporters covered the same seven male-designated topics as their print colleagues. They were urban affairs, outdoors, agriculture, police/courts, and science, as well as provincial and municipal government. Female television reporters, in contrast, covered only five of the seven topics designated as female in print. They were consumer affairs, social welfare, health, organizations, and education. The other two topics they covered were business and travel, topics that in print belonged to the male domain. The 10 topics covered by both genders in television included 3 from 1975: local, regional, and national politics. Among the remaining 7, 4 come from the female domain in print: human interest, minorities, entertainment and lifestyles and the remaining 2 come from the male domain: sports and weather, or represent "other" topics. These comparisons indicate that topic designations are not fixed but malleable, and that the Canadian print and broadcast newsrooms *do not agree* on the gendering of a given topic. Three conclusions regarding beat reporting follow from this evidence. First, in contrast to print journalism, beat reporting is not used as an indicator of professional status in television, because less than one fifth of television journalists covered a beat. Second, in television, beats do not function as restrictive barriers to the promotion for female journalists, because television newsrooms assign whoever is available to cover the story. Finally, although women reporters had access to more than 60% of all subject areas, those in which they comprise a substantial majority, like consumer affairs, social welfare and health, continue to be labeled "feminine" domains. In the following chapter, it is shown that this labeling is grounded in deep-seated dichotomies associated with appropriate "work" domains for females and males, which continue to underlie North American social consciousness.

SALARIES AND REMUNERATION

Salary statistics are extremely difficult to collect and are therefore usually presented in aggregate form for a particular media industry. One of the exceptional aspects of this survey is that I used position to correlate with salary information, which provides a more *detailed* salary picture than is usually available. Pritchard and Sauvageau's aggregate study notes that in 1995 television journalists garnered the highest salaries in Canada, an *average* of $59,100. This estimate is corroborated by my organizational survey, which found that journalists had a mean yearly salary of $63,388. Television salaries, just like those in print, were, however, heavily influenced by position and market size. Yet, in television, salaries were not linearly related to position in the newsroom hierarchy because small stations do not usually employ correspondents and news writers, who had mean annual salaries of $36,036 and $37,908 respectively. Researchers and reporters, the data show, were paid approximately the same. They had annual mean salaries of $36,815 and $35,256, whereas the desk head position was in the middle range, with a salary of $53,508. Only the top two positions in the hierarchy receive substantially greater yearly mean salaries: producer/directors $83,200 and executive producers $97,604. It is these high means that push up television salary averages over those in print.

Table 3.5 demonstrates that mean salary information hides substantial salary differences between television stations of different sizes and of different gender compositions. Together, these factors permit us to analyze in what type of institution female television journalists have the best salary and in what positions their access is greatest. Staff statistics at the bottom of Table 3.5 show that television stations in small markets (less than 100,000 viewers) where only 21% of all journalists were employed provide female television journalists with the *least satisfactory* employment opportunities. In Canada's 43 small stations (out of 119), one third (32%) of staff was female and as a minority, most of them were found in the lowest position, that of reporter. However, *within* this position, females constituted 38% of the total and were therefore, proportionally represented. Their input on the station's editorial policies was minimal, however, because males occupied between 80% and 90% of the positions as desk heads, producer/directors, and executive producers. Despite this hierarchical domination, female television journalists had one position in which they could earn a higher salary (e.g., as news writers where they earned a mean weekly salary of $687 as compared with the $437 for reporters). This anomaly is probably explained by the fact that there were only a handful of news writers employed by small stations. These findings constitute the exact opposite of what we discovered in newspaper employment, where female journalists had the best chances in small circulation dailies.

TABLE 3.5 Mean Weekly Salaries of Television Journalists in 1995 (by market size and position) (N = 1,305)

Town Population Thousands (K) Position	Small Stations (<100K)		Medium Stations (100–500K)		Large Stations (>500K)	
	Cdn$	%F	Cdn$	%F	Cdn$	%F
News writer	687	100	729	80	862	30
Reporter	437	38	502	43	854	41
Correspondent	449	0	693	10	937	46
Desk head	701	10	1,006	28	1,312	36
Producer/Director	749	13	1,600	22	2,500	46
Executive producer	812	20	1,877	11	3,000	18
Staff average % F		32		36		40
Staff (F/M)	271	(87/184)	250	(91/159)	784	(310/474)
% of all women in market segment		21%		19%		60%

Medium market (100,000–499,999) TV stations that employed only 19% of the total personnel provided even better female access because women constituted a little more than one third (36%) of the personnel in these stations. Yet, here too females were relegated to the two bottom positions. Table 3.5 demonstrates that 80% of all news writers and 43% of all reporters were female in Canada's 31 medium-sized stations. The table documents additionally that gender-equity improves across the newsroom hierarchy in middle-sized stations, indicating that 28% of desk heads and 22% of producer/directors were women. Once again, salary and gender are not linearly related because news writers, where females are 80% of the staff, make substantially better weekly salaries of $729, than reporters at $502.

As previously indicated, the best employment opportunities for female staff were in large stations located in metropolitan centers of more than 500,000 viewers, where 60% of Canada's TV personnel were found. In these stations, female personnel had above average (more than 40% representation) in three of the six positions: the reporter (41%), correspondent (46%), and producer/director (46%) categories. Their salary means were also double that of medium-sized stations. Reporters were paid $854 a week, correspondents $937, desk heads $1,312, and producer/directors $2,500. In all three categories of stations, however, the executive producer suit, with a mean salary of $3,000 weekly, was still virtually out of bounds for females.

Because 60% or 310 of all females in television were employed in metropolitan stations, their mean salaries were also higher than those in daily newspapers. All together, this evidence confirms that Canada's growth in private
television stations and networks throughout the 1980s and 1990s attracted a
proportionately larger group of younger, well-educated, and well-trained
professionals, whereas the U.S. broadcast sector stagnated. Canadian television stations also paid them more equitable starting salaries than south of the
border, indicating that female journalists in this sector had a chance to influence the TV programming of tomorrow.

REVISITING THE EXPLANATORY THEORIES

In concluding this chapter, it is important to revisit the four theories that
purport to explain the lack of women's' representation in the prestige media
professions. What has the Canadian print and television evidence contributed to modifying these theories and what are the questions that need
further investigation? The first theory, which argues that differences in
socialization patterns discourage women from entering journalism, was dis-
proved by Reskin and Hartmann (1986), who were able to demonstrate that
there are no links between gender-role socialization and occupational outcomes. Historical accounts have more generally shown that middle-class
American women's occupational choices were restricted at the turn of the
century to teaching, nursing, and social work. These restrictions were
imposed because of Victorian notions about the "proper" role of women in
the home. There is no evidence that differences in socialization caused these
choices. Instead, these practices are now recognized as having not individual, but social roots (e.g., the gender-stereotyping of jobs). Social changes
engendered by economic growth and the second feminist revolution in the
late 1960s began to change these assumptions. For the first time, both older
middle-class women with children, and younger women were forced to contribute to the family income and to contemplate "nontraditional" career
choices in new fields. One of these new fields, which has attracted great
numbers of Canadian students, is journalism and/or communication studies,
a trend that persists to this day (Robinson, 2000). It has fueled the improved
access to newspaper and television jobs, which the 1995 evidence confirms.

The second, or human capital theory, argues that women, because they
will bear children, will not choose to acquire the requisite educational capital to be eligible for media jobs. Here, comparative Canadian evidence for
newspaper and television personnel demonstrate that although there were
educational deficits on the women's side in the 1970s, these were eliminated
by the mid-1990s. Today, female journalists have, on average, higher educa-

tional qualifications than their male counterparts despite the fact that educational accomplishments have risen in the profession as a whole. Table 2.2 demonstrates that more than half of both female (56%) and male (55%) journalists have an undergraduate degree today. My gender comparison discovered furthermore that fully 71% of the females, but only 68% of the males had studied journalism. This shows that females, like other professional minorities, use higher educational qualifications to overcome entry biases.

The third theory, which has been called the sociostructural theory, ascribes the lack of females in the prestige professions to different opportunity structures for the two genders, which in turn, lead to different access and promotion patterns. In 1975, the CBC's Task Force on the Status of Women in the Corporation, discovered that male attitudes were an important barrier to female's entry into broadcasting. Among the findings were male administrators' beliefs that women and men were constitutionally suited to different kinds of jobs. It was assumed, for instance, that women's greater manual dexterity predestined them for secretarial jobs. Other male notions included the idea that females were less career-oriented and therefore would not agree to transfers. Finally, it was thought that women were too emotional and therefore unfit to become neutral reporters. Because the same investigation found that two thirds of female CBC broadcast personnel were unmarried and had no children, the prejudicial assumptions undergirding this 80% male profession at the time, were thrown into clear relief (CBC, 1975).

Differences in opportunity structures begin with the fact that in North America, females continue to be made responsible for family and child care. Journalism, with its long hours, is incompatible with these demands, as my representative gender sample of 1995 (see the appendix) corroborates. The survey shows that the discrepancy in the rates of marriage and total numbers of children between female and male journalists continues to exist. In 1995, only two thirds (65%) of female journalists were married or lived with a partner, whereas four fifths (81%) of males lived in a union. The continuing "dual-role" strain is manifested by the fact that female professionals have substantially fewer children than males. Nearly two thirds (59%) of all females have no children, whereas only one third of males (31%) are childless. Such statistics show that, even now, when both partners have to work to maintain a family's living standards, home responsibilities constitute a larger burden for female than male professionals.

Differences in access to media positions, as well as to timely promotion for female newspaper journalists, were confirmed by my comparative 1975 and 1995 newspaper studies. The mechanism used, as Chapter 2 showed, was female assignment to a soft news beat, which retarded promotion. Moreover, because females had greater difficulty in being hired in the first place, they were also disproportionately clustered in the lowest reporter position 20 years later. My first ever comparison of female and male occupants in the beat structure demonstrated that females had access to only 4 of the 30 beats, whereas males had access to three times that number: namely 13 beats. Only 7 beats were covered by both genders. The female beats included the "soft" areas of lifestyles (86%), consumer affairs (62%), religion (59%), and social welfare (50%). These topics rarely make it on to the front pages of Canadian newspapers and thus fail to function as springboards for promotion. The male-gendered beats were in the "hard news" categories and included government, economics, and sports. Another social barrier is the newsroom hierarchy itself, which is structured by gender. In 1995, an astounding two thirds (63%) of all female personnel continued to be reporters and thus at the bottom of the newsroom hierarchy, whereas overall, only about half (53%) of the total Canadian press corps was located here. Beyond that, females in the profession were not promoted as fast as males. This is documented by their dismal representation in the higher ranks in 1975. Only a minuscule 0.8% of star reporters, 13.6% of desk heads (Women's Department), 0.4% of day/night editors, 0.7% of assistant managing editors and 0.5% of chief editors/publishers in Canada's 106 newspapers were female in the mid-1970s (Robinson, 1981).

By the mid-1990s our evidence indicates, sociostructural barriers to the media professions had been substantially reduced, although they still exist. The 1995 female to male comparisons indicate that male administrators' attitudes changed, and equity legislation mandated more neutral promotion processes. In addition, female journalists acquired more than adequate scholarity in order to compete. Consequently, movement up the professional ladder became faster and more equitable, as both the daily newspaper and the television data show. Furthermore, newsreporting styles changed since the 1980s and generally became more "soft" news-oriented. The lifestyles, consumer affairs, travel, and social welfare beats became as high profile as the traditional prestigious "hard" news beats of politics, economics, and sports. The proportional representation of females across statuses in newspapers and television, consequently became more equitable, especially in Canada's large circulation papers and in metropolitan television stations. In both of these newsrooms, the so-called "glass ceiling" was moved upward to the assistant editor and the producer/director positions, where sufficiently large groups of females were waiting to move to the top.

The fourth theory, gender discrimination, as an explanation for the continued inequities in media jobs also receives support from the Canadian evidence. As noted at the beginning of Chapter 2, job segregation by gender is a primary mechanism through which male superiority is maintained in capitalist societies. In the professions, this economic self-interest is hidden behind claims to improve reportorial standards, with the result that females continue to experience subtle workplace pressures, which are virtually unknown to their male counterparts. These are explored from a gendered point of view in the next chapter. Here, the *cultural* approach helps me explore professional involvement from both a structural (organizational) and a hermeneutic (meaning) perspective, which permits me to unravel how the workplace social structure affects both interpretation and behavior.

Beyond that, my cultural theory of journalism notes that workplace activities themselves are vertically and horizontally stratified by power and gender, as the 1975 and 1995 newspaper comparisons indicate. Although females were disproportionally found in the less important beats in 1975, in the 20-year interval, they moved up in status to just below the editor/publisher position, indicating that gender is not a fixed category arising from biology, but a socially constructed one that changes over time. This happens because cultural understandings of gender change as well. As noted in the introduction, culture sets broad guidelines for what women and men should do in a given society. These guidelines not only affect the ways in which we interact with family, friends and co-workers, but most importantly, how we communicate with others. Because human interactions and social practices involve a classification into female and male categories, gender is constitutive of all social encounters, including professional encounters in the journalistic workplace. Gender must therefore be conceived not as a fixed property of individuals, but as part of an ongoing process of naming, by which social actors are constituted and relate to their environment. Epstein (1992) explains that language itself helps to create "boundaries" in this process, by providing the terms by which real and assumed behaviors and things are grouped and narrated. Language and thought are therefore not individual, but social achievements through which we learn to negotiate the world we grow up in. We do this through naming and labeling those features of the world that seem worth attending to. In this labeling process, gender is one of the most important categories, because it involves the four classificatory operations through which the deviant/inferior evaluation of females' worth and performance are created and sustained (Kessler & McKenna, 1978). How this gender inferiority plays itself out in the journalistic workplace is the focus of the next chapter.

chapter 4

GENDER IN THE NEWSROOM: AN INTERNATIONAL COMPARISON

Chapters 2 and 3 demonstrated that female journalists in Canada made substantial strides in entering the country's daily press and television newsrooms between 1970 and 2000. Despite this, it was found that women had greater difficulty being hired than their male colleagues and that their promotion and pay continued to lag. Yet, change has taken place despite the gender handicap. This requires us now to look more closely at the informal dimensions of working life and how they function as structural barriers for women and minorities in their organizational settings. Research has shown that working practices are ordered by gender scripts, which provide guidelines for how colleagues are supposed to interact with each other in the heterosexual newsroom. These scripts are not fixed, but change over time because they are part of an ongoing naming process through which we, as social actors, constitute ourselves and relate to our environment. Although the sociological theories mentioned in Chapter 2 were useful in explaining women's participation in the press and television professions, they implied that we, as social actors, were merely passive "role-players." Yet, communication scholarship has demonstrated that naming and interpretation turn social actors into active participants in social encounters, where they can exhibit creative and strategic behaviors. Such behavior takes account of the status and power of the other participants in the interaction situation. In order to uncover how female and male practitioners "make sense" of newsroom tasks and encounters, we therefore need to analyze both the differences in understanding, as well as the commonsense knowledge structures that female and male practitioners bring to their jobs. Beyond that, we will have to inquire whether and to what extent journalistic role definitions are an outcome of the historical and legal contexts in which North American and European practitioners do their work.

In her studies of the legal and medical professions, Epstein (1988) has found that biases against women and minorities are imported into the organizational setting through both structural and informal processes. The structural processes were investigated in Chapters 2 and 3. Now it remains to clarify the informal processes that regulate how female and male journalists *behave* in the newsroom. Because journalism is not a "proper" profession, because its expertise is not derived from systematic "training," as in law and medicine, but from "osmosis" and "fiat," it lacks agreed upon criteria for assessing journalistic qualifications. This permits a much more unrestricted importation of gender biases into journalism than is possible in the other professions (Zelizer, 1993). Under the circumstances, three attitudinal clusters based on gender distinctions acquire greater saliency. The first concerns journalists' definitions of their social roles as "mediators" between politicians and citizens and whether these are interpreted in the same manner by females and males. The second inquires into how females' and males' professional interactions are regulated in the heterosexual workplace. The third explores whether there are differential task expectations for female and male practitioners.

Since the 1930s, there has been an ongoing debate about whether journalism is a craft or a profession. These debates were revived in the 1960s, when the so-called "new" journalists like Tom Wolfe began to introduce fictional narrative styles into their news work. Thirty years later, it seems another narrative shift has occurred and novelists now employ journalistic conventions to appeal to mass audiences (Wolfe, 1972). Philip Elliott (1976) suggests that the craft–profession dichotomy continues to persist because journalists embrace a number of different and sometimes incompatible ideals. These include autonomy, creativity, working in a prosperous and culturally prestigious communication sector, and having access to large, diversified audiences. William Johnstone, Edward Slawski, and William Bowman (1976) were the first to empirically confirm this art–craft dichotomy. They found that in the 1970s U.S. practitioners had two contrasting conceptions of their professional role. They called the first group "straight" reporters because they were content to collect the facts through recognized channels and leave evaluation to the reader. The "participant" or committed groups of journalists, on the other hand, were of the opinion that more attention should be paid to investigation, background analysis, and evaluation. The Johnstone group hypothesized that the participant group of communicators not only challenged their peers' standards of professionalism, but were also likely to question their employers' motives. Consequently, they reasoned, the "participant" role interpretation would be neither as attractive, nor as prevalent among 1970s practitioners, as the neutral one (Johnstone et al., 1976).

In 1981, Weaver and Wilhoit revisited the Johnstone et al. (1976) study and 10 years later, in 1992, they carried out a third evaluation of professional attitudes in U.S. journalism. This survey attempted to find out whether technological changes in news work, resulting from computer and database uses, as well as satellite links offering instant replay of national and international events, had changed the social role definitions of U.S. journalists. It also sought to determine whether media concentration, with its emphasis on marketing, had changed outlooks. This re-study demonstrated that the impact of the so-called new technologies was minimal, but that journalistic role conceptions had become more diversified in the intervening decades (Wilhoit & Weaver, 1998b). By the 1990s, it appears, U.S. journalists subscribed to three different social role descriptions. The first may be called the *interpretive/investigative* role, which involves analyzing and interpreting complex problems and investigating government claims. The second, which they call the *information dissemination* role, aims at getting information to the public quickly and distributing it to the widest audience. The third, or *adversarial role* considers critique of government and business as its primary purpose. In this latest re-study, Weaver and Wilhoit (1998a) conclude that U.S. journalists in the 1990s subscribed to a plurality of media roles, with nearly one third embracing the joint, interpretive as well as the disseminator conceptions. How did Canadian communicators compare and were their particular role conceptions similar to or different from those of their U.S. cousins?

JOURNALISTIC ROLE CONCEPTIONS IN CANADA

Defining the social role of journalists and the media's mission in contemporary democracy have been matters of public debate for more than 50 years in Canada, since the time that both the media and the profession endorsed the social responsibility mandate in the late 1950s (Saint-Jean, 2002). Yet, the history of this debate, which pitted Anglo-American against Quebec-French traditions, is as yet only spottily documented. There have been accounts of reporting and ownership conflicts during the Quiet Revolution (Raboy, 1983) and analyses of the roles of the media in the 1980 and 1995 referendary campaigns (Robinson, 1998, 2000a). There are critiques of the embourgeoisment of professional values (Demers, 1989), but a coherent intellectual history of the profession has not yet been written. Before entering the debate, a definition is in order to ground the following discussion. When I talk about a journalist's social role conceptions, I am referring to the "mind-set and behavior of an incumbent in an organizational position." This means that the focus is on how a person thinks about and does his or her job. Because it is difficult to define the journalistic mediator position, which is located between politicians and their public in a democratic state, the most recent investigations, as we have seen, have employed a tri-partite model distinguishing among the adversarial, interpretive, and disseminator roles.

The Canadian proportional gender survey adopted Weaver and Wilhoit's (1986/1991) methodology and added gender as an important independent variable. Using a list of "things that the media do or try to do today," respondents were asked to rate the importance of eight media roles on a 5-point scale, ranging from *very important* to *not important*. Table 4.1 indicates that the U.S. and Canadian journalism corps' assigned different importance ratings to the eight media roles and that gender differences were more pronounced in the Canadian than in the U.S. sample. In the U.S. sample, two thirds of journalists assigned primary importance to *investigating government claims* (67%) and *getting information to the public quickly* (69%); whereas *avoiding stories with unverified content* was considered to be in third place by 49% of the group. Weaver and Wilhoit conclude that the dominant professional role of contemporary practitioners continues to be interpretive/investigative, and they find that two thirds (62%) of all U.S. journalists subscribed to this role. The disseminator role, in contrast, was embraced by half (51%) of the U.S. sample and the adversarial one, by less than one fifth (17%).

Table 4.1 demonstrates that in 1995, Canadian journalists made different role choices. About two-thirds of them place *analysis of complex problems* in first placed (63%), with *getting information to the public quickly* (60%) of nearly equal importance and *investigating government claims* subscribed to by one half (52%) of all professionals. This suggests that the Canadians favor the educational roles more than their U.S. counterparts, while at the same time stressing the distributive and investigative dimensions of their craft. Yet, in each case, the news agendas of the two countries may also have influenced these role choices. In the post-Watergate United States, the investigative function fell into abeyance, whereas in Canada the complex constitutional issues arising from Quebec's upcoming referendum on secession in 1995, accentuated the need for interpretation. No wonder that *providing analysis of complex problems* topped the list of media roles for Canadian professionals. All of these role comparisons are significant, except for *avoiding stories with unverified content*. Interestingly, *reaching the widest audience* was of little interest to journalists in both countries, with only one fifth (20%) of Canadians and of Americans considering it important. Weaver and Wilhoit (1998b) opine that the fragmentation of the mass audience by cable seems to have made reaching the largest audience a lesser goal than it was 20 years earlier. Canadian professionals shared this conclusion, as the comparative evidence shows.

TABLE 4.1 Canadian and U.S. Media Role Conceptions by Gender (in percentages)

Media Roles	Canada 1995 (N = 124)					United States 1992 (N = 1,156)			
	F n = 49 %	M n = 75 %	F/M diff. %	Total N = 124 %	χ^2 Signif.	F n = 338 %	M n = 661 %	F/M diff. %	Total N = 1,156 %
Investigate gov. claims	50	52	-2	52	0.0001	69	64	+5	67
Get information quickly	64	57	+7	60	0.05	63	58	+5	69
Avoid stories with unverified content	29	28	+1	29	n.s	58	46	+12	49
Analyse complex problems	61	63	-2	63	0.0001	49	49	0	48
Discuss national policy	39	27	+4	32	0.0001	40	39	+1	39
Reach widest audience	14	23	-9	20	0.05	n.a.	n.a.	0	20
Dev. intellectual interests	14	14	0	14	0.05	26	23	+3	18
Provide entertainment	2	10	-8	7	0.001	23	18	+5	14

Que: What importance do you ascribe to the following media functions?
Based on Weaver & Wilhoit (1998b) and Pritchard & Sauvageau (1999), and Canadian gender sample shown in the appendix. (Percentages derived from tasks considered extremely important on a 5-point scale.)

A second important point demonstrated in Table 4.1 is that gender seemed to have a stronger impact on Canadian than on U.S. professional attitudes. The table demonstrates that if one compares percentage spreads between the gender responses, one finds that these spreads are *smaller* (between 1 and 5 points) in the United States, than they are in Canada. Here the gender differences vary between 1 and 9 percentage points. The only exception is a 12-point gender difference concerning *stories with unverified content*. Here more than half (58%) of U.S. female staffers are concerned, whereas slightly less than half (46%) of their male colleagues shared the same attitude. Otherwise, U.S. attitudes show only 5-point gender spreads in two domains. In both, *investigating government claims* (69% female to 64% of male) and *getting information to the public quickly* (63% to 58%) female responses were higher than those of male professionals. Weaver and Wilhoit (1998b) note that these gender differences disappeared in the U.S. sample, if age differences and the media sector in which the respondent worked were controlled.

In Canada, gender differences in journalistic attitudes were not only significant, but also much more pronounced amounting to nine-point differences. Interestingly, Canadian female and male practitioners agreed on the top three role definitions, but disagreed on their order of importance. Almost two thirds of all females (64%) considered *getting information to the public quickly* most important, closely followed by *analysis of complex problems,* which an almost equal number (61%) endorsed. For them, *investigating government claims* (52%) came in third place. Male colleagues, in contrast, placed the *analysis* function first with 63% of support, followed by speedy information transfer (57%) and the investigative function (52%) last. Concentrating on reaching the widest audience was much more important for males (23%) than females (14%); as was providing entertainment, which got 10% of the male vote, but only 2% of females votes.

To explore whether the differences in social role conceptions had consequences for journalistic practice, respondents were asked to evaluate the importance of 14 reporting tasks. Table 4.2 records the top two responses to the question: "In your opinion, what tasks should journalists perform?" Once again, both genders assigned top priority to the same mix of four tasks, but they did not rank them in the same order. The four major journalistic tasks, all of which received more than 90% approval, include *report events, investigate, and critique events* as well as *explain in simple terms.* However, Table 4.2 demonstrates that there were three secondary tasks with 70% to 80% approval ratings, which differed by gender. The female group supported in declining order of importance, *giving background information* (85%), *educate* (79%), and the *watchdog* tasks (71%). The male group gave higher ratings to *play watchdog role* (77%) and *condemn wrongdoings* (66%). Although the evaluative differences between genders were not large,

TABLE 4.2 Canadian Respondents' Ranking of Journalistic Tasks by Gender (in percentages) (N = 124)

Journalistic Tasks	Females n = 49 %	Males n = 75 %	Total N = 124 %
Report events	100	99	99
Comment on events	40	40	40
Critique events	92	95	93
Raise controversy	33	38	36
Arbitrate social conflicts	7	10	9
Give background information	85	83	84
Investigate	96	96	96
Explain in simple terms	90	93	92
Educate	79	70	74
Favor new ideas	40	39	39
Play watchdog role	71	77	75
Condemn wrongdoings	42	66	56
Help sell	10	12	11

Que: In your opinion, what tasks should journalists perform? (Percentages derived from tasks considered extremely important on 5-point scale) Based on gender sample in the appendix.

it is interesting to speculate that "educating the public" is one of the ways through which women translate their social commitment into journalistic practice. Males, in contrast, showed a greater interest in watchdog and condemnatory tasks, which seem to grow out of the competitive and adversarial stances that are prevalent in the newsroom.

What does all of this add up to? A very broad interpretation of these data suggests that male practitioners were more interested in the business dimensions of media activity, whereas female journalists favored content-oriented media roles, which privilege the intellectual and social missions assigned to the media in democratic societies. Beyond that, factor analyses of these complex responses confirm that, in contrast to the United States, Canadian professionals subscribed to only two role conceptions rather than three. These can be described as the "interpretive/investigative" and the "educator" roles. The first encompasses investigation of government claims, report-critique and comment on events, explain simply and arbitrate. Two-thirds (61%) of all Canadian journalists subscribed to this role conception.

This confirms that the two North American journalism corps' *share* one aspect of what constitutes good journalistic practice. Canada's "educator" role conception, however, which was espoused by 39% of all practitioners, did not have a U.S. counterpart. Factor analysis reveals that it combines explaining events with fostering new ideas, offering background information, raising controversy, and helping to sell. One may hypothesize that this attitude cluster is influenced by the "public service" credo espoused by the CBC, for which there is no counterpart in the United States. As such, it signals the existence of *national* differences in the ways journalists in different Western democracies interpret their social roles. Such interpretations, the cultural theory suggests, develop within the *specific* sociopolitical contexts in which the profession operates in each country, a matter that is further explored in the next section.

Canadian evidence further suggests that, as in the United States, subtle attitudinal differences appear between media practitioners in different media sectors. Table 4.3 demonstrates that television journalists rated *speedy transmission* (getting information to public quickly) slightly more favorably (80%) than newspaper journalists (77%). The latter, in contrast, stressed the importance of the *analysis* (72% to 68%) role of their medium. This corresponds to the modern division of labor between the print and broadcast media, where newspapers are seen as providing in-depth backgrounding for daily events that unfold on the television newscast. In the Canadian setting, both broadcast and print journalists also agreed that the *investigative* role, vis-à-vis government claims was the second most important function of journalists (76% to 75%), with *discussing national policy* in third place. All

Table 4.3 **Canadian Broadcast and Print Roles Compared (in percentages) (*N* = 554)**

Media Roles	TV Broadcasting %	Print %
Investigate government claims	75***	76***
Provide analysis of complex problems	68***	72***
Get information to public quickly	80*	77*
Discuss national policy	60***	58***
Concentrate on widest audience	47	49*
Develop intellectual and cultural interests	26	27*
Provide entertainment	14	28**

*$p < .05$; **$p < 0.001$; ***$p < 0.0001$. Que: What do you consider the most important journalistic roles for broadcast and print media? (Averages computed on a 4-point scale for each role.)*

of these differences are significant at the $p = 0.0001$ level. The most striking difference that emerges is that television news people consider providing entertainment less important than newspaper journalists (14% to 28%). This seems to indicate that print journalists are deeply aware of the competitive advantages of television as an "entertainment" medium, with which they have to compete on a daily basis. The remaining print significances are less strong than the top three roles, registering only $p = 0.5$ on the chi-square scale.

JOURNALISTIC ROLE CONCEPTIONS IN EUROPE

Both the U.S. and the Canadian material on how journalists conceptualize their social roles demonstrate that what was previously viewed as a pan-cultural profession, may not be as global as was initially suggested. This is to be expected if the national and cultural contexts in which the profession functions, are taken seriously. Renate Köcher, who compared British with German professional outlooks, was one of the first to demonstrate that there are three important national institutions that affect journalistic activities. They are (a) the ways in which press freedom is codified, (b) how government and media relationships are institutionalized, and (c) the ways in which journalistic work is legally protected (Köcher, 1986). These social contexts furthermore suggest that journalists' understandings of their roles are not fixed forever, but may change over time. It has already been demonstrated that some of this change is accounted for by the recruitment of women into the profession and by the increased level of education of today's journalists, in comparison to those who entered the profession in the 1970s. Yet the politico-legal situation on both sides of the Atlantic also leaves traces on journalistic role conceptions.

Although it is difficult to compare the U.S. and Canadian role conceptions with Köcher's findings directly because differently worded questions were used, the comparison is never the less suggestive. Table 4.4 demonstrates that German and British journalists, like their North American counterparts, viewed their role as complex, but in their estimation it encompassed four, rather than three dimensions, judging by their five top responses. British journalists saw themselves as *neutral reporters* (90%); *guardians of democracy* (82%); *critics of abuses, proponents of new ideas* and *entertainers*; all three supported by 76% of the sample. In sixth place came *educating the public* (74%). Such an interpretation suggests that British professionals placed the greatest emphasis on the "channeling" roles of neutral reporting and entertaining, combined with the active role of educating the public and critiquing abuses.

TABLE 4.4 Comparison of German and British Journalistic Role
Conceptions (in percentages)

Journalistic Roles	Great Britain (1985) N = 405 %	Germany (1985) N = 450 %
Critic of abuses	76	95
Neutral reporter	90	81
Guardian of democracy	82	79
Raise new ideas	76	72
Spokesperson for underdog	60	70
Help people understand	61	58
Entertain	76	54
Mirror public thought	61	47
Educate	74	16
Exert political influence	24	12

Que: How do you view the job you do as a journalist? (In percentages answering most important on a
5-point scale). Based on Köcher (1986).

Such a role conception is closer to the Canadian understanding, which
also stressed the distribution and education functions. The Germans, in contrast, stressed the "critical" role of *ferreting out abuses,* which a full 95% of
all professionals supported, combined with three other roles. These were
neutral reporting, which 81% supported, plus two additional roles: being a
guardian of democracy (79%) and being a *proponent of new ideas* (72%).
Köcher comments that factor analysis revealed that British journalists viewed
being a neutral reporter and *mirroring public thought* as part of the same relatively passive channeling role. In contrast, German journalists interpreted
the *mirroring* function as part of *speaking for the underdog* (e.g., an active
advocacy role). These differences suggest not only that national press traditions affect the *importance* of different role dimensions, but also that the
interpretation and understanding of what it *means* to fulfill given journalistic roles is interpreted differently in different countries (Köcher, 1986).

Köcher suggests that the British preoccupation with the "neutral
reporting" role grew out of the hard-won fight against the Crown, which
had censorship rights until 1771. The right to report on parliament is thus
deeply imbedded in precedent, but has never been codified in British common law. Germany's 19th-century history of fragmented states, in contrast,

encouraged the legal protection of both the press and of journalists after unification in 1871. Even in conflicts with the government, the rights of journalists have to be weighed against the protection of state secrets in Germany. The development of Britain's press system from the London center to the peripheries is also different from that on the continent. It led to a pyramidal set-up, in which the London newspapers dominate. In Germany decentralization is reflected in the power and diversity of regional newspapers, all of which reflect different political points of view. Consequently, British journalists interpret the mandate for information diversity as a requirement to be fulfilled *within* each newspaper, whereas in Germany it is manifested by the differing political points of view that are demonstrated *between* newspapers. For British journalists this means that "objectivity" became a crucial professional criterion in the late 19th century, when, as in the United States, the penny press needed to present information to a mass readership with varying political outlooks. Because the majority of German newspapers, in contrast, are closely aligned with different political parties, journalists view their social role as being standard bearers for a particular political camp, a position that reinterprets and makes the Anglo-Saxon "objectivity" criterion less salient. Köcher (1986) argues that "freedom of the press" in Britain consequently means "freedom of social communication," whereas in Germany and on the continent generally, its meaning is defined individually, as a component of "the natural right of the individual to develop freely" (pp. 44-49).

ETHICAL UNDERSTANDINGS
IN NORTH AMERICA AND EUROPE

With the differences in the interpretation of journalistic roles clearly established between North American and European professionals, it remains to be seen whether these national differences also carried over into the ethical realm. Two different questions, which have not been systematically compared, need to be distinguished. They are (a) whether the individualist and action-oriented U.S. outlook tends to support exceptionally aggressive journalistic methods for information acquisition? And (b) to what extent does gender affect ethical understandings? Both of these questions are dealt with separately. Although it is difficult to evaluate a reporting tactic when it is removed from the context of a specific news story, Weaver and Wilhoit (1986/1991) have developed a 5-point scale on which to rate seven ethical practices.

Table 4.5, which compares the approval ratings by country, demonstrates that nationality is complexly interrelated with attitudes toward ethical practices. One of the most striking findings emerging from the table is

TABLE 4.5 Approval Ratings of Professional Practices by Country (in percentages)

Professional Practices	U.S. (1992) N = 1,156 %	Canada (1995) N = 124 %	Great Britain (1985) N = 405 %	Germany (1985) N = 450 %
Getting employed to gain insider information	63	36	73	36
Using confidential docs. without authorization	82	60	-	-
Badgering unwilling informants	49	31	72	8
Using personal documents without permission	48	17	-	-
Paying for confidential information	20	9	69	25
Claiming to be someone else	22	7	33	22
Agreeing to protect confidentiality and reneging	5	2	-	-

Based on Köcher (1986, p. 62). Que: Journalists have to use various methods to get information. Given an important story, which of the following methods do you think would be justified on occasion and which do you not approve under any circumstances? (Percentages derived by combining the two "justifiable" responses on a 5-point scale). Canadian data based on gender sample in appendix.

that on an attitudinal continuum, the British colleagues were the most aggressive and the Germans least so, with the North Americans in between. British journalists gave between 10 and 30 points more approval to such practices as *getting employed to gain insider information* (73%), *badgering unwilling informants* (72%), and *paying for confidential information* (69%). Nearly three quarters of all British practitioners approved of these two practices, whereas a surprising two-thirds (69%) favored paying for information. U.S. and Canadian journalists were in the middle, with the latter generally more critical of all professional practices studied. This is indicated by the fact that in Canada, six of the seven practices received approval ratings *below* 50%, whereas their U.S. colleagues approved with margins that were more than double.

The seven ethical practices can be divided into three different groupings according to their level of support. The two practices that were most strongly disapproved were *using confidential information without authorization* (U.S. 82% to Canada's 60%) and *being employed by an organization to gain information* (U.S. 63% to Canada's 36%). Eight out of 10 U.S. journalists, but only 1 in 3 Canadian professionals approved of these unethical practices. The second group of practices, which are approved by about half of the U.S. group and less than one third of the Canadians are: *badgering sources* (U.S. 49% to Canada's 31%) and *unauthorized use of personal documents* (U.S. 48% to Canada's 17%). Both American and Canadian professionals virtually unanimously disapprove three practices. They are *paying people for confidential information* (U.S. 20% to Canada's 9%), *claiming to be someone else* (U.S. 22% to Canada's 7%), and reneging on *confidentiality* (U.S. 5% to Canada's 2 %). Interestingly, slightly more than one third (36%) of Germans and Canadians agreed that it is legitimate to become employed for insider information. Yet, on two other methods, the Germans were closer to the U.S. stance than to the Canadian. These include *paying for confidential information* (Germans 25% to U.S. 22%) and *claiming to be someone else* (Germans 22% and U.S. 22%). Nearly one quarter of both of these groups approve of these practices, which as demonstrated earlier, were roundly rejected by the Canadians. The only practice where there is a huge attitudinal gap between the Germans and the other three groups is in the domain of *badgering informants*. The overwhelming majority (92%) of German practitioners rejected this, whereas nearly three quarters (72%) of the British practitioners approved. The Americans and Canadians were in the middle with 49% and 31% approval ratings, respectively.

How can these striking national differences in ethical outlooks be explained and why do the British professionals and our southern neighbors seem to be more aggressive? Part of the answer may lie in the corrosive effects of what critics like Max Frankel (1999) call the U.S. "media madness" of the 1990s in which media conglomeration, market declines, and competition from the Internet, seem to have eroded factual reporting approaches in favor of sensationalism. A similar trend has been noted in the increased 1990s competition of both London newspapers and the regional press, which was trying to boost sales through screaming headlines and populist angles (Tunstall, 1996). Beyond that, there is disquieting evidence from Germany and Britain that age may be contributing to the erosion of ethical outlooks, because it is the younger professionals, those under the age of 45, who seem more willing to pay and disclaim their true identity to gain information (Köcher, 1986). Meryl Aldridge (2001) makes a similar point when she confirms that British papers have undermined their in-house training programs and reports an editor commenting that ethical standards are today more subject to sardonic jokes, than to serious debate. The comparative data on ethical attitudes indicate overwhelmingly that competition has had a negative impact on professional behavior on both sides of the Atlantic.

The second question concerning the impact of gender on ethical outlooks has only been studied in the Canadian context. Table 4.6, based on my
proportionate gender sample, demonstrates that gender is less important
than nationality in affecting the ethical practices of the profession. Feminist
cultural research on women's psychology and workplace behavior suggests
that gender differences manifest themselves in a tendency for females to
comply with authority more than their male counterparts (Löfgren-Nilsson,
1994). One might expect, therefore, that formal socialization patterns might
lead them to reject actions that are legally or morally questionable, such as
using confidential documents, acting without permission, or *badgering
informants.* This hypothesis is borne out by the evidence.

Overall, the data show that both female and male professionals made the
same ethical choices about the justifiability of different professional practices but the male approval was higher than that of the females. Table 4.6

Table 4.6 U.S. and Canadian Approval Ratings of Professional Practices by Gender (in percentages)

Professional Practices	U.S.[a] 1991 $N = 1,156$ %	Canada[b] 1995 $N = 124$ %	Canada Females $n = 49$ %	Canada Males $n = 75$ %
Getting employed to gain inside information	63	36	37	37
Using confidential docs. without authorization	82	60	59	62
Badgering unwilling informants to get a story	49	31	22	38
Using personal documents without permission	48	17	15	19
Paying people for confidential information	20	9	11	8
Claiming to be somebody else	22	7	7	7
Agreeing to protect confidentiality and reneging	5	2	2	3

[a]*Based on Weaver & Wilhoit (1986/1991).*
[b]*Canada based on gender sample (see the appendix); (Percentages were derived by combining the two "justifiable" responses on the 5-point scale).*

indicates that both Canadian females and males strongly disapproved of professional methods that involve lies or deception, like *claiming to be someone else,* which garnered only a 7% approval rating, or failing to keep a *promise of confidentiality,* for which the approval rating was a mere 2%. The largest gender differences in approval ratings, with 4 to 14 percentage point spreads, were found in two practices: *badgering unwilling informants* to get a story, as well as *using personal documents without permission.* In the former there was a 16-point difference: only 22% of females vs. 38% of males approved this practice, whereas in the latter there was a 4-point spread: only 15% of female and 19% of male practitioners approved. Both of these practices have to do with overt and covert forms of coercion, which women, as underdogs in the newsroom power structure, tend not to condone. In the other domains, attitudes between female and male practitioners were quite similar. What this suggests is that, as in the other realms of professional practices, the relationships between gender and behavior are not linear, but *strategic.* Depending on their position in the newsroom hierarchy and the issues with which they are dealing, female professionals will insert gender considerations at specific times and on specific issues, to highlight an alternative sensibility or to clarify a different point of view. There is no evidence that there is a "gendered ethic" in the journalism profession, there are merely instances where female and male professionals react differently, by taking gender into account in their interpretations of the situation. This suggests that survey evidence on journalistic attitudes must be enriched by interview material, so that respondents can describe those instances where gender becomes a salient consideration.

GENDERED INTERACTIONS IN THE NEWSROOM: SOCIAL EXPECTATIONS

Despite the fact that gender studies are demonstrating that newsroom work is different for female and male personnel, communication scholarship continues to perpetuate the orthodoxy that women's different experiences are a result of their lesser numbers in the newsroom, rather than an outcome of gender biases in the organizational setting (Weaver & Wilhoit, 1998b). In all of these studies, gender is considered a simple biological attribute, which exists in isolation from other social characteristics like ethnicity, status, and education. Although this might have been a persuasive argument 30 years ago, gender studies have indicated that such a view is not only oversimplified, but also factually wrong. Newsroom work for women is different, because of *systemic* biases in the social reproduction of the profession. These

systemic biases are recreated through classificatory and evaluative procedures that use gender dualisms to define females and ethnic minorities as
"different" and then fall back on these classificatory differences as reasons
for the unequal evaluations of women's newsroom activities.

In Canadian society, as in North America and Europe, the systemic
biases that affect how female and male journalists will perform their jobs are
grounded in gender-based assumptions about how work and family obligations are to be combined. Traditional gender scripts on both sides of the
Atlantic organize work and family responsibilities by sex, giving females
responsibility for the "private" sphere of the home and males for the "public" sphere outside. By the end of the 20th century, married women's
increased employment began to integrate these two spheres. As a result,
there has been a reduction of women's family role, but as yet virtually no
increase in the husband's family involvement. As a consequence, Joseph
Pleck (1984) notes, employed wives face strain and exhaustion in combining
their work with their family roles. There are two reasons for this. The first
is the fact that the husband's family role is unresponsive to changes in the
wife's working role. Men do not take on more household tasks when their
wives work. The second set of strains for women develops out of the fact
that females are expected to place family obligations above their work roles.

These gendered work- and family-role expectations have visible effects
on how female journalists organize their working lives and why there are
fewer women than men in the profession. Four findings from the proportional gender sample (see the appendix) corroborate the gender-based difficulties women encounter in trying to combine their family obligations with
their professional ambitions in the media professions. They are differential
rates of marriage, differential numbers of children for female and male professionals, the strains of "meshing" work with family responsibilities, and
the effects of what may be called "masculinist" career notions.

Interestingly, work on women's involvement in professional careers and
family life has documented that high-achieving men tend to be married,
whereas high-achieving women tend to be single (Lee, 1992). These findings
are certainly borne out in the Canadian profession. Our comparative data
indicate that in the mid-1990s, only 65% of female journalists were married
or lived with a partner, whereas 81% of males were married. Even more
strikingly, nearly 59% of female journalists had no children, whereas a mere
one third of males (31%) were childless. Among the personnel with children, gender again made a difference in the number of children per couple.
Table 4.7 demonstrates that among the 41% of female journalists with children, the greatest number (27%) had only one, with the remaining 8% and
6%, respectively, having two and three and more children. Among the 69%
of male professionals with children, in contrast, the numbers were again
substantially higher. Contrary to their female colleagues, Table 4.7 shows

TABLE 4.7 Canadian Journalists' Number of Children by Gender (in percentages) (N = 124)

Number of Children	Females (n = 49)		Males (n = 75)		Total (N = 124)	
	No.	%	No.	%	No.	%
No children	29	59	23	31	52	42
One child	13	27	14	19	27	22
Two children	4	8	22	29	26	21
Three children or more	3	6	16	21	19	15

Based on gender sample in the appendix.

that 27% of male journalists had two children, another 21% had three children, whereas 19% of the males, had only one.

Evidence from the Canadian proportional gender survey additionally shows that the small group of female journalists with children also had greater difficulty reconciling work with family responsibilities. As expected, a greater proportion of female journalists, nearly one half (42%), mention that child-care arrangements and other obligations at times interfered with their work schedules. Among male professionals, only 31% voiced the same complaints. Interestingly, the 68% of men who saw no problem in combining work with family responsibilities were of this opinion, irrespective of whether they had children or not, indicating that their wives assumed all family-related responsibilities. Pleck points to this as a manifestation of the fact that work–family roles for women and men continue to be segregated by a dual market and also by what he calls "asymmetrically" permeable boundaries. Working women are expected to do most of the housework and their family roles are expected to intrude on their work role. This means that when there is a crisis at school, it is the child's working mother, rather than the working father who is called to take responsibility. For the husband, on the other hand, the work–family permeability is in the opposite direction. He is expected to manage his family responsibilities so that they do not interfere with his work efficiency. Consequently, as is seen here, male journalists are much more able than their female colleagues to participate in the after-hour "pub culture" and to benefit from the informal, mostly male networks created through these encounters.

Finally, I discovered that there is a fourth gender-typed arrangement that systematically discourages female journalists from entering the profession. This can be called the "masculinist" career model, which penalizes females, but not males, for work interruptions. The proportional Canadian gender survey shows that overall, 27% of all female journalists, but only 19% of the males at all levels of the newsroom hierarchy have interrupted their careers at least once. For females, these interruptions are overwhelmingly caused by the birth of a child, whereas the males listed study, travel, or relocation as their main reasons for the temporary interruptions of their journalistic careers. Interviews established that the *evaluation* of career interruptions is different for male and female personnel. For males, these interruptions are interpreted as career-*building* strategies, whereas for females, because they have to do with childrearing, they are interpreted as career *inhibitors.* Canadian cost–benefit analyses of women's career development show that all kinds of career interruptions, reduced hours, and part-time work have deleterious effects on the life earnings potential of women and on her potential for advancement (Lee, 1992). Doubtlessly these differential outcomes are closely connected to a traditional view of motherhood, which is also reflected in the miserly maternity leave policies in the United States, which, in contrast to Canada and Europe, offers only between 2 weeks and 3 months of paid family leave after childbirth.

All of these systemic gender biases, as argued earlier, tend to discourage females, but not males, from entering the journalism professions. Contrary to what is usually asserted, the profession consequently develops what Melin-Higgins and Djerf-Pierre (1998) call a nonhomogeneous "working" as well as "professional" culture. In it, female professionals and minorities are not equal participants, but are viewed as having "different" needs that are not as important as those of the male majority. Within this nonhomogeneous culture, the male understandings of professional practice are consequently, systematically advantaged and therefore dominant. Females within the working community, by reason of the work–family gender scripts, will not only have to develop different strategies for building their professional careers, but also create different understandings of how to perform their work roles in the heterosexual newsroom.

GENDERED WORK EXPECTATIONS
AS MANIFESTED IN NEWSROOM "CLIMATE"

Professional "climate" in the newsroom and the ways in which females are supposed to "enact" their working roles, are two additional attitudinal clusters that are culturally constructed and therefore gendered. According to Rosabeth Moss Kanter (1980) the "climate" at work refers to the spirit or atmosphere that prevails at a given time in the workplace and can be defined in terms of relations between colleagues. Although it was initially assumed that the newsroom's working climate was a relatively simple variable, which was conceived as a neutral "professional ethos," Monica Löfgren-Nilsson (1994) discovered that the workplace climate is made up of two aspects: the "perceived control" one exercises over one's work, as well as the "perceived community" that exists between colleagues. Both the levels of control and community, or egalitarianism, are not linearly, but complexly related in the hierarchically organized newsroom. How do the power imbalances affect female understandings of how they are expected to *enact* their roles? And, to what extent are female professionals aware of these power imbalances?

The newsroom is a professional setting where females and males tend to reproduce behaviors that are related to their gendered understandings of their social roles. The proportional gender survey requested that respondents rate the newsroom situation in terms of six indices that incorporate both the competitive and the cooperative dimensions of the work situation. Table 4.8 indicates that a larger proportion of female than male journalists consider work relations *very stressful* (78% to 69%). Both of these figures are remarkably high, indicating that 8 of 10 female and 7 of 10 male reporters

TABLE 4.8 Canadian Respondents' Ratings of Newsroom Climate by Gender (in percentages) (*N* = 124)

Statement	Females (*n* = 49) %	Males (*n* = 75) %	Total (*N* = 124) %	χ^2 Signif.
Very stressful work relations	78	69	72	n.s.
Strict operational control from management	36	58	50	0.0009
Good communication and relations among workers	87	83	84	n.s.
Tough competition between some individuals	57	58	57	n.s.
Shared values about professional matters	87	83	84	n.s.
Good opportunities for advancement	49	42	45	n.s.
Lack of support for one's own ideas	36	64	53	0.003

Que: How would you rate the following statements concerning the climate of the newsroom in which you work? Responses derived by combining the two highest categories on a 4-point scale (4 often, 3 sometimes, 2 rarely, 1 never). Based on gender sample shown in the appendix.

consider newsroom relations very stressful. Unfortunately, the generality of the question does not permit me to discriminate what aspects of the workplace trigger these responses, but the fact that both genders mention *tough competition between some individuals* (57% female to 58% male), indirectly confirms that the stresses of news work have to do with its confrontational style. Beyond that, Table 4.8 indicates that female reporters' second most important newsroom concern is *lack of support for their own ideas.* The significance test ($p = 0.003$) indicates that this is indeed a valid differential perception. Nearly two-thirds (64%) of female practitioners, but only about one third (34%) of males are of this opinion. Male incumbents, in contrast, decry their lack of autonomy when they mention *strict operational control by management* (58%). Overall, the significance tests (χ^2) confirm that competition as well as cooperation are part of the newsroom climate, yet, because they are perceived by both genders, there are no gender differences on most aspects.

Interestingly, there is virtual unanimity between the genders on the "cooperative" dimensions of newsroom functioning. Both females and males agree that they *share values on professional matters* (87% to 83%) and that they have *good communication and good relations* among each other (87% to 83%) indicating that the newsroom climate is indeed made up of both the competitive and the cooperative dimensions and that one needs to interview journalists under what circumstances one or the other set of values dominate. Beyond that, it is clear that female professionals are indeed aware that they work in a situation where power differentials affect their own understandings of their work roles. The comparative evidence shows that the circumstances in which gender becomes crucial is the lack of support for female editorial ideas (significant at $p < 0.003$), whereas male practitioners are more concerned about the control function of management (significant at $p = 0.0009$).

The importance of informal workplace practices in reproducing an exclusionary newsroom culture where females are conceived as interlopers, gave rise to studies investigating the nature of these exclusionary practices (Ross, 2000). Interviews with female television journalists in Sweden (Djerf-Pierre, 1998), British practitioners (Melin-Higgins & Djerf-Pierre, 1998), and German reporters (Klaus, 1998) all confirm that there are a number of practices through which male incumbents, irrespective of their competence, try to reinforce their power superiority. Three of these practices have by now been documented in both North America and Europe. The first is the unique "communicative style" between colleagues, which permeates the newsroom. Elisabeth Klaus (1998) refers to it as "Kumpanei," whereas Melin-Higgins and Djerf-Pierre (1998) call it "lockerroom humor," and other researchers refer to it as "banter." In Britain, this humorous banter focuses on team sports such as soccer, cricket, and rugby and also contains sexist and racist jokes. In Canada, it utilizes football and ice hockey as its vehicle, two sports in which women's teams are not yet widely legitimated. Because females are generally not as interested in contact sports, this informal communication practice turns out to be a not-too-subtle mechanism for excluding women reporters from informal workplace interactions and making them feel like outsiders.

Journalism's "competitive culture" is another symbolic practice that female respondents identified. It draws attention to the fact that story assignment is not cooperatively worked out, but struggled over. In such a setting, females have difficulties not only getting their story ideas approved, but also, as demonstrated earlier, in being assigned to high-profile beats and interview assignments. Louise Angerer (1995) of Austria comments that one third of all Austrian female journalists and 40% of the West Berlin press corps complained about this issue. Pierre Bourdieu (1991) explains this contest as an asymmetrical prestige exchange process, in which male incumbents are able to convert their *political capital* based on power, into *cultural capital,* namely desirable story assignments. In the heterosexual newsroom, this exchange process is tilted against female reporters, because their *cultural capital* will never be accepted as equal to that of the males in the hierarchy. Clearly, the gender typification of stories and sources places female practitioners into an attitudinal double bind, pitting their status against their competence (Klaus, 1998). One Canadian press reporter describes the competition for stories by remarking: "We have helped bring issues traditionally deemed 'women's issues' such as health, parenting and family or relationship concerns to the forefront. Not only do we ensure these issues get covered, we are getting them off the lifestyle pages and on to the front pages of newspapers. Although we still have a way to go."

A third and final aspect of newsroom culture, which has already been alluded to, also disadvantages women and thus helps to marginalize female reporters. It is the after-hour "pub" tradition. This extends the already long working day into the wee hours of the night and thus equates a reporter's "competence" with *total availability*. It is here that the informal male networks are created and that resource and personnel decisions are informally vetted. Rainer Paris (1991) calls this the building of a "Seilschaft," a term referring to those who are roped together in their quest for a mountain peak. Only female reporters without family obligations or children are able to participate in the drinking bouts, where the "old boys network" is created and sustained. The evidence shows that this network informally influences work assignments, affects promotions and also creates gendered work–role expectations, which are symbolized in film and elsewhere by the hard drinking, trench-coated reporter. Humphrey Bogart plays this character to perfection in *Casablanca.* Women become full members of this network only under special circumstances, as seen in the next section.

To test whether the gendered workplace expectations translate into differences in how females and males *enact* their newsroom roles, the proportional Canadian gender questionnaire asked journalists whether "women had to do more of the following work?" Six different domains of activity, all of them associated with "private-sphere" activities, where feminist researchers have suspected differential performance criteria, were presented to the group. Table 4.9 demonstrates that there is a surprising level of difference in the performance of three tasks: *comforting colleagues* (54% females to 19% males), *being a lightning rod* (41% females to 13% males), and *answering the telephone* (39% females to 8% males). Comparative responses additionally show that women are seven times as likely as men to *pick up after others* (22% to 3%) and four times as likely to *look for documents* (22% to 6%). On all of these tasks, the significance levels (χ^2) indicate that the differences are significant and that the quality of these significances vary. The gendered distribution of these tasks demonstrates that the heterosexual newsroom continues to assign the labor-intensive "relationship building," "mothering," and "housekeeping" roles to female professionals, even though both genders should be made responsible for the smooth functioning of newsroom relations and tasks. Only one traditional activity, that of *coffee making* has, over the years, become de-gendered, indicating that even in the newsroom, stereotypical task assignments can be shifted.

Table 4.9 Tasks that Canadian Respondents feel Females perform more than Males (by gender in percentages) (N = 124)

Task	Females (n = 49) %	Males (n = 75) %	Total (N = 124) %	χ^2 Signif.
Pick up after others	22	3	10	0.003
Answer the phone	39	8	19	<0.0001
Look for documents	22	6	12	0.023
Comfort colleagues	54	19	32	0.0006
Be a lightning rod	41	13	22	0.0017
Make or get coffee	6	3	5	n.s

Que: Do women have to do more of the following types of work? (Percentages derived by combining the two highest responses on a 4-point scale.) Based on gender sample shown in the appendix.

Another way of assessing the extent to which gender as an ideology structures the journalistic working situation is by comparing the organizational attitudes and practices in the newsroom. Six of these potentially discriminatory situations were submitted to the Canadian female and male respondent groups. The comparison in Table 4.10 demonstrates the expected: The two groups have very different levels of consciousness concerning discrimination. It shows that many more women than men acknowledge that they have frequently or sometimes been victims of discrimination. The three most prevalent forms of discrimination noted by almost half of all female journalists are "attitudinal": *male colleagues' attitude* (47% female to 4% male), *management's attitude* (47% female to 34% male), and *public's attitude* (41% female to 12% male). Among the male group, on the other hand, the top three situations in which discrimination is perceived have to do with "working practices." In decreasing order of importance they are *management's attitude* (34%), *discrimination in assignments* (28%), and *sitting on committees* (18%). Interestingly, not only the *domains* in which discrimination is perceived, but also the *strength* of these perceptions vary between the two groups of professionals. A larger proportion of female than male professionals are aware of the different kinds of discriminatory situations. This is to be expected in a working situation where a minority is ideologically gender-typed, but the majority is not. Despite these findings, only two of the perceived sources of discrimination are significant, male colleague's attitudes and the public's attitude toward female reporters. No won-

Table 4.10 Canadian Respondents Feelings of Discrimination on the Job by Gender (in percentages) (*N* = 124)

Sources of discrimination	Females (*n* = 49) %	Males (*n* = 75) %	Total (*N* = 124) %	χ^2 Signif
In assignments	39	28	33	n.s
Sources preferences	30	17	22	n.s
Sitting on committees	24	18	21	n.s
Management's attitude	47	34	40	n.s
Male colleague's attitude	47	4	23	<0.00001
Female colleague's attitude	20	12	16	n.s
Public's attitude	41	12	25	0.0016

Que: Do you feel you have ever been discriminated against in your present job (Percentages derived by combining the two highest responses on a 4-point scale). Based on gender sample in the appendix.

der that males, as a group, remain unaware of their own discriminatory workplace attitudes. Only 4% of male practitioners, in contrast to 47% of the female journalists, are aware that the workplace is imbued with and functions according to male norms. The same gender scripts also pervade the public's attitude, according to female reporters.

Despite increased recruitment of women into the field, the socially constructed gender scripts lead to differential behavior expectations for female and male newsroom personnel. They furthermore result in different work assignments as well as in different evaluation criteria by which the job performances of females and males are judged. The Canadian proportional gender survey demonstrates that workplace *expectations* continue to be unequal and gender-based. These gendered expectations force female professionals to *enact* their newsroom roles either in conformity with these expectations or in opposition to them. Even when they conform, the evidence shows, females are either systematically excluded through such negative symbolic practices as banter and competitive attitudes, or they have to do *more* of those types of tasks that are relationship and efficiency building for everyone on the job. Following the traditional gender script furthermore results in a double bind from which it is difficult to extract one self. Klaus (1998) notes that the more professional a female behaves, the more she offers opportunities for male projections to evaluate her as "unfeminine" or to denigrate her behavior as "masculine." All of these strategies are designed to reinforce the profession's male power structure.

Although gender researchers on both sides of the Atlantic are in agreement that increased numbers of women in the profession will not *by themselves* translate into changes in newsroom "climate" and practices, they do believe that a feminist-inspired politics, which strives for merit (based on equality of opportunity for all), will become more widely accepted in the 21st century, than it was a mere 30 years ago (Ross, 2000). I support this prediction on the grounds that the median age of Canadian professionals has decreased from 40 to 37 years since the 1980s. This means that the older generation of journalists, those over 55 years of age with a lower level of education, is beginning to retire from the field. What is increasingly left are a middle generation of Canadian practitioners who have, from the start, encountered female colleagues and have thus become sensitized to equity issues in the workplace.

RESPONSES TO GENDERED WORKPLACE PRESSURES

Despite the inequalities female journalists face in the newsroom setting, conventional questionnaire-based inquiries into the profession continue to proclaim that female professionals rarely feel discriminated on the job, and their

job satisfaction rates are consequently as high as those of their male colleagues. How can these findings be reconciled with the evidence that women
have less power in the hierarchy and are expected to perform their journalistic roles differently from their male colleagues? Part of the answer, as Table
4.8 indicated, lies in the fact that female professionals perceive this discrimination as *attitudinal*, whereas the male group understands it as having to do
with *working practices*. This suggests that if the surveys do not include gender as a relevant variable, they are comparing apples with oranges. Beyond
that, there are no simple answers to these complex queries, because gender
differences *alone* cannot explain the varied workplace strategies that female
journalists decide to employ in specific situations. Other relevant considerations, as we have seen, are social characteristics such as marital status, numbers of children, position in the newsroom, and supervisory responsibilities,
not to mention how each individual responds to the power structure. At
present, there are no studies that systematically interrelate these and other
social factors with gender. However, Scandinavian and German researchers
have begun to explore female responses to the power structure at work
through in-depth interviews, a strategy I also followed in the Canadian gender survey.

Scandinavian researchers have documented three types of coping
strategies that female professionals develop, depending on their status and
the type of organization in which they are employed. The females who
inhabit a superior position in the newsroom tended to adapt by becoming
"one of the boys." As such, these females become "honorary males" and are
initiated into the "sherpa" group, which informally "runs" the newsroom.
Their membership is not based on competence or gender, but on the organizational position they occupy in the newsroom hierarchy. Many unmarried journalists from the older generation, were co-opted in this way and
were therefore quite unaware of the informal gender barriers in their working environment, as seen in Chapter 2. Such women frequently proclaim
that they made their way up the career ladder and succeeded through sheer
hard work, like their male colleagues. Their presence in the informal power
group thus strengthens and legitimizes the status quo (Klaus, 1998). These
female journalists furthermore embrace the male values they see around
them and often employ the "objectivist" reporting style, which they learned
on the job.

Another way of adapting to the unequal newsroom culture, is to object
and to choose what Melin-Higgins and Djerf-Pierre (1998) call a "mission"
approach. Such female reporters follow an ethic of "making a difference to
people and society." One might call this group of professionals journalists
with a "feminist" outlook, even though they need not be overt members of
the women's movement. More is said about this in upcoming chapters. What
these women have in common is that they conceive of their reporting role in

light of equity criteria and are concerned with understanding and highlighting women's unique social existence. As political reporters these professionals explore both the social advantages and the barriers that female and male
incumbents face in local and national elections. Or they might highlight the
public health aspects of such "private" issues as rape and child abuse.
Because this group of professionals is often perceived as having developed a
female counter culture in the newsroom, their capabilities are frequently
undervalued and they face substantial promotion difficulties. A final strategy for female journalists is to "opt out" of the competitive newsroom situation and its long hours of work by becoming freelancers. This group of
females and males tends to want to combine work with children. They additionally wish to do more critical and in-depth analysis than is possible on
tight newsroom schedules (Melin-Higgins & Djerf-Pierre, 1998). Exactly
when and under what circumstances female professionals opt for one of the
three, or yet other coping strategies, requires further research.

The extent to which Canadian journalists chose to opt out and become
freelancers is extremely difficult to evaluate for two reasons. The first is that
the Canadian national census does not cover this professional option, and
second, it appears that freelancers rarely join professional associations. My
organization survey of Canadian female and male journalists (see the appendix) discovered that there were six times as many freelancers in the Canadian
press (298) as in television (54) in 1995. This means that they constituted
about 9% of the newspaper labor force of 3,451, but only a minuscule 4%
of that in television (1,305). The gender ratio among newspaper freelancers
is about equal: 53% women and 47% men, but in television, women are in
the overwhelming majority and constitute 74% of this group. These statistics suggest that the option of freelancing is not chosen by a great number of
female professionals. Clearly, more work needs to be done on this question,
in order to illuminate whether there are differences in social and work characteristics between the two groups and to determine the circumstances
under which females and males choose to become freelancers.

What this admittedly partial evidence indicates is that the majority of
female professionals *do not* choose to follow the two extreme alternatives to
mitigate newsroom inequalities: namely, becoming "one of the boys" or
"opting out" of the newsroom culture. Most carry on as though they were
equal partners in the heterosexual newsroom and use their gender *strategi-
cally* and merely under certain circumstances. This indicates that one cannot
speak of a simple bifurcated "female" or "male" journalistic role conception,
but has to acknowledge that human beings are *active agents* in the construction of their professional personas. Consequently, both females and males
fall back on their gendered socialization experiences to explain their professional behavior to themselves and to others. Yet, because they are symbolically marked as "different," it is easier for females and other minorities to

become aware of their status discrepancies in the male-dominated newsroom. Interviews in both Germany and Canada reveal that there are situations in which female journalists put their subordinate and conflictual status as "female" to strategic use, to gain otherwise inaccessible information. Klaus (1998) gives examples where a legal reporter compensated for her exclusion from the male only pub sessions by taking specific colleagues aside during working hours and appealing to their supposedly superior legal expertise to explain a court situation to her. This yielded hitherto unrevealed reportorial material, and provided her with a new angle for her story. Another "scooped" her colleagues through superior social connections and an invitation to an exclusive wedding, from which the press was otherwise barred (Klaus, 1998). In Canada I was told that the role scripts of "buddy"and "motherly confidant," were sometimes used by female professionals to acquire information not otherwise shared. A female reporter, furthermore noted that she combined her professional with her social instincts and often queried male politicians on their personal feelings about public issues, a strategy rarely employed by her male colleagues. These examples indicate that the bifurcated notion of a *gender-specific* journalistic role conception is an oversimplified notion, which can no longer be entertained. Professional role identities, just like gender identities, are not fixed but malleable. They are not something we "have" but something we "create" and change, depending on the social and the work environments in which we find ourselves.

chapter 5

THE "GLASS CEILING" AND ITS EFFECTS ON WOMEN'S MEDIA CAREERS IN CANADA AND THE UNITED STATES

Throughout the past few years, attentive North American readers have encountered articles entitled "Cracks in the Glass Ceiling," "Giving Women the Business" (Jones, 1997), or "Screen Queens"(Saunders, 1998). All of these purport to document that women are slowly moving into the management ranks of Fortune 500 industries, and that they are participating in newspaper and broadcast management. At the close of the millennium, three women, CBC's Phyllis Platt, Susanne Boyce of CTV, and Loren Mawhinney at Global, decided what shows went on the air in Canada's largest television networks. What is the import of these articles and are they signaling a real change in industrial and media management? More specifically, are these articles in fact the harbingers of change predicted in Chapters 2 and 3, which document that Canadian female professionals now make up 28% of all newspaper and a full 37% of all broadcasting staff and are thus poised to move into middle and upper management jobs? Unfortunately, this chapter shows that these staff gains do not automatically translate into trouble-free promotion for women and minorities into the management suits of industrial and media corporations. A U.S. Senate Committee on women and the workplace, convened by President Bush senior, discovered in 1991 that despite workplace gains and the fact that females comprised 61% of all Fortune 500 industries, they held only 4.6% of corporate officer positions (Senate Committee on Labor and Human Resources, 1992). In Canada, the February 2000 *Report on Business* found similar discrepancies. It reported that two thirds of the top 500 Canadian companies had no women directors at all and that women were holding only 6.2% of board seats in the final one third of companies (Mallick, 2000). Even in crown corporations that have to comply with federal equity regulations, women constituted a mere 8.7% of the executive category in the federal public service in 1987 and have been making only slow gains since then (Morgan, 1988).

Although the term *glass ceiling* is widely used, it covers a variety of attitudinal and social processes that are neither well understood nor well defined. On the surface, the term seems to refer to a barrier through which women and minorities can "see" what lies ahead in their careers, but they cannot in fact "attain" management-level positions. The U.S. Department of Labor defines the term as "those artificial barriers based on attitudinal and organizational bias, that prevent qualified individuals from advancing upward in their organization into management level positions" (Women and the workplace: The Glass Ceiling, 1992, p. 46). Even this definition, it turns out, is too broad to be useful because it masks the specific behaviors, practices, and attitudes that women encounter in their attempts to reach managerial positions. The definition furthermore lumps together three social practices, which were documented in Chapter 4. These include the fact that there are barriers to advancement at *every level* of the hierarchy, not only at the top and that there may also be differential *speeds* with which females and males are promoted, as well as differential monetary *benefits* associated with promotion for the two genders. Also not included in the terminology, as documented in Chapter 4, are gendered social expectations for female journalists, concerning how to balance work with family roles (Pleck, 1984). The most crucial outcome of these expectations for North American media professionals is that they have to accept the elastic definition of the "working day" historically developed by male professionals, as a *norm,* even though it has higher social costs for females only. Under Norwegian law, in contrast, family needs are recognized as the responsibility of both genders and the "working day" is therefore statutorily limited to 7.5 hours, leveling the social costs of a media career for both female and male professionals.

THE "GLASS CEILING" IN THE CANADIAN AND U.S. NEWSPAPER INDUSTRIES

To determine where the glass ceiling is located in Canadian daily newspaper management proves to be a difficult task for two reasons. To begin with, there is ambiguity about what constitutes the "top" editorial position, because a variety of editing titles are used, especially in large circulation papers. Yet, there is agreement that editor, executive editor, and editor-in-chief are counted as top positions. More difficult to unravel, according to Lois L. Wolfe (1989), is whether assistant and associate editor's positions rank over or under those of managing editors. The American Society of Newspaper Editors (ASNE) seems to place managing editors on the third level, a practice that I follow here in order to ensure comparability with U.S. figures. The second problem in determining the location of the glass ceiling, has to do with the size at which a group is considered to be a "token" minority, without impact on the existing power structure. Epstein (1992) notes that what she calls "boundary maintenance" mechanisms contain physical as well as symbolic processes. What this means is that cultural designations (like gender or ethnicity) are not necessarily more powerful than organizational- or social-psychological designations, but rather that there is an *interaction* between all three, which tends to reinforce their combined effects (Epstein, 1992). This raises the following question: At what *degree* of presence in upper management positions women are no longer viewed as "tokens," but as threats to the power structure? Sociological investigations have placed this boundary at one third of a given group, suggesting that at this point a minority can change the operating rules by making strategic deals with the majority. This means that one can use a figure of less than 30% in a particular management position as a rough indicator of the existence of a glass ceiling.

Table 5.1, which is based on the organizational survey of the daily press, indicates that although the top editor-in-chief position is still out of bounds, the Canadian glass ceiling has been raised to the editor's level since the 1970s. According to the table there were 22 female editor-in-chiefs in 1995, compared with 173 males, representing 13% of the total group in this position. The second management level, according to Table 5.1, was made up of three titles: assistant, associate, and editors. Here, females have made the largest inroads. In 1995, there were 272 females and 703 males in this position, constituting a 39% female representation and showing that they were poised to move to the top in the 21st century. Even the managing editor's level, where there were 33 females and 109 males for a ratio of about 30% overall, showed progress. And on the lowest or desk head level, there were 35 females to 95 males, for a ratio of about 37% females overall, enough to make a difference in decision making. Why was the Canadian pace of promotion in the daily press slower than that in broadcasting? Two types of answers have been offered. The first notes that in the 1980s, concentration in press ownership led to the closing of 76 of the smallest properties, as well as to management rationalization and circulation reductions (Dornan, 1996). The elimination of positions suggests that qualified female managers were available to fill some of the remaining slots in the metropolitan papers, which saw the greatest circulation gains. The comparison with organizational data from 1975 shows additionally that females who had only a 10% representation at the desk head level in the mid-1970s finally were able to enter the management suits (Robinson, 1981).

Table 5.1 Female Representations in Canadian Newspaper Management in 1995 (by circulation in percentages) ($N = 1,442$)

Circulation thousands (K)	Small Circulation <50K		Medium Circulation 50–100K		Large Circulation >100K		Totals
Position	Staff No.	% F	Staff No.	% F	Staff No.	% F	F/M No.
Editor-in-chief	124	8	31	10	40	13	22/173
Editor assist./Assoc.	297	26	124	19	554	31	272/703
Managing editor	46	41	34	20	62	11	33/109
Editorial chiefs Desk heads	30	8	17	6	83	28	35/95

Before inquiring into what female managers experienced as tokens in the executive suite, it is important to peruse the second portion of Table 5.1, which breaks down the gross management position figures by a newspaper's circulation. As demonstrated in Chapter 2, this breakdown indicates where female managers had the best opportunities for promotion. Table 5.1 indicates that women were not only promoted across the board, but that they could now claim near parity in small circulation papers in two positions: that of editors and assistant editors, as well as managing editors. In these management positions, they constituted 26% and 41% of all incumbents. Females did least well in medium circulation (50,000–100,000) papers, where they represented only 20% of the editorial group. In metropolitan dailies, located in cities like Toronto, Montreal, and Vancouver, there was only one position, that of editor, where Canadian female journalists cracked the glass ceiling. Here, they held 31% of all editorial positions, but only 11% of managing editors. From the perspective of career strategies, this means that female print journalists did best in small and large circulation management in the past 20 years where they have pushed the glass ceiling up by a full two levels. The reason for this, Chapter 2 suggests, is the fact that in the small circulation papers, managerial levels were frequently combined to save money and in the large metropolitan dailies, younger highly educated females were hired, who have moved up the management ladder as fast as their male counterparts.

The U.S. data in Table 5.2 show how Canadian female newspaper managers compared with their U.S. counterparts in 1995, enabling me to illuminate the glass-ceiling phenomenon from an additional, rarely considered

Table 5.2 Female Representation in Canadian and U.S. Newspaper Management (in percentages)

Circulation thousands (K)	Canada 1995 (N = 1,442)			U.S. 1989 (N = 3,055)[a]		
	Small <50K %	Medium 50-100K %	Large >100K %	Small <50K %	Medium 50-100K %	Large >100K %
Editor in chief	8	10	13	0	0	0.8
Editor & assist./assoc.	26	19	31	14	0.7	0.9
Managing editor	41	20	11	16	0.8	13
Editorial chiefs, news, lifestyles, sport, etc.	8	6	28	13	0.8	0.5
Staff Total: F/M	156/341	76/130	210/529	294/1606	30/348	103/674

[a]*U.S. source: Lois Wolfe (1989).*

perspective, namely that of national differences. Aggregate figures for the top three positions show that Canadian newspaper journalists were ahead of their U.S. sisters in managerial clout. There was an average of 10% female editors-in-chief in Canada in all circulation types versus a minuscule 0.8% in the United States. The same discrepancies were found in all of the other management levels, where the U.S. figures were about half of those in Canada. At the editor and assistant/associate editor levels, Canadian females held an average of slightly less than one third (27%) of these positions, whereas their U.S. sisters registered only 14% in small circulation dailies with proportions of less than 1% in the other two circulation categories. On the third management level, that of managing editors, Canada's female proportion was between 11% and 41%, depending on circulation, whereas it ranged between 13% and 16% in the United States (Marzolf, 1993). These wide variations in managerial clout are surprising and difficult to explain. The hypothesis that the discrepancy is due to the 6-year time difference in data collection is invalidated by the fact that the global figures for "supervisory" personnel, which include all of the top positions, were roughly the same in both countries. In 1995, females held 33% of all supervisory positions in Canada and 31% in the United States (ASNE, 1997). More probably, greater unionization and more effective equity legislation have propelled Canadian females toward the top, whereas the Reagan administration ceased to pursue equity issues in the United States in the 1980s. The next chapter explores this issue in greater detail.

The U.S. data in Table 5.2 demonstrate another interesting point about national differences in career advancement. In contrast to Canada, where females did better in both small and large circulation dailies, U.S. female print journalists had better promotion chances in small circulation papers only, where they constituted 14% of the editor and 16% of the managing editors positions. Surprisingly, in large circulation U.S. papers, women made inroads in only one position, that of the managing editor, where they constituted 13% of the group. Above that, they continued to be tokens, with infinitesimal representations of 0.5% among editor-in-chiefs and 0.9% among editors (Ogan, 1983). This suggests that the U.S. glass ceiling is still functioning as a substantial barrier, which protects the press' top management suites from women and minorities. Surprisingly, similar newspaper management conditions pertain on the European continent, where females are also finding it difficult to enter the top ranks in the six countries for which data are available. Why this difference between the Canadian and U.S. managerial situations? A 1998 study by the Media Management Center at Northwestern University, which surveyed 228 female senior managers at newspapers with circulations of 85,000 or more, provides some initial insights (Hemlinger, 2001). Respondents pointed out that newspapers had been more passive than broadcast stations about diversity. Furthermore, they decried the fact that they had failed to address work–family balance issues and failed to recognize that female managers are an asset newspapers cannot afford to lose (Bulkeley, 2004). The concluding section of this chapter discusses these matters in greater detail and recommends strategies for corporate and individual action.

Table 5.3 extends national comparisons from North America to western Europe. These figures come from a 1997 study by Margaret Lünenborg (1997), which compared the status of female and male journalists in Germany, Denmark, Spain, and Italy. To achieve comparability between the different editorial structures in the four countries, Lünenborg unfortunately collapses what we have called the second and third management levels, which include managing editors and editors. This means that the comparisons are only indicative, but despite this, they highlight a number of additional perspectives concerning the variability of the glass-ceiling phenomenon in different societies and how long it takes females to move from middle into upper newspaper management positions. The first observation is that the glass ceiling is manifest in Europe, just as it is in North America, indicating that the sidelining of females is practiced in all countries and constitutes the greatest challenge to female career progress in the highly developed world. This is a very important discovery because it has been argued that countries with socially liberal policies and strong unionization, like Denmark and Sweden, would favor female managerial progress. The comparative Table 5.3 demonstrates that this is not true. There are no female newspaper publishers

Table 5.3 Female Representation in North American and European
Newspaper Management (in percent females)

Position	Canada (1995) %	U.S.[a] (1989) %	Germany[b] (1997) %	Denmark[b] (1997) %	Spain[b] (1997) %	Italy[b] (1997) %
Editor/Publisher[c]	10	6	0	0	0	0
Editors (assist. & assoc.)	25	14	N/A	N/A	N/A	N/A
Managing editor	24	15	19	15	8	13
Editorial chiefs[d]	14	13	20	18	20	14

[a]*U.S. figures: Lois L. Wolfe (Jan. 1989, p.10).*
[b]*European figures from Lünenborg (1997).*
[c]*Editor/publisher include executive and senior editor.*
[d]*Editorial chiefs include city ed; news; editorial page; features; lifestyle; etc.*

or editors-in-chief in any of the European countries and they thus lack even the "token" status, which they have achieved in North America. Only one German alternative newspaper, the *taz,* had a female editor-in-chief at the turn of the century, according to Gisela Brackert (1992). This means that the unique managerial talents of a Katherine Graham at *The Washington Post* and a Joan Fraser at the *Montreal Gazette* in the 1990s, have not yet been acknowledged on the continent.

Second, the European figures demonstrate that the glass ceilings are located at the *bottom* of the managerial hierarchy, at the level of what we have called editorial chiefs, such as city editors, news editors, and editorial page editors. At this level, Germany and Spain register 20% females, Denmark 18%, and Italy 14%. This means that in contrast to North America, European female print journalists are just beginning their climb into the managerial ranks. Their glass ceilings are located two to three positions below the Canadian levels. Lünenborg cautions that this global figure hides the fact that female heads direct gender-typed content areas such as lifestyles, feature, and entertainment desks (Lünenborg, 1997). At the managing editor's level, furthermore, Table 5.3 indicates Canada has the highest rate of female representation at 24%, with Germany, Denmark the United States, and Italy in the middle (between 13% and 19%) and Spain at the bottom, with a female representation of only 8%.

Lünenborg's interviews with European personnel, to understand why there are so few females in newspaper management, elicited heavily gendered perceptions among female and male personnel. This is illustrated by the fact that even the egalitarian Danish males were of the opinion that there was a "lack of qualified female candidates" available for promotion. Chapter 4 demonstrates that this is a typical sexist response by a member of the gendered majority. German and Danish female respondents were closer to the mark, opining that the inordinate length of the 10-hour reporting day was probably at fault because it made it impossible to combine work with family needs. Consequently, the older generation female professionals did not seek management jobs and the requisite pool of mid-level female managers failed to materialize (Lünenborg, 1997). The strong gender bias in the Italian journalistic profession, in contrast, is explained by the fact that too few female recruits entered the profession until the 1970s, and that those who had chosen to become journalists, had accommodated to the pervasive sexism in their newsroom. Younger Italian professionals did not begin to raise gender-equity issues in the workplace until 1993, 10 years after their German and a full 25 years after their North American colleagues (Lünenborg, 1997). This is remarkable considering that equity legislation has been on the books of the European Economic Community (EU) since the 1957 Treaty of Rome. In Spain, finally, it appears that female professionals *expect* to have their journalism careers curtailed when children are born. This country is one of the few that has not promulgated laws to ameliorate work–family conflicts, nor does it provide training facilities for the professional improvement of its newspaper staff (Lünenborg, 1997, p. 197).

If social legislation and progressive political systems have not aided women in reaching management positions in Europe, there must also be informal barriers restricting their promotion. These, according to Lünenborg (1997) are the anti-female attitudes of the male-dominated "old boys" networks in the press of western Europe. Her interviews have demonstrated that the binary "gendering process" acts as a systemic "position marker" for female, but not for male career expectations. I demonstrate in Chapter 6 that female journalists were unthinkingly classified as "not having management potential" on the European continent, where equity initiatives failed to bring about change until the early 1990s (Lünenborg, 1997). The ambivalence of European print professionals is understandable, considering their one fifth (20%) representation in the lowest management ranks, which has not yet enabled them to change the working practices of the heterosexual newsroom. Three of these working practices were singled out by female respondents, who decried them as gender stereotyping. They are what Chapter 4 called the newsroom's "confrontational culture"; the profession's unreasonable time requirements; as well as its lack of transparency in the promotion process. The newsroom culture presently interprets "competence" as "total availability" and is based on the *hours* spent at work, rather than the *quality* of the work produced. As we have already demonstrated in

Chapter 4, this requirement favors male personnel, who need not make time concessions for family responsibilities. In addition, female professionals decry the lack of courses for professional upgrading, including management training on the continent. As a result, females who frequently have more scholarity, have difficulty demonstrating and legitimating their managerial potential. And finally, European female journalists question the need for a 10-hour working day to produce a newspaper, when technological innovations like databases and software programs have drastically reduced the time required for news production (Lünenborg, 1997). All together, these cultural practices disadvantage female practitioners and reinforce the existing and unequal power structure.

THE "GLASS CEILING" IN THE CANADIAN AND U.S. TELEVISION INDUSTRIES

To explore the glass-ceiling phenomenon in broadcasting turns out to be even more difficult than to tackle the issue in the print industry because the management structure is even less well-defined. This results from the fact that the hierarchical organization of the television newsroom is not nearly as uniform as that in print. Vernon Stone (1997) mentions that there is great variation not only in the number of positions, but also in the responsibilities assigned to these positions between stations. These differences are particularly marked between small news outfits of less than 10 people and those with 50 or more personnel. In the small stations, the managing editor position is often absent and an executive producer may handle these duties. Even in large stations, however, the managing editor may also serve as the assistant news director or vice versa. As a result of these position variations, promotion is also not linear from a defined bottom to a defined top status. Interviews show that potential steps in the hierarchy may be skipped for appointees to a news directorship, depending on perceived "qualifications." This practice results in a promotion process that is far from transparent and leaves lots of room for the "old boys network" to be activated. The description and analysis of the glass ceiling in U.S. broadcasting is finally made more difficult because there has been no systematic scrutiny of gender issues. Even Stone's (1997) article "Women Breaking the 'Glass Ceiling' in TV News" continues to define gender biologically and thus fails to raise questions about the gendered power differentials in the newsroom and how these might affect female promotion into management positions and their differential pay.

My Canadian organizational survey, which places "gender" at the center of the research design, is able to trace the interrelationships between gender and *social* characteristics like marital status and children, as well as such *cultural* features as North American society's expectations about how females and males are supposed to combine their personal with their professional lives. Furthermore, it is sensitive to the fact that the professional career paths of females need to be constructed differently and that the male model should not be used as the norm from which the female is perceived as deviating. The refusal to embrace this negative binary opposition stance clarifies the fact that criteria like "age" and "experience" in terms of which females are typically found to be "wanting," are in fact *not neutral,* but male-privileging criteria. Experience measured as numbers of years in a professional position will always disadvantage a female broadcaster, who has had to take leaves for childbearing, which as Chapter 3 showed, diminishes her total working credits. It also fails to account for the fact that females may encounter difficulties in career planning because of marital obligations. On the broadcast management level, a more relevant, as well as neutral criterion for experience would be documented "skill enhancement," which could include management courses or other relevant work activities. What emerges from these considerations is an understanding that the glass ceiling is not about demographics alone, but about power and deep-seated gender biases. It furthermore concerns the top managerial elite's ability to exclude equally qualified candidates who differ from themselves merely by virtue of their gender or their race.

Table 5.4, which compares female representation in Canadian television management, indicates that four different positions are involved in the management of the television news production process. They are the news direc-

TABLE 5.4 Female Representation in Canadian TV Management 1995
(by market size and position) (*N* = 486)

Market Size Thousands (K) Position	Small TV Stations <100K Staff No.	% F	Medium TV Stations 100–500K Staff No.	% F	Large TV Stations >500K Staff No.	% F	F/M No.
News director	20	10	32	28	107	35	49/110
Producer/Director	15	13	23	22	155	46	74/119
General manager	2	0	10	10	24	49	14/22
Executive Producer	40	20	18	11	40	18	17/81
Staff sub-total	77		83		326		154/332

tor, producer/director, general manager, and executive producer. Of these, the general manager position is prevalent in only about one third of the stations, as the small staff numbers (36) indicate. It has already been noted that station size affects the management structure of the press, and this analysis has additionally demonstrated that females had a better chance at promotion in small, rather than large media institutions. To test this finding for the Canadian broadcast markets, these were divided into three groups roughly following the circulation sizes of daily newspapers. They are small markets with less than 100,000 viewers, medium with up to 499,000, and large metropolitan centers with up to a few million viewers. Table 5.4 demonstrates that contrary to the print experience, Canadian female broadcasters had a much better chance to enter the management cadres in the large and medium, rather than the small television stations. To our great surprise we found furthermore that the glass ceiling had just about been eliminated in Canada's largest broadcast stations, where females held an unbelievable half of two of the top three positions. In the largest markets, 35% of all news directors, as well as 46% of the producer/directors and a full 49% of general managers were female. Only the executive producer post eluded them, but even here almost one in five (18%) of the staff were female, indicating that the television management suites are full of qualified candidates of both genders in large markets.

Table 5.4 demonstrates that females were nearly at the one-third influence level in the top two positions in medium-sized markets. Within the hierarchy, they moved into a solid one quarter of all news director (28%) and producer/director (22%) positions. The absence of female representation on the general manager level (10%) results partly from the fact that medium-sized TV stations eliminate this position or combine it with others. Consequently, the executive producer position, Table 5.4 shows, became more gender-typed and had only 11% female participation. Finally, it is surprising to note that female professionals did worse in the management structure of small market stations. Not only did they have the smallest share of total management positions in small station staffs, an average of 10%, but they also had only a 10% and 13% representation in the top positions. Surprisingly, however, female staff began to penetrate the coveted executive producer suites, where they filled one-fifth (20%) of these positions in 1995.

Exactly the opposite trend seemed to be operating in the much larger U.S. television market, although it is impossible to make an exact comparison because these types of statistics are lacking. Vernon Stone's long-range surveys note that even though females began to move into the broadcast profession in increasing numbers in the 1980s, they were unable to penetrate the management ranks. According to his data, females garnered an astounding 36% of all broadcast jobs in both television and radio between 1979 and 1994, yet the management glass ceiling continued firmly in place. Between

1981 and 1986, female news directors grew from less than 10% of the management staff, to a miserly 14% (Stone, 1987). After that, they had 5 excellent growth years, in which they reached the 24% mark by 1996. Interestingly, these news director positions were, however, not located in the large affiliate markets (9%), but disproportionately concentrated in the small independent markets (41%), a segregation pattern that did not begin to change until the late 1990s. Although U.S. female broadcasters, just as their sisters in print, had a better chance to advance in small markets, Stone claims they were distributed across stations of all sizes and located in all markets. Yet, by 1996 only 18% of female news directors were at independent stations compared with 13% for the males. This is partially a result of differences in staff supervision sizes between the genders (Stone, 1994, 1997). In 1987, female supervisors headed a median staff of only 9 people, whereas male TV news directors were in charge of about three times that number, that is, a median of 24 people (Stone, 1987). By 1996, females supervised more than half (17) the median numbers of personnel, to their male colleagues' 26 (Stone, 1997). With these supervisory changes came increased access for females into the general manager position, where, in 1995, women now held 10% of these positions.

What does all of this evidence tell us about the glass-ceiling phenomenon in U.S. broadcasting, as compared with the Canadian situation in the mid-1990s? Three observations come to mind and are illustrated in the following tables. First of all, the comparative evidence in Table 5.5 indicates that the glass ceiling continued to exist in both countries, but that it moved up to the assistant news directorship, just one level below the top in Canada but not in the United States. After 30 years of recruitment, Canadian female staffers filled almost one third (30%) of the total pool of desk heads in 1995, which means 49 of the 110 staff. More importantly, Canadian females also reached the 30% level in one position, news directorships, which was similar to the U.S. figure of 27%.

The second observation is that the gender barrier seems to have been more deeply entrenched in the United States, than in Canada. In contrast to their southern sisters, Canadian female broadcasters reached virtual parity in the most important, large television markets (see Table 5.4). Females now constituted well over one third of news directors (36%) and almost one half of all producer/directors (46%) and general managers (49%) in large stations, guaranteeing promotion to the top. Although detailed U.S. evidence is lacking, Table 5.5 suggests that on both sides of the border, TV women have an alternative route to success in the performance sector. In the program presentation sector, females held 40% of all positions in Canada and 45% in the United States. Stone's U.S. reviews show that this trend began in 1976, when one in every five U.S. anchors was a woman. By 1989, anchors were 39% female and the trend leveled off at close to parity in the 1990s, when

Table 5.5 Female Representation in Canadian and U.S. Television Production (in percentages)

Position	1995 Canada N = 1,305 Female %	1997 U.S. N = 1,622[a] Female %
Reporters	34	52
Program presentation	54	54
9% announcer/hosts	(40)	(45)
10% reporters	(52)	(49)
Desk heads	30	22
News directors/Ass. dir.	30	27
Executive producers/Producers	18	12
Subtotal: F/M	154/326	459/797
Technical: M	N/A	330
Total Staff: F/M	486/819	459/1,127

[a]*U.S. data from Stone (2001).*

the Federal Communications Commission (FCC) began to ignore ethnic and gender-equity concerns which Commissioner Fowler had introduced during his chairmanship (Stone, 1990).

A third observation concerns the diminishing salary differentials between female and male staff. Stone comments that as news became more central to station profits in the United States, salaries increased for the people charged directly with bringing in the ratings. At a growing number of stations, anchors were paid more like entertainment stars and news directors like impresarios. Median salaries overall increased by market size in the 1990s, providing substantial differences in take-home pay. In small markets, the rank-and-file anchors in the early 1990s averaged between $19,500 and $28,100. At medium-sized stations, the average was $34,100, with the really big money being paid to anchors in major markets like New York, Chicago, and Los Angeles. Here, the anchor salaries ranged between $104,000 and $197,000 (Stone, 1990). These averages, however, hide substantial salary differences between female and male personnel, amounting to a median of 16%, less income for female professionals, according to Stone.

Why should these salary differentials continue to persist into the 21st century, even though pay-equity legislation has been introduced in both Canada and the United States? The conventional answer is that female incumbents earn less because they have less seniority and because they are younger. Stone's television pay analysis demonstrates that years of experience emerges from multiple regression analyses as the strongest predictor of salary level. In second place are position held, size of the news operation, and finally age and market size, all of which are significant at the $p = 0.001$ level (Stone, 2000a). Stone, like many U.S. researchers, concludes: "TV news-women's median salaries were found to be 16% less than men's. But within categories of age and experience, the differences were not only smaller but also mixed. Women earned less than men in some categories and more in others. As multiple regression has told us, it pretty much evens out" (Stone, 2000a, p. 2). This sanguine conclusion fails to point out that gender is an *interactive* variable that reinforces the negative effects of gendered differences in years of experience, position held, and market size. Stone's aggregate salary analysis shows that female TV staff with up to 5 years and/or 5 to 10 years of experience, drew better pay than their male contenders by 3% and 6% respectively, whereas those who were older and had been in the field longer than 10 to 16 years, were paid lower median salaries of -1% and -3%, respectively. Much of this has to do with the higher educational qualifications of younger female professionals, according to Canadian data. In the United States, young female recruits (aged 20 to 29) are paid 5% less than their male colleagues, whereas they draw equal salaries in the 30- to 39-year age group and made 8% more by the time they were age 40 and up (Stone, 2000a, p. 3). Unfortunately, Stone has not indicated how these median pay scales vary by market size. Other researchers, however, have corroborated that U.S. female personnel, like their Canadian counterparts, have better pay chances in the larger markets. Beyond that, Smith, Fredin, and Nardone (1993) agree with Stone that systemic pay discrimination has been significantly reduced by equity legislation in the United States, but qualify this by pointing out that certain female personnel groups (office and wardrobe) continue to receive less pay and that 2% of this statistically significant variance is gender-related.

CONCLUSIONS: GENDERING AND PROMOTION

The comparisons of Canada's two media industries, the daily press and television, with those in the United States and western Europe demonstrate that barriers to the promotion of female staff exist in all countries and that gender combines with and reinforces these barriers. This glass-ceiling phenomenon is, however, not as uniform as the metaphor suggests. The comparative evidence shows that the barriers are located at different managerial levels in the daily press and in the broadcast industries and that they vary as well by country. In the Canadian newspaper industry, the barrier moved up two levels to the directing editor's level in small and large circulation papers. Although females were still a minority of 12% in the top editor-in-chief positions, they were gaining ground on the second level. Here they held 26% of the country's assistant/associate editorships in 1995. Beyond that, females did almost equally well in large circulation papers, where they were 31% of all editors and 28% of editorial chiefs. In the United States, the situation was quite different. Here, Table 5.2 demonstrates, they held a very small 13% and 16% of the four management positions in the small circulation papers only and were virtually excluded from management positions in U.S. medium and metropolitan dailies. This means that U.S. female newspaper managers remained in a heavily "skewed" position (less than 15%), unable to affect policy. The very rough European comparisons (Table 5.3) suggest that female print journalists on the continent shared the same fate as their U.S. counterparts. They, too, continued to be excluded from the top management jobs, although they made progress into middle-level management and into the offices of content chiefs.

A second conclusion emerging from the sector comparisons is the fact that female promotional opportunities were better in broadcasting than in daily print in Canada. To our great surprise, we found (see Table 5.4) that although here too the glass ceiling protects the very top or news director's position, female broadcasters made impressive inroads in both medium and large television markets. In the former, they held a healthy 28% of all news directorships and in the latter they approach parity, in the producer/director (46%) category. The depth of their managerial influence is further attested by the fact that 49% of all managing editorships in large TV markets were female, even though the executive producer level still eluded them.

Unfortunately, there is no fully comparable data to determine the situation in the United States. However, two surveys by Stone (1997, 2001) corroborate the Canadian findings and confirm that U.S. females also had better promotion opportunities in the electronic, than the daily print media. These data suggest that the glass ceiling was probably located at the executive producer and news director levels, as in Canadian broadcasting, even though Stone collapsed these two position statistics. Beyond that, Table 5.5 provides corroboration that about 40% of all Canadian and about the same percentage of U.S. female personnel (45%) were involved in program presentation as announcer/hosts, whereas only 13% of all males were found in this domain in the two countries. Instead, male broadcasters were dominant in the technical desk head domains of photography and video as well as sports and weather, which employed 22% of all U.S. male broadcasters. In contrast, females were dominant in such "soft" news areas as lifestyles and the environment, which garner less pay. It is difficult to account for the much less polarized professional work situation in Canada, than in the United States, except to mention that Canada never introduced affirmative action quotas similar to those advanced by the FCC. Instead, Canadian equity legislation uses crown corporations (among them banks and the CBC) as testing grounds for advancing qualified women, aboriginal people, and visible minorities into positions where they are traditionally underrepresented. To fulfill this mandate, the CBC set up an Employment Equity Office in 1986, although it had begun to monitor women's status in the corporation as early as 1975. In 1994, the CBC articulated its corporate point of view by noting that it does not practice reverse discrimination; it instead believes in *reversing discrimination* (CBC Equity Newsletter, 1994, italics added). The effectiveness of these initiatives is assessed in greater detail in the concluding section of this chapter.

Even though the Treaty of Rome (1957) has enshrined equity between women and men in the European Union, broadcasters were relative latecomers in addressing the glass-ceiling phenomenon in their profession. The European Commission (EC) waited until 1983 to fund research that led to the establishment, in 1986, of a Steering Committee for Equal Opportunities in Broadcasting. At about the same time, in 1984, the Council of Europe adopted a Recommendation on Equality Between Women and Men in the Media (Recommendation No. R [84] 17 of the Committee of Ministers to Member States). In a parallel development in 1987, the European Parliament passed a resolution on the Depiction and Position of Women in the Media (Resolution A2/95/97, Official Journal of the European Communities, No. C305, 14.11.87). Yet, it took until 1990 for the first female broadcasting studies broken down by professional category to become available. They indicate that the proportion of women in the 71 organizations in the 12 EC Member states was 35%, and that 52% of all of these women worked in administration. Another 23% were production assistants. The Equal Opportunities Report elaborates that women were secretaries, receptionists, and personal assistants, or managers in sales, personnel or public relations (European Commission, 1992). As in North America, female staff was a tiny 6% of all technical and 7% of crafts personnel as well as 6% of senior managers (Table 4.3). Unfortunately, these positions are not further described, although there is mention that females occupy about 12% of Level 2 and 11% of Level 3 positions. The same figures reappear in the 1992 European Committee for Equal Opportunities in Broadcasting Report presented in Brussels. It shows that women made up approximately 15% of the members of external governing bodies, 11% of top management committee members, and in the great majority of organizations studied, less than 20% of senior management (European Commission, 1992, p. 26). In all the major broadcasting companies of the EC, there was only one female director general at the beginning of the 1990s.

The Canadian and international evidence on the glass-ceiling phenomenon suggests that there are two very general sets of social factors that inhibit both career development and planning for female journalists. The first consists of the difficulty of combining professional with family responsibilities. Clearly, the solutions to this problem depend partially on a given country's social legislation, including rules about maternity and paternity leave, the availability and cost of day care, and society's options for the care of elders. Interviews with media personnel have additionally revealed that the journalism profession itself provides challenges for female staff. Two of these have aroused attention in Europe, but are rarely mentioned in North America. They are associated with the profession's *interpretations* of "availability" and the notion of "writing skill." Depending on the medium and the position one occupies in the newsroom, European interviews show, journalists spend from 7 to 10 hours a day on the job. Lünenborg (1997) was the first to demonstrate the linkage between time spent on the job with the professional self-understanding of "competence." The unique interpretation of writing ability as an unteachable "gift," furthermore, grows out of the "craft" origins of the journalism profession. In both print and broadcasting, this conception has inhibited the rationalization of reporting practices, as well as the movement toward collective time management. With new technologies like computers, databases, cell phones, and instant video-recording capabilities, the newsroom's collective time requirements can surely be compressed into an ordinary 7- or 8-hour working day, providing more time for family needs.

Another set of factors affecting female's career options result from the profession's horizontal segregation by gender *within* the newsroom itself. In this chapter, we have explored one of the most important of these barriers, the glass ceiling, and the ways in which it affects females' access to the different management levels in the print and broadcast industries. The Canadian, U.S., and European evidence on female promotion are both positive and negative. On the positive side, it appears that in the past 30 years, the North American glass ceiling has moved up at least into the middle management ranks and attracted more female staff. In Europe, unfortunately, this movement has not yet occurred. Interviews on both sides of the Atlantic additionally demonstrate that female professionals qua females have greater difficulty in planning their careers and that only the young, single group of female professionals matches the promotion speed of their male colleagues. Furthermore, in some countries like Italy and Spain, female managers lack advanced training programs, which are widespread in Scandinavia and North America. Together, these social expectations and professional barriers propel a larger proportion of female than male personnel either into freelance work or into public relations. Both of these provide regular hours and have made public relations the most popular career alternative for North

American media people (Stone, 1994). Stone's surveys of television news personnel consequently suggest that the imbalance between female and male personnel is a matter of turnover. Women, he documents, leave television at some point up to their mid-careers, whereas males do not (Bulkeley, 2004; Stone, 2000b). The reasons for this are explored in the next section.

THE "GLASS CEILING": WHAT DOES IT MEAN?

A 1996 mail survey of 1,251 U.S. female vice presidents and 1,000 male CEOs identified six barriers to female advancement into corporate leadership, which graphically illustrates how gender affects the way in which female and male managers *perceive* their activities. According to female executives, the most important barrier is *interpretive* and consists of gender stereotyping of female managerial capabilities. More than half (52%) of the females, but only one quarter (25%) of the males consider this barrier most important. The second barrier identified is exclusion from informal networks (females 49%, males 15%). A third barrier has to do with what counts as "professional experience." Here 49% of the females, as compared with 82% of males, consider the lack of line experience an important barrier to female promotion. The final three barriers in descending order of importance according to female executives are inhospitable corporate climate (females 35% to males 18%), lack of mentoring (females 30% to males 34%), and length of service in the institution at 29% for females and more than double that figure (64%) for males (Catalyst, 1995). These responses suggests that female executives consider male stereotyping and exclusion from informal networks the greatest barriers to career progress, whereas the males consider lack of experience and lack of years in management the most important barriers to female success. These conclusions were echoed by the Media Management Center findings at Northwestern University, whose 2001 study of female managers listed exclusion from informal networks, male stereotyping and lack of general line experience, as the three top barriers to female managerial progress (Bulkeley, 2004).

No wonder that interviews in Canada and Germany indicate that female media personnel, in contrast to their male counterparts, have very ambivalent attitudes toward promotion into management positions. There seems to be, first of all, a reluctance to exchange the journalistic writing tasks for the responsibilities of managing a team. Beyond that, some female respondents have commented that they are reluctant to be promoted, because it means losing their support "network." Still others have cited examples of female managers being criticized for either being too "feminine" or not "feminine enough" in their news jobs. In addition, there have been concerns with exposure created by being the "only" or "first" female to inhabit a top managerial position. Is there any way in which these statements can be explained and furthermore, do they signal yet another dimension of the glass ceiling phenomenon that has not yet been discussed?

Since the 1980s, sociologists and management professors have suggested that professional women's reluctance to move into top management positions is a realistic response, which grows out of the exclusionary practices that affect the "token" women at the top (Agocs, 1989). Rosabeth Kanter (1980), a Yale University sociologist who has studied gender rules *within* organizations and professions, explains that these rules are grounded in the *cultural* understandings of the mostly male managerial elite. Gender rules must thus be seen as a social construction, rooted in hierarchy and not in biology or internalization (Epstein, 1988, p. 15). Virginia O'Leary and Jeanette Ickovics (1992) elaborate that there are two attitudinal processes, which are involved in elite selection. The first process consists of gender stereotyping of work, which is found in all North American and European societies and is grounded in sex-role stereotyping. The researchers define sex-role stereotyping as "sets of beliefs about the *personal* attributes of a group of people and their behaviour" (p. 9). This belief formation about groups is not the result of a single experience, but of a continuous process that occurs with little or no conscious awareness throughout life. It most often occurs when a given characteristic of an individual is particularly obvious, such as gender and race and thus can be easily used to differentiate the minority from the group. Stereotyping is also a reflexive process because the stereotypes in turn serve to rationalize this division of labor, by attributing intrinsic personality differences to the two gendered groups (O'Leary & Ickovics, 1992).

The impact of social role preconceptions on behavior is particularly strong, as noted above, in settings like top management, where role-related expectations conflict. Here, few females are present to offer counter-examples to stereotypical expectations and they therefore have drastically different leadership experiences than their male counterparts. The dearth of females in top management triggers an additional process, namely the right of only one group (males) to define and interpret the behavior of the other group (females) in the heterosexual workplace. This leads to bizarre situations where female professionals are accused of both "acting too much like a woman," interpreted as being sensitive, emotional, and family- rather than career-oriented, and at other times acting "too much like a man," interpreted as being competent, deceitful, and aggressive. In both cases, it is a male manager making the interpretation, not a mixed group of gendered individuals. Sissy de Maas, a German female sports reporter, was caught in this interpretive double bind when she was relieved of her TV sport show on the grounds that she "lacked a unique female perspective" in her coverage, which would distinguish her from her male colleagues. It turns out that the male executive producer was looking for a "less professional and more emotional approach" to sports reporting to boost his ratings (Klein, 1986, p. 53).

The 1996 management survey mentioned earlier indicates that the association between sex-role stereotyping and management characteristics continues to exist in the 21st century. O'Leary and Ickovics (1992) offer a number of reasons why *culture*-based interpretations are so difficult to change. To begin with, there is the finding that both genders prefer to work for male bosses and that there are radically different interpretations for female versus male "successes" and "efforts" at work. Two in-depth comparisons show that managers of both genders ascribe the successful performance of a female manager to "effort" or "luck," whereas that of a male is ascribed to "ability" (O'Leary & Ickovics, 1992, p. 13). Moreover O'Leary and Hansen (1985) discovered when a female boss is perceived to exert effort on a test with a successful outcome, her "effort" is interpreted as being compensatory for her *lack* of ability, whereas a males' effort in the same situation is interpreted as *intentional* and thus diagnostic of his ability. The authors conclude that to the extent that "perceived effort" is pivotal in the performance evaluation process, female bosses will continue to reap *lesser rewards* than males, for the same performance outcomes (O'Leary & Ickovics, 1992).

All of these attitudinal processes result in a recruitment bias in favor of male managers in the media industries, as they do in corporations generally (Kagan, 1986). Beyond pay, as we have seen, preferential treatment for male media personnel has been documented in hiring, job placement and promotion. According to O'Leary and Ickovics (1992) these effects are even stronger when the job in question is male-dominated, because the so-called "rational bias" theory encourages managers to make personnel decisions on the basis of their own self-interest, rather than on the abilities of their subordinates. This helps explain why gender discrimination continues in what a *Harper's* editor dubbed the "schmoozocracy," where one advances because of who one gets along with at the office, rather than on the basis of merit (Jones, 1997). Male managers continue to harbor three preconceptions that underrate the management competencies of female personnel. Each of these preconceptions is refuted by the proportional Canadian gender sample, as they have been in studies elsewhere (see the appendix). The first refers to the male managers' mistaken belief that female personnel will drop out of their careers to get married or have children. My Canadian gender sample demonstrates exactly the opposite. In 1995, female Canadian professionals were less likely to be married than the male sample. Only 31 out of 49 (65%) of the female personnel were married or lived with a partner, whereas an overwhelming 60 out of the 75 (81%) of the male professionals were married.

My evidence also contests another attitudinal preconception that states that females will choose to be mothers rather than managers. It highlights the reality of the "dual-role strain" and the fact that combining the long journalistic hours with child care is virtually impossible. Consequently, my proportional gender sample shows that 29 out of 49, or nearly two thirds (59%) of the Canadian female professionals had no children. On the male side, this strain did not exist and consequently only 23 out of 75 males or 31% were childless. Beyond that, Table 4.7 demonstrated that the small group of females who were parents had smaller numbers of children than their male counterparts. Among the 20 female professionals with children, 27% had only one child and the remaining 14% had two or three. Among the 52 males with children, 14 (19%) had only one, whereas 29% had two and a remarkable 21% of the group had three or more children. The difficulty of reconciling work with family responsibilities has furthermore been documented in the gendered responses to the scheduling of work and family obligations. As expected, a greater proportion of female media personnel — nearly half (42%) — mentioned child-care arrangements and other obligations, which at times interfere with work schedules. On the male side, slightly less than one third (31%) voiced the same complaints. Interestingly, the 69% of male media personnel who had no problem combining work with family responsibilities were of this opinion irrespective of whether they had children, indicating that their wives assumed all family-related responsibilities, an alternative not available to female professionals.

The final male managerial gender stereotype, that female journalists are not career primary workers, has already been refuted by the large proportion of unmarried female media personnel who hold positions throughout the hierarchy. Furthermore, it is an unwarranted assumption, which is never raised with respect to male workers. Males also sacrifice time to devote to their wives and children, while pursuing a demanding career, but they are never asked to give up family life all together. Our comparative evidence from Europe suggests that the salient question to ask is not whether one gender group is more career-oriented than the other, but rather, how can newsroom work be restructured so that the work–family interface can be accommodated for both female and male professionals. Beyond that, it is important to expose the supposed "rational" biases in terms of which management elites select their candidates as what they *really* are: irrational gender stereotypes. One way of minimizing the problem of sexual stereotyping is to make another identity salient, such as that of the manager, thereby avoiding the gender stereotypes attached to it.

Another way of probing the meaning of the glass-ceiling phenomenon for female professionals, is to analyze what Kanter calls the "token" phenomenon that females and ethnic minorities encounter in top positions. For Kanter (1980), this means visibility on the basis of difference and treatment by others as a member of a category, rather than as an individual (p. 311). The token status affects not only the power a person is able to marshal in a position, but also the personal feelings of singularity and vulnerability that one encounters. Kanter uses power, opportunity, and relative gender concentrations to explain the different types of token status that females encounter in different organizational settings. Her comparison of professional behavior demonstrates that this status affects all subgroups, which make up less than one third of a given population. In such a situation, an individual will become the subject of special scrutiny, derived not from their performance, but from their very *presence* in a given environment. As Christine Doudna notes, "the major issue for women in management today is often not whether they can perform as well as men, but whether they will be *allowed to*" (Harpers, 1997, p. 55, italics added).

Power within a corporation is viewed as the ability to mobilize resources of money, materials, time, information, as well as support, and to use these to accomplish one's goals. Opportunity is defined as access to personal growth and development, especially career development and mobility. These two attributes of structure tend to be empirically linked and tied to positions in the organizational hierarchy. For Kanter, tokenism in senior management signifies marginality and powerlessness; the token is at the periphery, not really accepted as a member of the core elite or dominant coalition and network, empowered to make decisions for the organization. Kanter furthermore found that tokenism as a powerless status contributes to dysfunctional individual behaviour, because of the role ambiguity and the role conflict the "token" suffers. The German television sports reporter who lost her job is a case in point. Thus, the powerlessness of the token is detrimental not only to herself and her career, but also to those who report to her. I have already documented these role conflicts in Chapter 4, where I describe them as part of the exclusionary strategies that the dominant coalition imposes on certain female colleagues and how these strategies affect the "climate" of the journalistic workplace. The power and opportunities associated with a managerial position tend to increase as one moves up the organizational hierarchy, as does the scope to exercise *discretion*. At the managerial pinnacle, Carol Agocs (1989) argues, there are few rules to control behavior, performance standards become vague and diffuse, and there is little supervision. Internalized norms of behavior and cultural controls, therefore, play a larger role in structuring behavior, than they would elsewhere in the hierarchy. Mutual trust among peers becomes essential to the exercise of management power and is a critical criterion in management recruitment. Furthermore, interpersonal communication occupies more of the top manager's time than any other activity, reinforcing the importance of being part of the "schmoozocracy." For these reasons, elites tend to reproduce themselves (Mintzberg, 1975).

Given the importance of relative gender concentrations and the scarcity of female managers in the top newspaper and broadcasting positions, every managerial woman above the glass-ceiling range of media positions will become an "isolate" and her daily reality is transformed into an eggshell existence of high visibility. Recent investigations have discovered that there are three unpleasant results of isolation at the top. They are the token status, sex-segregated work assignments, and sexual harassment on the job. Each of these will be separately investigated in order to tease out the ways in which they reinforce each other and make life at the top difficult for female managers. One of the most important discoveries is Kanter's (1993) finding that the sex ratio of a group affects the degree of isolation female professionals experience in their work settings. Her organizational research discovered that there are *two* types of tokenism, rather than just one and that they are related to the *group situation* in which a woman finds herself. She calls these the uniform, balanced, skewed, and tilted group situations. Token status, which is based on personal characteristics, rather than capacities, is thus not universal, as was initially assumed, but is the outcome of only two group situations, the skewed and the tilted. In gender-uniform groups like librarianship, there is no token status, because all members of the group tend to be of the same gender. In balanced groups it is also absent, because the genders are approximately evenly represented. In the last two groups, however, different kinds of token effects occur. For skewed groups, where the ratio of females or minorities to males is about 35% to 65%, the token effects are less pronounced because minority group members can align themselves with the majority and thus protect themselves and wield some power. My evidence suggests that most middle-level media managers in North American newsrooms find themselves in this skewed situation and therefore generally do not consider themselves discriminated on the job. It is only in the top managerial newspaper and broadcasting positions, where female incumbents hold less than 15% of the management positions, that the tilted token effects are felt most acutely. Here, the behavior of one token is perceived as *representing* all tokens, which means that these top female managers are not only excluded from the informal power networks, but also side-lined from getting their ideas accepted or marshalling the necessary resources of time and money to implement them.

Applying Kanter's sex ratios to our Canadian and U.S. data in Table 5.2 suggests that Canadian female newspaper managers will feel less isolated than their U.S. sisters because their proportional representation is larger. Even though the Canadian editor-in-chief position is still protected, the majority of Canadian female managers have moved out of the tilted position by occupying well over 15% in three out of the four top positions in all types of dailies. In the United States, in contrast, Table 5.2 documents that there is substantial female isolation in the top two management positions (editors-in-chief and editors), because females hold less than 1% of these positions, except in small circulation dailies. In broadcasting, Table 4.5 demonstrates that both Canadian and U.S. managers have escaped the extreme tilted position even at the top, where they hold 17% and 21%, respectively, of the executive producer levels. One level down, among the news directors, furthermore, females have nearly achieved the balanced status, with proportions of 41% for the Canadian and 47% of the U.S. staffs. No wonder that most female media personnel do not consider themselves discriminated in the workplace.

There is only one study by German media scholar Susanne Keil (2001) that explores what it *means* to work in a tilted management environment. Her interviews reveal that German female broadcast managers are aware that they are unable to change the formal structures of their newsrooms in such a situation, although they do feel that they have informal power to influence the organizational *culture*. German female news directors try to achieve change in the organizational culture by being more democratic in decision situations, and by trying to convince, rather than dictate to their heterosexual staff. For instance, they introduce an "issue" focus in editorial meetings in order to undermine the competitive power rituals, which usually pit female against male staff (Keil, 2001). These managers also consciously try to restructure the gendered beat structure by encouraging all staff to report in a variety of different domains. The German news directors comment that external factors, like increased competition between Germany's public and private stations and the requirement to attract new viewer groups, have aided them in changing their newsroom cultures (Keil, 2001). Despite these examples, Keil cautions that longitudinal, not snapshot studies, are required to assess the impact of females on management practices. For the time being, German female managers continue to lack leverage in the country's broadcast organizations (Keil, 2001).

Another way in which isolation at the top manifests itself for female managers is through sex-segregated work assignments. Sex segregation of work has been a stable feature of the North American and the European workforces throughout the century. As it stands, females are disproportionately represented in the clerical and service occupations. These jobs are called "female-intensive" because they are not as productive as other industries, and consequently tend to be less well remunerated (Armstrong & Armstrong, 1986, p. 24). Even though managerial positions are today considered gender-neutral, my organizational media data have revealed that occupational segregation *within* the management category continues to exist. As a result of ongoing gender barriers, female and male managers have different median ages, social characteristics, and are drawn from different professional specializations. Stone's (2000) millennial survey of U.S. "Television News People" demonstrates that females' mobility into top management depends on their level of recruitment in prior decades. In Canada, this recruitment did not occur until the 1980s, whereas in the United States it began in the 1970s, when the FCC mandated equity in hiring. Yet, the gains that were made in the earlier decade were reversed by the Reagan administration in the 1980s. Consequently, U.S. female managers are younger than those in Canada. In 1995, the Canadian median age for female editors-in-chief or executive directors was 41 years old in the daily press and 38 years old in television. For the males, the median ages were 4 years older in the press (45) and 2 years older in broadcasting (40). In the United States, in contrast, female news directors had a median age of only 31 years, to their male companions' 39 years (Burks & Stone, 1993).

Canadian management research furthermore indicates that female managers have worked less number of years in their company or profession than their male compatriots. Consequently, the males are more often promoted from within, whereas female managers tend to be recruited from outside (Agocs, 1989). This means that male managers have their informal networks well established when they move up in the hierarchy, whereas the females who are recruited from outside lack such support. The available findings (Table 3.4) suggest that Canadian females have a median of 12 years of experience in the broadcast profession, to the males' 16.5 years. In the United States, the median experience was once again lower than in Canada because of their earlier recruitment. It stood at a median of 9 years for female managers and 10 years for male staff. This indicates that the broadcast profession saw much greater turnover in the United States than in Canada, a difference that may have something to do with the steadying influence of Canada's public broadcasting corporation (CBC), which provides better career options for all personnel.

An additional point to note is that media manager personnel have higher educational qualifications than the managerial elites in industry. My own proportionate gender survey of print and television journalists indicates that 67% of female staff and 65% of the males have completed college degrees. If one adds to this the group that took some college courses, it turns out that fully 77% of female and 72% of male staff are highly educated. This is close to the figure of 85% for all U.S. television news staff, which the American Society of Newspaper Editors (ASNE, 1997) found in the early 1990s. A final gendered difference appears in the areas of expertise of the two groups of senior managers. In the United States, the older, over 40 generation of general managers of both genders did not take management courses, but learned their skills in the newsroom. Among the younger recruits, those in their 30s, in contrast, female general managers acquired experience in TV sales (Stone 1997).

A final manifestation of isolation at the top is sexual harassment, which only began to be studied in the media domain in the 1990s. In the United

States, three studies began to lay the groundwork for estimating the prevalence of this workplace phenomenon, which had been previously documented in other professions. The first, an Associated Press Managing Editors Association (APNE) survey of 640 male and female journalists from 19 U.S. newsrooms, discovered in 1992 that the prevalence and importance of harassment activities were vastly underestimated. This is evidenced by the fact that only 30% of the surveyed newsrooms had harassment guidelines for filing complaints and that 95% of the victims were females (Kossan, 1992). At about the same time, a national survey of television news directors showed that about half of the female directors reported having faced some form of sexual harassment on the job, most of which was verbal and never reported (Stone & Forte Duhe, 1992). Kim Walsh-Childers, Jean Chance, and Kristin Herzog's (1996) study "Sexual Harassment of Women Journalists" began to fill the lacunae by developing the first definitions of these complex behavior patterns. It also inquired whether demographic characteristics such as age and marital status as well as organizational variables, such as position, size of newsroom, and percentage of females, affect harassment behavior. The research, which is based on a proportionate sample of 311 females in 120 small, medium, and large circulation papers, found that "sexual harassment" has two court-defined meanings and three respondent defined meanings. The first legal definition is known as *quid pro quo* (something for something) and refers to situations in which an individual promises a subordinate some sort of tangible benefit, such as a raise, in exchanged for sexual favors. The second legal definition, "hostile environment" discrimination, reflects circumstances in which an employee is subjected to a pattern of behavior, such as unwanted sexual advances, degrading sexual comments about the employee, that interfere unreasonably with an employee's ability to perform his or her job (Walsh-Childers et al., 1996, p. 559-560).

These legal definitions specify situations in which litigation is possible, but fail to distinguish between different kinds of harassment behaviours. Instead, the respondents distinguished between harassment that did not involve physical contact (sexual comments, jokes, pictures) and harassment that did involve physical contact (unwanted touching), although they also implicitly recognized a third harassing situation, such as pressuring a coworker for a date (Walsh-Childers et al., 1996). I call these situations verbal, physical, and psychological harassment, respectively. The study's cross-tabulations show that age and percentage of females in the newsroom are the only demographic and organizational variables that are related to harassment experiences. Younger women (23–30 years) are more sensitive to and consider harassment a more serious problem than the older (41–74 years) group. Furthermore, in newsrooms with the lowest percentage of female employees (up to 33%), 45% of the female respondents had experienced psychological harassment by coworkers, whereas in newsrooms with between 34% and 50% females, only 24% had been harassed (Walsh-Childers et al., 1996). This confirms Kanter's (1980) discovery that the sex ratio of a position or a work group is positively associated with the incidence of sexual harassment.

Most researchers who have studied the subject, including Kanter and myself, argue that sexual harassment is more about power than about sex. Theories based on power differences grow from a feminist view of sexual harassment as one more way males exercise power in our society—as men's way of putting women in their place at work. Cindy Brown and Gail Flatow's (1997) "Targets, Effects, and Perpetrators of Sexual harassment in Newsrooms" investigates which of the two power difference models are best able to explain the harassment experiences of 198 journalists in Indiana dailies. The sociocultural model suggests that sexual harassment results from and helps sustain the patriarchal distribution of power and status in society. According to Brown and Flatow, it is made up of two subtheories that are interrelated. The cultural subtheory assumes that women with the least power in our culture are the most vulnerable to sexual harassment, and would predict that younger, unmarried, and minority women are most vulnerable. This chapter on the glass-ceiling phenomenon has offered little confirmation for this theory. The social control subtheory, in contrast, is stronger and more useful in explaining the use of male power in media organizations. It is, for instance, able to explain the reluctance of female media professionals concerning their promotion into the management cadre. As demonstrated, they feared being cut off from their informal networks, which an external move into another organization involves. Male managers, in contrast, are overwhelmingly internally recruited and thus retain their networks. Beyond that, my study has demonstrated that these macro-theories are capable of clarifying the different forms that harassment activities take in Canadian newsrooms. For this one requires a micro-analysis, stratified by gender, position, and market size, as in my Canadian proportionate gender sample. Responses from this sample demonstrate that by the late 1990s, both gender groups were aware that there are at least three types of sexual harassment activities and that these mostly male practices interfere with female's ability to do their journalistic work. Overall, the inquiry demonstrates, as expected, that more female than male media professionals have encountered harassment practices. Nearly half (49%) of all female staff, but only 39% of males answered "maybe" to the question "Is sexual harassment a problem for female journalists?" One quarter of both female and male staff answered "yes," whereas more than one quarter (27%) and more than one third (38%) of male personnel responded "no."

In order to clarify harassment activities in greater detail, feminist scholarship suggests they be divided into three categories: verbal, physical and psychological. Table 5.6, which records responses to the question: "Have

you ever been sexually harassed in your work environment?" indicates that
female practitioners were most prone to verbal harassment: 60% of female
staff has encountered it at least once. This is close to Gail Flatow's (1994)
Indiana newspaper study, which documents that 62% of females but only
7% of male editorial staff experienced verbal harassment. Psychological
harassment came in second place with 43% of female media personnel having experienced it at least once. In the Indiana study, this figure was somewhat lower and stands at 30% of the personnel. Even physical harassment
has been experienced by an astounding 20% of Canadian females at least
once with Flatow's findings in the same range (22%) and U.S. respondents
mentioning that male colleagues had grabbed their breasts or buttocks. As
expected, percentages of male professionals experiencing harassment are
much lower among Canadian and U.S. staff. Table 5.6 shows only 13% of
male staff experienced verbal harassment at least once versus 7% in the
United States; 9% experienced psychological harassment and a mere 1%
experienced physical harassment in Canada. The U. S. figures for physical
harassment were 7%. This evidence shows that both Canadian and U.S.
feminist researchers' hunches about gender differences in the experience of
the three types of sexual harassment are confirmed by the significance tests.
The Canadian and U.S. data furthermore clarify that the quality and degree

Table 5.6 Respondents Who Have Been Victims of Sexual Harassment
(by gender and in percentages) ($N = 124$)

Type of Harassment	Respondents' Answers	Females ($n = 49$) %	Males ($n = 75$) %	Total ($n = 124$) %	χ^2 Signif.
Verbal harassment	Often/a few times/once	60	13	30	<0.00001
	Never	40	87	70	
Psychological harassment	Often/a few times/once	43	9	21	0.0002
	Never	57	91	79	
Physical harassment	Often/a few times/once	20	1	8	0.0064
	Never	80	99	92	

*Que: Have you ever been sexually harassed in your work environment? Responses derived by combin-
ing three highest responses on a 4-point scale (4 often, 3 a few times, 2 once, 1 never). Based on the
gender sample found in the appendix.*

of differences decreases from the top of the table to the bottom. Beyond that, witnessing the harassment of others at work is more common than experiencing it personally for both genders. This indicates that sensitization campaigns in the workplace have been effective where they exist, although they currently cover less than 30% of the newspaper outlets in both countries. Finally, my investigation demonstrates that the proportions of female and male respondents who have *witnessed* harassment are extremely close. About one half of all staff witnessed verbal harassment; 27% of females and 28% of males witnessed psychological harassment; 26% of female staff but only 11% of males witnessed at least one case of physical harassment. This is an expected outcome because most Canadian female media professionals do not work in what Kanter (1980) calls a severely tilted environment (less than 15% of the total group being female), but in a more comfortable skewed situation. Here females constitute more than one-third of the group and thus have the power to affect the working culture.

CANADA'S FIRST FEMALE BROADCAST MANAGERS

Although there are no systematic and comparative historical analyses of Canadian female and male broadcast managers, there is interesting interview material on what it felt like to be the "first women" in a top media position. These accounts provide an illustration of the six barriers to female advancement discovered in the 1996 executive survey. They also suggest strategies for adapting or overcoming the tilted token statuses of some of Canada's top broadcasters such as Dodi Robb, Margaret Lyons, Marge Anthony, Joan Schafer, and Trina McQueen, all of whom began their careers before the second feminist revolution, in the years between 1950 and 1970. Susan Crean (1985) divides these top media managers into three generations and demonstrates that even the first generation, despite being in an extremely tilted (less than 15%) gender position in their workplace, were able to lay the foundations for greater gender equity in the 1980s. They accomplished this by increasing their status through "networking" with their male superiors, who initially were reluctant, but ultimately promoted them into senior broadcast positions in both the public CBC and the private CTV networks. The second broadcast generation, including Barbara Frum, Adrienne Clarkson, and others, who came on the scene in the 1970s, benefited from their experience and sometimes from their mentoring, as did the 1980s group, which included Wendy Mesley and Diana Swain (Gazette, 2001). Barbara Frum became the first female host of *As It Happens*, an innovative Monday evening current events show, conceived in 1968 by Val Clery, a former British army commando, turned broadcaster. Using no reporters, cameras, crews, or microphones, this show interconnected Canada's five regions by telephone and became popular almost overnight. By the early 1970s it had expanded to 5 nights a week, as well as innovated the anchor "couple" idea, pairing Frum (1971-1981) with Alan Maitland (1974–1993). In 2003, it celebrated its 35th anniversary and continues to delight listeners in Canada and the United States (Budd, 2003).

Dodi Robb, from the first generation, was important because by 1965, when she became the head of CBC daytime information programming, hers was the top position held by a female in the corporation. In this position, she began to create an institutional space where females could learn and develop their own broadcast talents. Robb remembers that the decade between 1965 and 1975 was one of expansion for the CBC, and for the women working in current affairs. Two programs, *Women Now* (1968) and *Market Place* (1972) owe their existence to her initiatives and her preference for working with women. Her substantial managerial talents were recognized by network chief Peter Herrndorf who next promoted her to director of television in Winnipeg, and then to the first female regional directorship of CBC's Maritime Region (1982–1984), after which she returned to a less high-pressure situation as head of children's programming in 1984. Just as the air gets thinner when you scale a mountain, Robb found the environment thinning of women the higher she moved. At the same time, she told Crean: "Life at the giddy heights of senior management was not quite so deadly dull as expected, as long as you don't take it too seriously or go by the rules instead of walking around them, as I have always done." And in a wry aside she notes, "There is one thing men are nervous about in women: their intuition and character-assessing ability" (Crean, 1985, pp. 320–321). Herrndorf also promoted another "self-made" pioneer, Margaret Lyons, up the CBC management ladder. To her, however, the corporation's glass ceiling remained invisible until the CBC's 1975 International Women's Year inquiry, which for the first time investigated the status of females in the corporation. As a consequence, she did not begin to mentor female colleagues until she was appointed the first female head of radio current affairs and director of AM services in 1982 and was elevated to be vice president of English Network Radio, a year later. This made her the CBC's first woman vice president and the highest-ranking appointment since Nellie McClung was named to the first board of governors in 1936 (Crean, 1985).

In the 1970s, another important broadcaster, Trina McQueen, started her meteoric rise to the top by becoming the first female executive producer (1976) of *The National*, the CBC's flagship news program. McQueen had started as an on-air reporter at CFTO Toronto and then became the first female co-host of CTV's *W-Five* before she became a writer and editor for CBC's *The National* in 1969 (Damsell, 2001). Seven years later, in 1976, she was promoted to the executive producer suite, an elevation that created a classic double bind. Ann Medina recalls: "She took over the *Newsmagazine* pure and simple; she had the executive producer, if not fired, then pushed aside" (Crean, 1985, p. 335). This created controversy in both gender groups. To the men whose turf she threatened, she was an unwelcome agent of change by suggesting that the carefully drawn lines between news reporting and longer, documentary items could be relaxed, whereas women in the corporation decried her seeming lack of interest and solidarity in equity issues. Yet, she too became a symbol for the managerial talents of female broadcasters when she was appointed the first director of TV programming for the English Network in 1980. Echoing the typical experiences of the token, McQueen commented to Crean that contrary to widespread belief, "management is creative and can be a tremendous source of excitement and energy . . . [Yet even though] I didn't think about it in the early years, now that I look back on it, I must have been lonely" (Crean, 1985, pp. 338–339). McQueen's last position at the CBC, before she left for CTV, was as vice president of TV news (1988–1992), where she launched the highly popular "Newsworld" Channel.

In the early 1990s, when the Canadian Radio-Television Commission (CRTC) mandated that the public broadcaster (CBC) eliminate virtually all non-Canadian content, private networks too were entering a new era. To receive specialty licenses, which would further fragment the Canadian viewing public, the CRTC mandated that private stations too, had to produce more Canadian programming. This shift provided an opportunity for three, second-generation female broadcasters to move into top management positions. Susanne Boyce at CTV, Phyllis Platt at CBC, and Loren Mawhinney at Global became top executives at Canadian networks on the basis of their production experience. They were responsible for almost $422 million worth of Canadian-content programming, or the lion's share of prime-time TV produced in the country in 1998 (Saunders, 1998). Meanwhile, Tina McQueen had moved from CBC to CTV in 1993 and was offered the founding presidency of yet another specialty channel by Ivan Fecan, a colleague and CEO of CTV's Bellglobe Media. McQueen headed the "Discovery Channel" until 1998 when she was made president and CEO of CTV Inc. She retired in 2002 after a 35-year career in broadcasting and has now been appointed consul general in New York by Prime Minister Chrétien. In an interview with Doug Saunders, McQueen comments on the differing career paths of female broadcasters noting: "when I look at the power structure today, it's far less male-dominated than it was. . . . The women who occupy these positions are women of power and skill, but they probably came up through the ranks, when the financial or legal side was not attainable" (Saunders, 1998, p. C1).

COMBATING THE "GLASS CEILING":
CORPORATE RESPONSES

This chapter's discussion has demonstrated that resistance to women in top managerial positions has begun to decrease in North American broadcasting and print, but remains strong in Europe. Research has furthermore shown that this resistance is grounded in sex-role stereotypes, which are particularly strong in settings like senior management, where role-related expectations conflict. These stereotypes, which grew out of the sexual division of labor, attribute intrinsic personality differences to the sexes that in fact do not exist. Beyond that, the discussion has documented that sex-role stereotyping affects all social domains, including such professions as journalism. In order to dismantle the glass-ceiling phenomenon, O'Leary and Ickovics (1992) argue, it is important to make another identity, that of "manager," salient, by highlighting the overwhelming *similarities* in managerial behavior by both genders. Unfortunately, however, external circumstances like globalization and corporate takeovers have, since the 1990s reduced the size of the managerial pool, and thus once again made it more difficult to get to the top for everyone. Using Fortune 500 figures, E.C. Arnette (1987) notes that in 1987, 1 person in 20 was promoted into top management, whereas by 2001 the ratio would be only 1 in 50.

My more detailed comparisons of Canadian and U.S. female progress into top media positions have shown that the situation in the Canadian press and in both countries' broadcast management are substantially better than the progress registered in the economic sector of the Fortune 500 companies. Yet, these gains for female media personnel must not lull us into believing that the glass-ceiling barriers have been eradicated. Instead, it is important to remember that the complex ways in which gender stereotypes operate in everyday life demand continued vigilance and informed action. Feminist scholars and others have suggested that these actions need to be multilevel and that they have to encompass both the organizational and the individual levels of behavior. Both of these types of initiatives will now be discussed in greater detail.

In addition to affirmative action initiatives at the federal level in both Canada and the United States, which are assessed in Chapter 6, organizations can also make changes to encourage the mobility of qualified female staff. One of the most widely used corporate strategies in the federally supervised Canadian and U.S. broadcast sectors consists of setting up a task force to institute diversity and implement change. In Canada, this mandate includes women, visible minorities, aboriginal people, as well as people with disabilities and uses crown corporations, like the CBC, as sites for change. As a result, the CBC formally constituted an Employment Equity Office in 1986. By the late 1980s the CBC also initiated outreach activities at each location, and implemented an applicant tracking system to exchange information among CBC locations about potential designated group candidates and to ensure that these candidates were included in a more transparent hiring procedure for new positions. In addition, a Help Fund for the training of designated minorities was started in 1989, but discontinued 2 years later because of government cutbacks. It was re-established in 1994 with $400,000, to support CBC apprenticeships, workplace modification for people with disabilities, and developmental activities for the designated groups. These apprenticeships range from 2 months to 1 year and provide technical and creative job training in all broadcast roles (CBC Equity Newsletter, 2000).

Since the early 1990s, the dearth of females in the technical sector has also been addressed through recruiting two female engineering students per year to work as maintenance technicians at the Sackville Transmitting Station. Toronto Women in Film and Video, furthermore, sponsors courses to teach females video production and editing, as well as camera work. Other outreach projects involve the Department of Indian Affairs, which helped set up an Aboriginal Trainee Program in various broadcast roles. Among these was "Collaborative Visions," a workshop for series writing, which culminated in the creation of the popular *North of Sixty* program, about life in Nunavut, edited by Jordan Wheeler, an aboriginal writer (CBC Equity Newsletter, 1994). Finally, personnel diversity was fostered by providing visible minority internships to two young British Columbians to contribute to the *Canada Now* news show, while the "New Voices" initiative of 2001 added 3,000 new recruits for casual or freelance work. All together, these initiatives have begun to better reflect the regional, socioeconomic and ethnic realities in Canadian radio and television programming (CBC Equity Newsletter, 2001).

What was the success of these CBC initiatives for female management aspirants in the 8 years between 1993 and 2001? Table 5.7 indicates that the public broadcaster indeed served as an example for providing improved management access for female staff. The results for visible minorities and aboriginal people, however, were not nearly as far advanced. In the CBC's manager category, the proportion of females almost doubled from an overall representation of 17% in 1993, to a 26% representation in 2001. Company records reveal that this global figure includes an astounding 57% majority of females in the third-level management positions of chief and associate editors. Women also did very well on the three producer levels. Here, Table 5.7 indicates, that female professionals achieved virtual parity (moving from 40% to 45%) among producers and also 34% of all executive producer chairs. Among associate producers, Table 5.7 indicates, females increased their virtual parity (48%) in 1993, to a majority of 60% in 2001. Beyond that, 2001 figures show that 14 females moved into directorial positions, for a representation of 42%. All together, these figures are only slight-

Table 5.7 Canadian Broadcasting Corporation's (CBC) Top Management Profile (by gender in percentages)

| Position | 1993 (N = 799)[a] | | 2001 (N = 824)[b] | |
	Female %	Staff Total No.	Female %	Staff Total No.
Directors	n.a	n.a	42	33
Creative heads	n.a	n.a	29	7
Chief editors/Assoc.	n.a	n.a	57	7
Managers	17	82	26	39
Executive producers	34	70	33	79
Producers	40	467	45	490
Associate producers	48	73	60	78
Program presentations Hosts/Anchors	38	107	40	91
Total F/M	300/499	799	359/465	824

[a]CBC Workforce Semi-Annual Report to CHRC (1993).
[b]CBC Workforce Semi-Annual Report to CHRC (2001).

ly above my own management findings, which include both the Canadian public and private television sectors and thus confirm that the crown corporation has indeed been functioning as a model for facilitating female managerial progress.

There was also movement on the senior officer level of the public sector CBC. Here, Annual Reports show that in 1995, when Perrin Beatty was president and CEO, there were 11 positions at the top, only 2 of which were held by women, for an 18% representation. They were senior vice president of resources, Louise Tremblay and one of four operational vice presidents: Michèle Fortin for French Television. In 2001, the senior management group had been enlarged to 12 positions under Robert Rabinovitch as CEO. Of these, 25%, were held by female managers. Two of these women, Louise Tremblay and Michèle Fortin, were still in place in 2001, whereas the third, Sally Southey, had meanwhile been appointed senior director corporate communications, a position not available until the 2000 restructuring (CBC Annual Reports 1995 and 2001). These public sector CBC figures are considerably better than those for the boards of Canada's 52 major communications companies, where only 12.7% of all directors were female at the turn of the millennium (CBC Equity Newsletter, 2000).

O'Leary and Ickovics (1992) note that a second strategy for change employed by both commercial and broadcast institutions are education and training programs to manage diversity. Examples are Du Pont's "Men and Women Working Together" and a similar program at the Gannett Corporation, America's largest newspaper chain, which owns *USA Today*. These programs provide fundamental information on managing diversity and reducing discrimination at all levels of the organization. Although many of these programs were originally targeted to women only, the trend is now to have both women and men train together (O'Leary & Ickovics, 1992). In the United States, no other media company has a better track record of hiring and promoting women and minorities than the Gannett Corporation. Gannett achieved this leadership role by implementing three types of strategies that are designed to eliminate and monitor gender-stereotypical managerial hiring practices. They are establishing top-level supervisory bodies; offering technical training opportunities for female professionals, and making all management levels "accountable" for recruiting females and minorities. This includes line managers who are given bonuses and incentives to provide mobility for female personnel to move from "staff" to "line" positions, which the 1996 executive survey highlighted as a prerequisite for promotion. Jose Barrios, the vice president for staffing, claims that the company achieved equitable representation by 2001 because "senior managers and executives know what is expected of them and have to provide monthly, quarterly and annual reviews" (Papper & Gerhard, 2001, p. 3).

At the CBC, too, a blue-ribbon Steering Committee on Equity, which includes the president, was created in 1993. The committee is made up of the managers of Employment Equity and Equity in Portrayal, as well as the four operational vice presidents of English and French Television and English and French Radio. Between 1993 and 1995, this committee amended hiring and promotion procedures to include both merit, as well as, in the case of comparable qualifications, preferential hiring of designated group members (CBC Equity Newsletter, 1994). In the 1996 restructuring of the CBC, the Equity Committee was reduced to three people and included representatives of official languages and relocation. An audit by the Human Rights Commission in 2002 determined that the CBC had fulfilled all of its obligations and that equity concerns could remain decentralized, as they are today.

In her detailed study of Germany's first generation of women in top broadcast positions, Keil (2001) concludes that there is now sufficient evidence to demonstrate the merits of equity legislation for female media personnel. Although the pioneer generation of female managers got to the top without the benefit of this type of legislation, it has had two positive results for the current generations of female professionals. The first is its important symbolic value in introducing equity concerns into the public debate. As a result, equity values have become widely accepted by people of all kinds of political persuasion since the 1980s. Beyond that, this legislation draws attention to society's unfinished business and makes public institutions, among them the media, *accountable* for redressing the ongoing imbalances within their own organizations. The CBC initiatives mirror Keil's findings that the top directors of broadcasting organizations must be assigned personal responsibility and thus become the chief actors in the transformation process (Keil, 2001; Robinson & Hildebrandt, 1993). Considering that the media professions were heavily male-dominated until recently, it is no wonder that in Germany, as in Canada, such high-ranking males as Fritz Pleitgen of the WDR (Westgerman Radio) and Mark Starowicz or Peter Herrndorf of the CBC, have spearheaded the female promotions of the first two generations of female media managers, but that there are now institutional bodies and specially designated equity officers to develop company-wide initiatives and to make managerial recruitment more transparent.

A third and much more radical suggestion for corporate and newsroom change comes from Lünenborg's (1997) interviews with mid-level female managers, who ascribe their lack of promotion to the European television profession's reluctance to modernize. As Table 5.3 indicates, there were no females in the top two German broadcast positions and only 1 of the 10 networks (Nordwestdeutscher Rundfunk) had an infinitesimal 8% female representation in its 1994 management cadre. In Europe, as in Canada in the 1970s, it is the less prestigious radio domain, where female staff had the best chances. Here, 29% of the management positions were filled by women at the turn of the century. The top position figures for the three other European countries are even more discouraging. In Denmark there were no top managers, whereas Italy's RAI had a 5.6% representation and Spain's public broadcaster RTVE had an infinitesimal 2.4% female managerial cadre (Lünenborg, 1997). These figures indicate clearly that the male managerial power structures in European broadcasting continue to be entrenched. Lünenborg comments that even in the much larger Italian broadcast bureaucracy, which employs substantially more top personnel, female access continues to be severely restricted. No wonder European female journalists are calling for a restructuring of the profession and more energetic removal of the access and promotion barriers identified in the North American setting.

COMBATING THE "GLASS CEILING": INDIVIDUAL RESPONSES

It is finally important to review what individual female managers can do to overcome their isolation in top management positions, which we have called tokenism. According to management consultants O'Leary and Ickovics, two strategies are most effective: *networking* and *mentoring*. Networking usually involves contacts with a variety of colleagues for the purpose of mutual work benefits (O'Leary & Ickovics, 1992). In her German analysis of this practice, Keil (2001) found that the importance of networking lies in its reciprocity and in that it involves favors, persuasion, and connections to people at various levels of the organization who have varying degrees of influence. Her interviews show that the first generation of European female managers, like their Canadian counterparts, primarily networked and legitimated themselves within the male, rather than the female, power structure. This explains the often stated ambivalence of these pioneer managers to be sensitized to the barriers confronting females and minorities and to connect with them across the media hierarchy. In Chapter 4, I identified this strategy as becoming "one of the boys" to increase one's influence.

One German manager explained that she only learned about the power of networking *across* organizational levels after she had tried unsuccessfully to convince her incredulous male executive board members that female voices were virtually absent from German news reports. The immediate response was that there were no qualified female experts available. Yet, when she turned to middle management female broadcasters, they instantly comprehended her concern and supported her initiative by developing an alternative speaker list (Keil, 2001). Interestingly, interhierarchical networking among female media personnel is not automatically fostered by gender, Keil found, but depends on mutually recognized qualifications, common working concerns, and/or similar task domains. Networking *across* the broadcast hierarchy offers five types of advantages to managers. The first is information exchange about the functioning of the corporation and its informal operating procedures, which provide insights into "how things are done." Networking also helps with career planning and strategizing by offering information on how others have achieved their goals. Very importantly, networking furthermore provides professional support and encouragement, a hugely important way for the tilted token to counteract her isolation at the top. Of course, this support and encouragement from selected female and male colleagues also increases a manager's visibility and thus may enhance her upward mobility. Herminia Ibarra (1993) found that female and male networks within a corporation are of equal size, but that both genders tend to interact only with their own gender-segregated networks. This points to the absolute necessity for female managers to seek out other women in the organization when they are aiming for the top.

In addition to networking, mentoring is another important informal process that helps to assuage the loneliness of the pioneer generation female managers. Mentorship is not new, but what is new about it today is that females are beginning to serve as mentors themselves. The historical evidence on CBC's first female bosses, as well as interviews in Germany, show that mentorship is now recognized as a formal component of overall career and human resource development. Mentoring can be divided into two functions according to O'Leary and Ickovics (1992): its "career" function to enhance learning the ropes and preparing for advancement and its "psychosocial" function to enhance the sense of competence, clarity of identity, and effectiveness in one's professional career. Both of these functions are demonstrated in the Canadian and German experiences. The most critical element in a successful mentor–mentee relationship is the recognition of *reciprocal professional benefits,* not sexual favors. Unfortunately, attractive younger professional women continue to be harassed by gossip that they have "slept" their way to the top. Consequently, mentor relationships are harder to manage and often provide fewer benefits for females and minorities than for males. Although most advocates of mentoring recommend that mentor and protégé be of the same gender, there is some indication that female professionals both prefer and attain their greatest benefits from male mentors (O'Leary & Ickovics, 1992). This is an easy to understand outcome in what Kanter would call a tilted corporate situation, where females constitute less than 15% of the group. Many of the CBC's second- and third-generation female managers, the previous section demonstrated, were mentored by such people as Dodi Robb and Helen James, who entered the corporation before and during World War II, when males were drafted. Since then, second- and third-generation female media managers in North America have done particularly well in the public broadcast institution (CBC/Radio Canada) and in heading cable's new specialty channels in Canada and the United States (Crean, 1985).

The final issue that needs addressing is how male journalists are coping with the increased presence of females in managerial positions and the fact that almost 27% of news directors in the U.S. television industry were female by 1997. Are the White male managers feeling threatened in any way and can one call this a form of "backlash" within the profession? Although it is not "politically correct" to state such feelings, a number of U.S. studies from the late 1990s suggest that the scramble to reshape the newsrooms to better reflect their communities does make White male journalists anxious, particularly in the newspaper industry. For the first time, these professionals believe they have to overcome the handicaps of race and gender that have traditionally worked against women and minorities. Although they acknowledge that past injustices need to be remedied, they feel threatened, frustrated, and in many cases angry. Minorities conversely, deride White male "angst" and maintain that newspapers, in particular, are still not doing enough for equity (Shepard, 1993). Can these starkly differing assessments be verified? A 1993 survey by the American Association of Newspaper Editors (ASNE) suggests that White males have little to worry about, at least in the press. This survey of 987 U.S. papers (out of 1,535) estimated that

10.3% of newsroom professionals were gender and ethnic minorities, less than half of their 26% representation in the general population. In 1978, that figure was only 4%. As in Canada, integration is happening much faster in large metropolitan papers like *USA Today* (21%), *The Los Angeles Times* (18%), the *Detroit Free Press* (21%), the *Miami Herald* (30%), and the *Seattle Times* (26%), which have high concentrations of Asian, Hispanic, and other minorities in their cities. Although this minority hiring pattern mirrors women's integration into the press since the 1980s, it does not reflect it in terms of numbers. Where in 1993, there were no Canadian newspaper newsrooms without female managers, 45% of all U.S. newspapers, representing nearly one third of the country's total circulation, continue to have no minority staff in their newsrooms at all (Shepard, 1993).

The backlash in the United States seems to be primarily focused on the ways in which management implements gender and ethnic diversity criteria in hiring. Three complaints were most frequently heard. The first notes that managers are too harried by daily production pressures to be sensitive to diversity criteria and that they are motivated by bonuses, rather than by convictions. This problem is compounded by the fact that most top managers are White and male. In 1993, ASNE reported that 85% of newsroom executives in the United States were male and 96% were White. Not only were they White and male, they had also been in the business for a long time to reach these positions. Consequently, as one respondent put it, "the people that [avoided] hiring minorities for so long are the very same people who are now in charge of doing it" (Shepard, 1993, p. 24). This is a compelling argument and suggests that the corporate strategy of making line managers responsible for integration and promotion *without* combining it with a set of company-wide personnel training and education courses and a designated equity officer, is counterproductive. It also falls short, if there is no monitoring from the top, as the Gannett and CBC initiatives showed, where the presidents and vice presidents, as well as the line managers were involved in ethnic and gender initiatives. Without such corporate commitment, the "backlash" phenomenon is exacerbated. Canadian media initiatives like that of the CBC feature company-wide strategies and involve males as well as females, an educational approach that conforms with the "best practices" recommended by the Gannett Corporation. In Europe, in contrast, the small (between 2% and 8%) female representation in management is not yet threatening to the male power structure and is therefore not yet resulting in resistance, although EU directives on broadcast equity are planning for a possible backlash.

A similar survey of television stations by Vernon Stone shows that the Federal Communication Commission's (FCC) diversity requirements for license renewal has borne fruit, but that the gains in the early 1990s were small, a 3-point increase from 15% to 18%. This means, as we have seen, that female managers overall still find themselves in the tilted token situation of a 15% minority (Stone, 1995/2000b). Under these circumstances, it is difficult to argue that White male broadcasters need to fear for their jobs. A comparison of total workforce figures in 1990 and 1995 demonstrates that White males lost two percentage points, dropping from 56% to 54% of all broadcast jobs. According to Stone, this drop did not benefit minorities but women, who increased their share of the TV workforce from 26% to 28%. Moreover, the losses in male broadcast jobs were made up by growth in the television sector, which recruited 700 more male and 1,000 more female staff by the mid-1990s (Stone 1995/2000b). The very slow rate of growth of minorities in both the print and broadcast media did not bode well for ASNE's goal that newsrooms should reflect the 30% minority composition of the U.S. population by the year 2000. Similar concerns are expressed in Canada, whose population of 32 million has a birth rate, which does not replace the population, and will therefore increasingly have to look to growth through immigration. Luckily, this Canadian immigration is today overwhelmingly non-White, ethnic, and includes minority females, boding well for more equitable ethnic representation in the media jobs of the next millennium.

Another newspaper study by Carolyn Byerly and Catherine Warren (1996) assesses the backlash phenomenon from a larger perspective. It inquires whether and under what circumstances journalists themselves are willing to become activists and initiate newsroom change. The survey found that activism is episodic as well as institutionalized. Episodic in the sense that it was retriggered in the early 1990s, by the Anita Hill case, the Los Angeles race riots, and the first Gulf War. All of these cases involved sexual harassment, assignment discrimination against Black journalists, and the lack of foreign correspondent postings for female staff. Institutionally, the study found that journalistic activism goes back to the 1970s and 1980s, originating in both management initiated "diversity groups," as well as journalist-initiated groups, to address discrimination problems. Byerly and Warren (1996) found that activism was practiced by only 31% of all respondents, especially in unionized papers, where groups already existed. On the efficacy of activism, 49% of the respondents said that in-house gender groups improved pay equity and promotions, an issue investigated in greater detail in the next chapter. Even in papers with a chilly environment for female journalists, however, a significant three fourths of respondents believe that activism has benefited them in a *personal* way, in the sense that it encouraged them to take part in organized attempts to challenge newsroom policies. About one third mentioned they are much better informed about ethnic and gender issues as a result of their activism, with another 20% mentioning that participation deepened their convictions to work for change, and another 13% stating that they feel more personally connected to others like themselves (Byerly & Warren, 1996). These explanations seem to confirm the private rewards that females and minorities derive from networking in their organization, a process that was discussed earlier.

THE FUTURE OF FEMALES IN MEDIA MANAGEMENT

What do these findings about the glass ceiling add up to and what do they mean for the future of females in media management? The differences in social characteristics and professional backgrounds between female and male editors-in-chief and general managers demonstrate that it is at present impossible to assess whether females in senior management will behave differently in their jobs or not. As we have seen, females in power roles are still so rare that it is impossible to design research that allows for the systematic analysis of gender differences in recruitment to senior management and in the performance of the executive role. Furthermore, if female representation at the top is to increase, vacancies must be filled by external recruitment. To increase this recruitment, concerned groups like the Canadian Women in Communications (CWC) headed by CBC's Pamela Wallin, must continue to agitate for female management representation. They are helping the cause by circulating their database of qualified female broadcasters and experts and by agitating for half of all upcoming media board vacancies to be filled by female managers (CBC Equity Newsletter, 2000). Because respondents indicated that the most important consideration in making executive appointments are senior management's evaluation of a candidate's performance in previous organizational positions, female outside candidates are once again at a disadvantage. Many of these, as we have seen, will be recruited from other organizations and thus lack the ready-made networks that their male colleagues can call on, who are recruited from within.

According to Carol Agocs (1989), who monitored employment equity regulations for the Federal Contractors Program (FCP), three organizational characteristics are positively associated with more equitable access to top management posts. All of these have been corroborated by my Canadian organizational surveys. The first is employment equity activity by the employers themselves, who understand the positive contributions that females and minorities make to the workplace. Another turns out to be a greater than 30% representation of females in middle management ready to move up. The third characteristic, a low level of gender segregation across job classes, refers to what Kanter calls the importance of female representation in all working groups. The Canadian and U.S. evidence shows that all three of these structural prerequisites are today more present in the broadcast than the print sectors. Broadcast stations since the 1990s have been more aggressive in putting employment equity regulations in place, whereas the newspaper industry, as was shown here has been slower in hiring females and minorities to reflect their readership characteristics more accurately (Shepard, 1993). Yet, even here, U.S. figures show that 24% of all news directors in the daily press are female, as are 25% of the vice presidents at the country's four networks (ABC, CBS, CNN, NBC). Together, this evidence suggests that we are at a crucial cross roads, where most North American (although not the European) media organizations have sufficient females in the middle-management ranks poised to move up to the top. Here, they will finally be able to give voices to the unrepresented half of their country's populations.

chapter 6

EQUAL OPPORTUNITY LEGISLATION IN NORTH AMERICA AND EUROPE

ITS IMPACT ON MEDIA EMPLOYMENT

In the discussion on the glass ceiling, references were made to the fact that female personnel in the media corporations of North America and western Europe were making use of equity legislation to further their cause. This chapter investigates three broad issues that are complexly interrelated with each other. The first concerns the varieties of equity legislation, which were introduced in the different countries and how they differ from each other. In assessing this legislation, Sandra Burt (1986) argues that it is important to distinguish between what she calls role-equality and role-change legislation. She defines the difference by noting: "Role equality has as its goal to equalize the opportunities for men and women to compete for public roles. Role change has as its goal, change in the dependent female roles of wife, mother, and homemaker, holding out the potential of greater sexual freedom and independence in a variety of contexts" (p. 115). It will become evident that Europe lagged behind North America both in the time it took to initiate the programs, as well as the types of equal opportunity legislation it embraced for its female staff. Why this is the case is at present not well understood.

Another closely related issue concerns the efficacy of equal opportunity legislation. Has it provided greater access for women into different media sectors and/or improved their working conditions? No one has yet broached this difficult question, but material in the previous chapters provides a basis for such a comparison. These chapters suggest that there have indeed been improvements in female media employment in North America since the 1970s and 1980s, and that these improvements are not nearly as great in western Europe. There is spirited debate moreover, as to whether

these improvements in media employment result from labor-market expansion, the growth or stagnation of certain media industries, and/or the
requirements of equal opportunity legislation (Coates, 1986). The fact that
the rates of change were much slower and much less for ethnic minorities
tends to discredit the labor market explanation. Yet, as is seen here, labor-
market expansion conditions in a particular media sector, as well as equity
legislation seem to be interlinked. The third and final issue to be addressed
in this chapter deals with whether equity programs have improved the promotional opportunities of female staff. Much has been written about the
complexity of this issue and of the need for a feminist explanation that is not
"essentialist." This means that the explanation must not assume the fundamental identity of gender with biological traits. Various chapters have
already demonstrated that the majority of female media practitioners are
ambivalent about the efficacy of equity legislation, although many feel that
it has raised their consciousness (Cunco, 1990; Kelly, 1988).

EQUAL OPPORTUNITY LEGISLATION IN CANADA

Burt (1986), who is an authority on the second-wave women's movement,
points to the social and work changes in women's lives since World War II
as the source for equal opportunity legislation in Canada. On Canada's
100th birthday in 1967, liberal feminists began agitating for a Royal
Commission on the Status of Women to survey women's changing life conditions and to make recommendations for the future. Two processes in particular were on women's minds at the time. The first concerned the problems
females were facing in the industrialization processes after World War II,
where they had limited access to jobs and were routed into gender-segregated types of work, which depressed their earnings. The second resulted from
the unwillingness of Canada's political parties to give females an equal voice
in the political realm. There were, in the late 1960s, still separate women's
auxiliaries within the Canadian Liberal and Conservative parties, which had
very little input into party councils. Both of these processes reinforced a
search for remedies, in what Burt called role-equality initiatives, which have
as their goal to equalize the opportunities for men and women to compete
for public roles.

Burt, Code, and Dorney (1988) suggest that two events in 1970 signaled
a transition in legislators' thinking about women's roles. They were the
addition of maternity leave provisions to the Canada Labor (Standards)
Code, and the publication of the *Report* of the Royal Commission on the
Status of Women. She points out that although the *Report* was not implemented in its entirety, it contributed to a realization that the role of "work-

ing mother" needed to be incorporated into future legislation, a fact that led to improvements in women's equality rights in the public sphere (Burt, 1988). A number of government initiatives were undertaken to respond to the Royal Commission's recommendations and to set up a federal framework to integrate women's concerns into national policymaking. This federal structure encompasses three components: the Minister for the Status of Women; a government department known as Status of Women Canada (SWC) to coordinate and review existing legislation; and the Canadian Advisory Council on the Status of Women. The latter is an independent organization, funded by the government to conduct research and to disseminate information of concern to women. Their deliberations added an anti-discrimination clause to the Unemployment Insurance Act of 1972 and thus, for the first time, gave unemployed women the same benefits as males.

The second governmental initiative, to guarantee females equality rights in the public sphere, started with the passage of the 1977 Canadian Human Rights Act. This act makes it discriminatory not to pay equal wages to men and women performing work of equal value in the same establishment. In 1976, moreover, the Cabinet adopted the principle of affirmative action for hiring practices in crown corporations (such as banks and the CBC), as well as those industries benefiting from government contracts. In 1979, finally, the Cabinet set up an Affirmative Action Directorate to promote voluntary adoption of affirmative action in the private sector and to improve the representation of three target groups: women, native people, and disabled persons at all levels of the workforce. Since the late 1980s both levels of government accepted the principle of "affirmative action," which affirms that women and men should be treated equally when they do the same work. Burt (1988) observes that this principle improves women's access to the public sphere, but requires them to behave like men and compete on men's terms for jobs that men have created and defined. Affirmative action was extended in 1986 by Bill C-62 to cover federally regulated companies, as well as crown corporations with more than 100 employees. This turned out to be an ineffective initiative because there were no provisions made to enforce compliance on the part of private contractors. Although the Canadian Human Rights Commission was designated as the watchdog for this initiative, this organization lacks the human and investigative resources for effective supervision and had a backlog of more than 1,500 cases by the early 1990s (Burt, 1988).

The third initiative, implementation of equal pay for work of equal value laws, have been much more difficult to accomplish because they challenge the traditional notion that women's work is less valuable than men's. At the core of equal pay for equal value legislation is the feminist argument that women should be allowed to remain different from men without being economically penalized for their differences (Burt, 1988). As already mentioned, the federal government passed the Canadian Human Rights Act in

1977, which established the principle of equal pay for work of equal value in the federal public service. On the face of it, this was a great leap forward for women, but the federal guidelines for equal value were poorly written and the program, therefore, had only limited effectiveness. So, in 1984 the national Equal Pay Program was initiated to ensure that employers under federal jurisdiction adopt the principle of equal pay for work of equal value. The success of this program, it turns out, depends on the provincial legislatures and their interpretations. In Canada, Quebec was the first (1975) to implement it for their public employees, followed by Manitoba (1986). In Ontario the legislation applies to *all firms* with more than 100 employees, and mandates that wage adjustments come into effect between 2 and 4 years from the date of proclamation of the act. However, the Neilson Task Force (1987) points out that the equal pay initiatives have not been very effective to date, and that the significant wage gap between full-time employed females and males has remained virtually unchanged since 1978 (as cited in Burt, 1988). The reasons for this failure lie with the fact that labor-force equality for women requires improved access to affordable and reliable day care, pensions for housewives, maternity leave rules, and spousal allowances. Only child care was addressed through a National Strategy in 1987, which promised to finance 200,000 new child care spaces and to increase the child care expense deduction to $4,000 per year. As a result, Canada's Plan of Action for the United Nations Women's Decade of Action (1975–1985) focused primarily on ethical, rather than substantive issues. These included action on rape, sexual harassment, and wife-battering. The only substantive issues addressed were pension reforms for women, whose employers had to treat them like male employees, and a requirement that crown corporations, among them the media, serve as testing grounds for what Burt (1986) calls "role-change" legislation.

Although the Plan of Action laid the groundwork, the shift in the goals of equity legislation received an unexpected boost from a coalition of women's groups in 1982, who demanded that the newly drafted Canadian Charter of Rights be made more inclusive. According to lawyer Lise Gotell (1990), the crucial change, which they achieved, is found in Section 15 (1), which expands the procedural guarantee of equality contained in the Bill of Rights, to include equality "under the law." As a consequence of these legal additions, the Canadian Charter of Rights and Freedoms now protects not only equality in the *administration* of the law, but also equality in the *substance* of the law. Moreover, Section 15 (2) of the Charter, the affirmative action clause, protects programs that address the conditions of disadvantaged groups and thus reaches beyond the conception of equality as "sameness." It now potentially recognizes the necessity of different treatment to compensate for women's historical disadvantages. Finally, the sexual equality clause, Section 28, operating outside the override provision of the

Charter, acts to enhance the guarantee of sexual equality included in Section 15. In sum, the equality sections of the Charter convey a clear antidiscriminatory intent (Gotell, 1990). Catherine MacKinnon (1987), an American legal scholar, asserts that these Charter provisions are far advanced beyond any comparable instruments in the United States and Europe, in guaranteeing Canadian women full citizenship rights and access to the public sphere.

The final major piece of legislation is the Employment Equity Act of 1986, which was designed to supersede the ineffective Canadian Human Rights Act of 1977. It mandates that all government-owned and regulated corporations, as well as large contractors with more than 100 employees have to report annually on the employment and salary levels of women and other minorities. To enlarge the groups covered, an employment equity bill for the public service was introduced in 1994, because even here, although women constitute almost half of all employees, they were concentrated in the lowest-paying jobs (Saunders, 1998). The past two decades demonstrate that employment equity is well on the way to being achieved for female employees in the public and broadcasting sectors, despite the fact that the other designated groups, such as native people, ethnic minorities, and the handicapped have made few gains. By the mid-1990s, native people made up a paltry 2% of Canada's federal workforce, disabled workers 3%, and visible minorities an infinitesimal 4%. Most importantly, the advances in female workforce representation raised the public consciousness on equality issues just as it has in Europe. Moreover, it led to the formal recognition of women as a legitimate and named constituency in the newly rewritten Broadcasting Act of 1991, in which fair employment and representation are reaffirmed (Robinson, 1992).

Hannah Pandian (1999), past editor of the *Media and Gender Monitor*, considers the Canadian gender and media policy model to be the best developed gender communications policy system today. She justifies this assessment by pointing out that guidelines and recommendations on self-regulation exist at several levels, both judiciary and voluntary, and in different domains of the communications industry. She ascribes the success of the media policy to Canada's preoccupation with preserving the country's cultural identity through promoting local talent, which has been at the heart of Canadian regulatory policy since the 1920s. Beyond that, Pandian observes, in contrast to the United States, the hierarchical relationship between the different regulatory bodies makes self-regulation a viable option for broadcasters (Pandian, 1999). Within this framework, the independently operating CRTC is the top institution and is responsible for implementing policy under the Broadcasting Act. It lays down broad requirements for license renewal, such as providing programming for a variety of designated viewer/listener groups (including women) and fostering local over foreign-created shows in prime time in both official languages. The Canadian

Broadcast Standards Council (CBSC), a nongovernmental organization (NGO), constitutes a second tier within the national framework. The CBSC, which was created by the Canadian Association of Broadcasters, functions as a self-regulating body with five regional councils. As the lobby organization of Canada's private broadcasters, it administers industry-generated codes regarding programming content and managed to get the highly rated American "Howard Stern" radio program off the air for breaching the sex-role portrayal code (Pandian, 1999). Section J of this code requires that freedom of expression be tempered by gender-equity concerns in media programming. A final component of the national framework introduces procedures for regular public hearings, which offer media access to consumers, and facilitate communication between the public and it's policymakers. The impact of these rules on broadcast content is further assessed in Chapter 7, which deals with programming.

EQUAL OPPORTUNITY LEGISLATION IN THE UNITED STATES

In the United States, pay equity was mandated by the 1963 Equal Pay Act, required by Title VII of the 1964 Civil Rights Act and supported by a 1980 Presidential Executive Order and a 1981 Supreme Court ruling. It thus preceded the Canadian act by 7 years, but emerged within a completely different political context. This context was the country's preoccupation with the inferior status of Black Americans, both politically and socially, which the Civil Rights Act was designed to address. This act therefore focused on providing all Americans with voting privileges, access to public accommodations, and equal educational chances, as well as employment opportunities. The 1960s Civil Rights Movement, which particularly targeted the southern states, organized, marched, and confronted the federal government of President Kennedy with demands for major political changes in voter registration, desegregation of public spaces such as buses and restaurants, as well as access to integrated public schools. On the social side, Title VII of the Civil Rights Act, in contrast, was less driven by racial preoccupations. It acknowledged that discrimination in employment existed not only in the south, but everywhere in the United States and that it affected many other groups in society, such as women and minorities. Comments by Ohio Senator Stephen Young at the time indicate that the push for employment equity had a similar origin as in Canada, namely the changing workforce requirements that the postindustrial revolution was unleashing. He described employment discrimination as ranging from absolute rejection to more subtle forms of invidious distinctions and concluded, "most frequently it manifests itself through relegation to 'traditional' positions and through discriminatory promotional practices" (as cited in Stevens, 1985, p. 1). Title VII, making workplace discrimination illegal, was not passed until 1972. It specifically prohibits an employer of 15 or more employees to (a) fail or refuse to hire or to discharge any individual, or otherwise to discriminate . . . with respect to . . . compensation, terms, conditions, or privileges of employment, because of such individual's race, colour, religion, sex, or national origin; or (b) limit, segregate, or classify employees or applicants for employment in any way which would deprive . . . any individual of employment opportunities or otherwise adversely affect his status as an employee, because of such individual's race, color, religion, sex, or national origin (Stevens, 1985). The majority of lawsuits by women and racial minorities were consequently not filed and settled until later in the decade. The U.S. Supreme Court, furthermore, did not recognize sexual harassment as a violation of Title VII until 1986 (Byerly, 2004).

In 1964, Congress chose not to enumerate specific discriminatory practices, nor to elucidate the parameters of such activities. Therefore, the determination of what constitutes a violation has been left to the courts in the United States. The courts, moreover, have considerable discretion in deciding what remedy to impose if the plaintiff is successful. George Stevens elaborates that to establish a case of disparate treatment, the plaintiff must provide evidence that the defendant treated him or her differently from other similarly situated persons who are not members of the protected class, and that one or more adverse employment decisions or conditions resulted from that treatment. These interpretations indicate that Title VII constitutes what Burt (1986) calls "role-equality" legislation. It is designed to eliminate discrimination, it does not require that underrepresented persons be hired, retained, or promoted. Court decisions have furthermore elaborated that under Title VII a media employer may fire a qualified employee to hire an even better one if the employer's behavior is not motivated by animosity toward a protected group or its members. And considerable latitude is allowed an employer in deciding who is a "qualified" person. The employer may, for instance, place more value on work experience than a journalism degree, or vice versa, in making employment decisions (Stevens, 1985).

Two issues of gender discrimination, as indicated in the previous chapter, weigh most heavily on female media personnel: the fact that they are paid less than similarly situated male employees and how "comparable work" is defined. On these issues, the U.S. court decided that the crucial issue is not what skills are possessed by a media applicant, but whether the duties *actually performed* require or utilize those additional skills. It also regards as unimportant the fact that job titles might differ, reasoning that the focus should be on "actual job requirements and performance, not on job classifications or titles." Comparable work furthermore permits the employer to apply different standards of compensation "pursuant to a bona fide seniority or merit system, or a system which measures earnings by quantity or quality of production, or when the plaintiff's work requires less 'skill and effort, and responsibility' than that of a male employee" (Stevens, 1985, pp. 9–10). Stevens concludes that because equal employment opportunity law has developed in a blue-collar context, the courts have tended to defer to the judgments of employers to resolve professional employment disputes. This means that Title VII may provide little direct help to many minority and female job applicants in the media professions, unless the watchdog Equal Employment Opportunity Commission (EECO) takes an activist stance. Its impact on the newspaper industry is discussed in the next section. Despite these drawbacks, minority and female communicators have benefited in two domains according to Stevens: They cannot legally be paid less than a White male for work of similar value and over time, furthermore, the antidiscrimination injunction will diversify the media work force and thus provide women and other minorities with more equal chances. Such an evaluation relies heavily on a voluntaristic "trickle down" effect that, as Chapter 5 demonstrated, has left female staff in the press in a less desirable situation than their sisters in broadcasting because the FCC, in the 1970s, mandated equity for license renewal.

EQUAL OPPORTUNITY LEGISLATION IN THE EUROPEAN UNION

Although the six west European countries (Britain, France, Germany, Italy, Spain, Denmark) that have been compared in this book introduced equal opportunity legislation at different times during the late 1970s or early 1980s, their membership in the European Community (EC) provides them with a common framework for antidiscrimination legislation. These supranational rules, however, do not prescribe implementation strategies, which are informed by each country's unique legal and political structures. In Britain, for instance, the implementation of equality of opportunity legislation is focused on the organizational level, and assumes a gradualist approach. In Denmark, in contrast, gender neutrality is the starting point for implementation of equal opportunity strategies and thus involves preferential treatment for the minority group in a variety of professions. In addition, Denmark sets aside positions and thus countenances "positive discrimination," where imbalances in personnel groups have been established (Egsmose, 2001). How have these initiatives played themselves out in the European broadcast and print industries?

According to European Community records, the EC has a long history of commitment to equality between women and men. In the 1970s, EC legislation on equal pay and equal treatment pioneered a common standard of rights for individuals in all member states. The next phase of the Commission's work started in 1982, with the adoption of a series of Community Action Programs on Equality. Their goal, according to Commission member Vasso Papandreou, was to promote equality not only in law, but also in reality. The Commission's first equal opportunity legislation was passed in 1983, when a comparison of female and male broadcast personnel uncovered substantial imbalances in various job categories, especially in the technical and management sectors. These disturbing findings led to the establishment, in 1986, of a Steering Committee for Equal Opportunities in Broadcasting. At about the same time, in 1984 the Council of Europe adopted a Recommendation on Equality Between Women and Men in the Media (R [84] 17 of the Committee of Ministers). Parallel concerns encouraged the European Parliament in 1987 to pass a resolution on the Depiction and Position of Women in the Media and the institution, in 1988, of the Prix NIKI, aimed at promoting a better image of women in television programs (Commission Employment, Industrial Relations and Social Affairs "Guide," 1991).

In order to understand the European implementation strategies, the EC's interpretations of such key terms as *discrimination* and *positive action* need to be clarified. Interestingly, in contrast to North American legislation, the Commission makes a distinction between what it calls *direct* and *indirect* discrimination. Both of these are illegal under the 1976 EC Directive on Equal Treatment, which requires "both men and women to be treated equally as regards access to employment, vocational training and promotion, and working conditions." In light of this directive, employers may be guilty of indirect discrimination "if they create requirements or conditions, which adversely affect a greater proportion of women than men" (Guide, 1991, p. 3). Examples given of indirect discrimination are among other things, deciding not to promote people who have child-care responsibilities, excluding part-time workers from training opportunities, or imposing unnecessary age limits or mobility requirements on certain jobs.

According to the Equal Opportunities in European Broadcasting: Guide to Good Practice (1991) booklet, avoiding discrimination is only a start. The spirit of the EC legislation calls for a much more active approach. The 1984 EC Recommendation on Positive Action explicitly encourages *positive* measures to eliminate inequalities that affect working women. Positive action does not mean "reverse discrimination," but has two purposes: "to create opportunities to allow women to 'catch up' with men . . . right through to giving women the edge in a 'tie-break' situation especially in appointments to senior management positions" (1991, p. 3). Although 36%

of the EC's broadcasting workforce in 1990 was female, males held 94% of
the top decision-making jobs in radio and television stations. These disproportions, as demonstrated in Chapter 5, have primarily to do with two factors: male managers' ingrained misconceptions about female workers' competencies and the fact that many of the senior-level positions are never
advertised, either internally or externally. Research in 1989 showed that men
were 15 times more likely than women to be "directly" appointed to management posts in the EC broadcast stations (Guide, 1991, p. 9). Fair selection and promotion practices are therefore of the essence in bringing about
change. To operate effectively, fair-selection practices require the presence of
females on interviewing panels, guidance, and training for these panels and
adopting methods, such as tests to minimize subjectivity and be sure that the
initial short list disadvantages neither female nor male applicants. Finally,
research has shown that women are more likely to apply for jobs if these
applications specifically target women or indicate that preference will be
given to a female applicant in the case of a tie. BRT Belgium, DR Denmark,
and most German and Dutch, as well as some British broadcasting companies practice such positive action in selection. The Dutch national public
system, NOS, ran an ad with the following content: "Because in NOS
women are under-represented in this kind of job, in the case of equal suitability, preference will be given to a woman; therefore we explicitly invite
women to apply" (Guide, 1991, p. 10).

Progressive broadcasting companies have, since the 1980s introduced a
variety of initiatives to equip all staff with the confidence, skills, and experience that will enhance their talents. Among these are training courses to
increase personal self-confidence and professional development (WDR &
ZDF Germany, DR Denmark, BRT Belgium). Other companies have developed what are called *familiarization* courses in the production and technical
areas, in order to familiarize female staff with production jobs. Included are
sports and music production as well as electronic engineering (BBC &
Thames, Central, and LWT Britain; RTE Ireland and RTP Portugal). In
addition, management training, which is widely supported in North
America, has also been introduced in Europe to prepare females to negotiate the glass ceiling into upper management. The BBC and the Independent
Television Association (ITVA), both of Britain, launched the first women in
management courses in 1986 with excellent results, and Dutch, Greek, Irish,
and Danish stations are following suit. Beyond that, other EC countries
have followed the Scandinavian lead in work/family coordination initiatives.
All of these countries have generous maternity–paternity leave arrangements, they also provide support for child care either on the premises or
near by and limit the working day. Danish Radio furthermore, has experi-
mented with flexible working conditions by permitting individual production teams to decide how resources of personnel and money are to be used.

British broadcasters have additionally explored "job sharing," which divides a full-time post between two employees at *their request*. In the BBC, job-shares exist among producers, vision mixers, floor managers, costume designers, as well as more obvious categories such as secretaries and administrators (Guide, 1991, p. 13). The only domain where virtually no progress has been made is in equal pay for work of equal value, where only Denmark had launched an analysis by 1990. Such an exercise requires two things: the examination of female and male salaries in identical occupations and a review of the salary scales for all jobs, based on a re-evaluation of the skills, responsibilities, and educational requirements involved (Guide, 1991, p. 13). The effect of this lack of a comparative salary scrutiny is further discussed in the next chapter.

In looking to the future, European broadcasters who are facing increased competition from private stations, have committed to two initiatives to improve the conditions of female employees. The first consists of reinforcing existing legislation at the national and the supranational levels, and the second is more effective implementation of equal opportunity initiatives. The British Broadcasting Act of 1990, for instance, empowers the Independent Television Commission to grant and renew licenses on condition that the broadcaster arranges to promote "equality of opportunity between men and women" in its employment and to periodically review progress. This sounds similar to the Canadian legislative initiative under the Broadcasting Act of 1991, which also mandates that equity issues be addressed. Beyond that, the supranational European Commission itself supported positive action in its Third Action Programme for equality between women and men (1991–1995).

In 1995, Margaret Gallagher was asked to investigate the effectiveness of equity legislation in European broadcasting. In the nearly 10 intervening years since her earlier 1984 and 1986 studies, Gallagher found that access for females had indeed improved in the 15 states, with the average size of their female staff increasing from 30% to 33% (Gallagher, 1984, 1986; Gallagher, 1995). Although females continue to be segregated into a much narrower range of broadcast jobs, change is beginning to happen even here. This is evidenced by the fact that there has been a 12% drop of females in administration from 60% to 48%, whereas they have tripled their presence in the technical and crafts areas (camera, sound, lighting) from an infinitesimal 4% to 14%. More importantly, females have also made gains in the editorial sectors, where they held 20% of positions in 1986 and have advanced to 24% 10 years later. This progress, as shown previously, follows the North American pattern by a decade.

Gallagher is more cautious in her assessment of the promotional and management opportunities for female staff in European broadcasting. Although about 20% of television producers were female in 1986, they were found primarily in two gender-segregated program areas: education (25% of all staff) and children's programming, where they had a remarkable 38% of all producer positions. Conversely, females were underrepresented in the more prestigious departments, such as news and current affairs, where they held only 14% of the producer, director, and editorial jobs (Gallagher, 1995). Ten years later, varied equity initiatives had increased this figure to an average of 24% of all editorial staff. Yet, as already documented, there were great variations between countries on both sides of the Atlantic. Three groups of countries had less effective equity initiatives judging by their small proportion of females in editorial positions. They were Belgium, Germany, and Spain, where the averages varied between 10% and 13%. The middle group of countries, with better promotional opportunities, include Britain, the Netherlands, and Italy, where the editorial proportions are around 30%. The best promotional opportunities are found in the Nordic countries, with more than 40% female representation in the editorial domain (Gallagher, 1995).

Only the management suites of the European broadcasting institutions remain virtually out of bounds for female broadcasters. In 1986 there were a negligible 6% of females in the top three grades of senior management, and they were found at the lowest level of the hierarchy (Gallagher, 1986). Ten years later, these figures hardly budged and still hover around a regional average of 11% females in top management. Interestingly, France had nearly double that figure (24%), whereas Britain had 14% and Germany a dismal 4% (Gallagher, 1995). In general, Gallagher's analysis of the European situation found that on average, males are seven times more likely than females to reach the top of the power pyramid. Yet, once again there were country variations in what we have called the glass-ceiling phenomenon. Britain's more detailed breakdown shows that Channel 4 had the highest proportion of female managers at a healthy 33%, followed by Grampian Television at 25%, Granada Television at 18%, and the British Broadcasting Corporation (BBC) at a mere 15% (Gallagher, 1995). This finding suggests that Britain's younger broadcast organizations, rather than the public service institutions, have been most open to giving their female personnel a more equitable share of responsibility. Only detailed, country-by-country comparisons will be able to determine whether making equity concerns mandatory for license renewal is a more effective strategy than letting each organization implement its own rules, as in the European Community.

More effective implementation of equality regulations requires the design of a multifaceted implementation strategy for each broadcaster. Experience has shown that this entails detailed planning, administration, and coordination across the organization as a whole. Different broadcasters approach this task in different ways, but the suggested initiatives are similar on both sides of the Atlantic. The EC Commission guidelines make four recommendations. First, that a senior executive take responsibility for policy design and be ultimately made accountable for its implementation. In the CBC in the 1980s, this was the president of the corporation, who consulted with lower level executives and monitored annual progress reports. Experience also shows that coordination and implementation will be more effective if it is entrusted to a designated equality officer with special teaching and mediation skills. Thames TV (UK) was the first European broadcasting organization to appoint an equality officer in 1981, followed by the BBC in 1986. Finally, it is desirable to have a group or committee to support and advise the equality officer, and share responsibility. At the Gannett newspapers in the United States, as seen earlier, these were heads of departments, who furthermore received bonuses for improving equity targets in their domains. Finally, the Guide points out that a monitoring and reporting system is essential so that progress can be traced. This involves regular collection of statistics concerning the number of women and men in all job categories, salary bands, and/or hierarchical levels, including senior management. Furthermore, it is important to register the number of women and men involved at each stage of recruitment (applications, interviews, appointments) for all advertised vacancies, as well as the number of women and men involved in company financed training courses (Guide, 1991). Together these initiatives provide a framework for "good practice" in the implementation of equal opportunities in European broadcast stations and in assessing future progress.

Lisbeth Egsmose (2001) is one of the rare researchers who have compared antidiscrimination initiatives in different countries. She makes the interesting suggestion that there seem to be at least two different implementation philosophies among broadcasters. She calls these the "liberal" and the "corporatist" perspectives. The liberal perspective has as its goal to change behavior through an authoritative, top–down governance structure. Her research shows that behavior change is initiated through rule-setting, which establishes equitable conditions for individual women to compete for jobs and promotions. To achieve these results, whole departments are monitored and receive positive or negative sanctions depending on their progress (Egsmose, 2001). The "corporatist" perspective, in contrast, has as its goal to change attitudes with respect to discrimination. To achieve these attitude changes, a participatory bottom–up model of governance seems to be called for because the majority group has to be persuaded to yield some power. According to this implementation philosophy, legislative equality will be achieved through quotas that guarantee "fair distribution" of rewards for the disadvantaged minority.

To her surprise, Egsmose found that the two public broadcasters, BBC and Radio Denmark, which she assumed were going to follow similar equity strategies, in fact subscribed to different implementation approaches. The

BBC, her interviews showed, followed the liberal and Radio Denmark the corporatist model (Egsmose, 2001). In the BBC, where 33% of the staff in 1991 were female, the first equity officer was appointed in 1986 and located among the top 12 corporate decision makers. The unit printed a carefully researched brochure, laying out the corporation's policy in the following words: "The BBC is committed to equal opportunities for all, irrespective of race, colour, creed, ethnic or national origins, gender, marital status, sexuality, disability or age." According to the equity officer, the corporation's goal is to reflect the gender and ethnic composition of the nation, a goal similar to that voiced by the American Association of Newspaper Editors in the United States. To achieve this goal, in an organization with a male-dominated command structure, the corporation aimed at having 30% of all senior- and 40% of all middle-level management positions filled by females by the end of the 1990s (Egsmose, 2001). These targets proved, however, to be unrealistically high and impossible to achieve in the short space of only 6 years, even though the BBC followed all of the EC implementation recommendations. The corporation assigned top-level responsibility, designated an officer, set targets, and introduced monitoring mechanisms.

To increase the 30% female participation rate, Radio Denmark's corporatist model called for collective decision making and collective responsibility. Consequently, when the implementation was moved to the personnel office, the status advisor position was abolished. Attitude change toward women in the workplace, it was argued, would be achieved through a bottom–up enlightenment and persuasion campaign. As in the BBC, official targets were set at 40% "in all professions, occupations and levels in the hierarchy . . . and that [this figure] will be respected when members for boards, committees and working groups are selected" (Egsmose, 2001, p. 484). Yet, no time limits or monitoring provisions were included in the implementation project. Consequently, interviews with professionals revealed that the action program did not create new job opportunities for female personnel in Radio Denmark. They also showed that in a 5- to 7-year period, only 7 out of 98 job advertisements encouraged women to apply. Finally, her interviews confirmed that positive action, although implied, continued to be thwarted by managers with opposing views. Egsmose concludes that "the modest and cautious approach at DR was surprising . . . in a country where rules and regulations are . . . administered with great zeal" (p. 488). She furthermore wonders whether the emphasis on equality at the political level tends to be interpreted by the broadcast organizations, as relieving them of responsibility for the amelioration of equity imbalances in their own organizations. Although the importance of the national political set-up must not be underestimated, an additional reason for Radio Denmark's disappointing performance may be the fact that it totally ignored the EC's implementation advice. Its organization fails to make a top executive responsible for equity concerns, it does not use a designated facilitator, and although it sets goals, their implementation is not mandated in a specific time frame, nor are there monitoring practices in place. Radio Denmark's experience should serve as a warning that organizational responsibility is indispensable in implementing equity concerns, because "disestablishing privilege" is fiercely resisted. I explore these resistances in the next section.

HAVE EQUITY POLICIES HELPED FEMALE MEDIA EMPLOYMENT AND PROMOTION?

To try to assess whether equity policies have helped female media employment, a number of distinctions have to be drawn. First of all, there is the distinction between the media sectors themselves (e.g., the daily press and broadcasting), where previous chapters have indicated that the private print industry lags behind broadcasting in implementing equity legislation in most countries. Beyond that, Chapter 5 indicated that raw employment data need to be supplemented with managerial and promotional information to assess how different firms have fared. Finally, there is the question of equal pay for work of equal value, a very thorny issue on which the least progress has been made in both North America and in western Europe and which is scrutinized in Chapter 7.

In the Canadian media, equity legislation has increased daily print employment only marginally because of the sector's stagnant growth, except in large metropolitan papers. Equity legislation has, however, added substantially to the number of women employed in broadcasting in both Canada and the United States. Chapter 3 indicated that there were 2,450 print journalists employed in 110 daily newspapers in the mid-1970s. Of these papers, seven had no female staff. Twenty years later, only 1,000 additional staff had been added in the country's 114 dailies. Of these people, 25% were female in 1975 and a mere 28% were female 20 years later. There is, however, a slight silver lining to these aggregate figures in that the majority of the new hirees were female, indicating that the *pool* of female journalists had nearly doubled in the interval. Of the nearly one thousand new persons hired since the early 1970s, 962 were female, an increase from 504 in 1975. Paul Audley (1983) and Christopher Dornan's (1996) assessments agree that two factors have contributed to the lack of growth in the Canadian newspaper sector. The first is media concentration, which increased overall circulation but reduced per capita circulation. The other is circulation growth, which did not keep pace with either the growth in adult population or the number of households in Canada. Between the 1970s and mid-1980s the adult population in Canada increased by 20.3% and the number of Canadian households by 30.5%, whereas aggregate weekly circulation increased by only half that amount, 16.5% (Audley, 1983).

Two additional factors, according to Chapter 2, affect female recruitment: regionalism and market size. Table 2.6 demonstrates that women have much better employment access possibilities in Ontario dailies (+9) and the Maritimes (+4) than in Quebec and the Prairies, where the number of women hired, between 1975 and 1995, dropped by 7 and 4 percentage points, respectively. These regional differences are reflected in differential production costs, which can be decreased only in those papers where circulation can be increased (Audley, 1983). Furthermore, I discovered that regional variations are modified by the size of the newspaper enterprise and the market it serves. Table 2.7 indicates that in the past 20 years, Ontario, with the largest number of large circulation papers, had the greatest increase in proportional representation of women in editorial positions. Here, the proportion of women in editorial positions increased by a full 12 percentage points from 20% to 32% of the staff. Only one other region, the Maritimes, increased their proportional representation by 8 percentage points, whereas the other three regions had growth rates of only 3 to 4 points. This indicates that a final factor affecting female rates of access to newspaper jobs is circulation size. In 1975, most female staff worked in small circulation dailies, whereas by 1995, the opposite was true, with the majority of female print journalists (like their male colleagues) found in large metropolitan dailies that employed nearly half of Canada's 3,451 editorial personnel.

Quebec, in contrast, is the province with a substantial decline in both female and male print employment since the 1970s. Here, my comparison shows, only 30 additional women were hired to editorial positions and the overall increase in the 20-year period was a meagre 156 people overall. Most of these found work in Montreal's large circulation papers *La Presse, Le Journal de Montréal,* and *The Gazette.* Quebec's unique situation is explained by its greater concentration of print ownership and its loss of small circulation dailies, both of which reduced the number of personnel in the intervening quarter century. Overall, this means that the Francophone province continues to have a much lower newspaper to population ratio than the nine provinces in English Canada. These print statistics suggest that affirmative action legislation has had little effect on reducing the existing recruitment barriers facing female staff in Canada's dailies. Meryl Aldridge (2001), who queried Toronto female journalists at the onset of the new millennium, corroborates this assessment. She found that none of her interviewees believe that equity legislation has had a direct influence on job access. The only thing equal opportunity legislation has done is to "expand women's horizons" (Aldridge, 2001, p. 618). Female personnel ascribe this to the fact that "the conditions of print employment in the 1990s were not determined by those at the head of the creative hierarchy like editors, . . . but by shareholder value and that implied doing more with less personnel." In a climate of concentration and cut-backs, they furthermore commented, internal agitation for change becomes muted because "meetings, drawing up codes of practice; embedding and monitoring the changed approaches to the organization and to their work, are simply too time-consuming and therefore too costly (to undertake)" (Aldridge, 2001, p. 621). This echoes the U.S. findings of Carolyn Byerly and Catherine Warren (1997), who discovered that only one third of editorial personnel, especially in unionized papers, were willing to spend the time to agitate for change, and furthermore agreed that these activities had raised their consciousness, rather than their equitable status.

Equity legislation is much more effective in Canadian broadcasting because television stations are subject to the Employment Equity Act of 1986. This mandates that all government-owned and regulated corporations, as well as large contractors with more than 100 employees have to report annually on the employment and salary levels of women and minorities. Information on female and minority staffing is additionally required as a condition of license renewal by the CRTC under the 1991 Broadcasting Act. The cultural sovereignty philosophy which is at the core of this act (section 3) highlights three key points: (a) the linkage between identity formation and exposure over time to television; (b) the linkage between television and cultural diversity, as audiences from different regions and ethnic, gender, and linguistic backgrounds are included in a fluid national mosaic; and (c) the linkage between political unity and a broadcasting system that is predominantly Canadian-owned (Canada, House of Commons Standing Committee on Communications and Culture, 1992). Liss Jeffrey (1996) comments that "this technological nationalism—as it has been disparagingly called—may be unfashionable, liberal, or romantic, yet it offers a historical ground and a principled inspiration for a Canadian broadcasting system that serves all Canadians" (1996, p. 215).

My evidence suggests that female access to television work has improved in both the public and private networks. Chapter 3 shows that 37% of Canada's total television personnel were female by 1995, a slightly higher percentage than in the United States, where they constituted 33% of the editorial workforce. In the 20 years, the total number of Canadian stations grew from 111 to 119 (Audley, 1983, p. 262), whereas the public sector CBC network shrank from 62 to 50 stations. Yet, the addition of 25 specialty channels since 1983 has further enlarged and diversified this network (Jeffrey, 1996). In Canada, the majority of television stations are located in Ontario (28), Quebec (31), and the Prairies (33), which are also home to more than 80% of the Canadian population. Chapter 3 has furthermore shown that the increase in private stations has provided younger broadcast journalists with better educational backgrounds, greater entry into all television newsrooms, as well as better promotion opportunities in large stations serving metropolitan markets. Table 5.4 demonstrates that female television managers have, consequently, nearly eliminated the glass ceiling in these stations. In metropolitan markets, with more than 500,000 population, females held an amazing 46% of assistant news directors and 49% of general managers and about 35% of the top news director positions. The same table demonstrates that females had nothing like the same influence in medium and small markets. In medium-sized markets (up to 499,000 population), they held only 22% of all management positions, with even less, 16% management representation in small stations (less than 100,000 population). This startling discrepancy, I have suggested, results from the fact that news editors in small and medium markets take on the duties performed by executive producers and managing editors in the large stations.

Equity legislation has been promoted more aggressively in the U.S. print industry than in Canada, although both countries have been equally effective in the broadcast domain. Part of this difference is accounted for by U.S. legal practices. More important, however, is the fact that the United States has an activist Equal Employment Opportunity Commission with the mandate and resources to enforce Title VII of the 1964 Civil Rights Act. As previously mentioned, this act prohibits discrimination in employment on the grounds of gender, ethnicity, age, and so forth. The EEOC has filed thousands of complaints and has been aided in determining culpability by human rights commissions in the individual states. According to Maurine Beasley and Sheila Gibbon (1993), who provide the most detailed assessment of the effects of antidiscrimination activities in the U.S. print media, the concessions typically made by employers are pledges to institute affirmative action programs and career training and integration of job categories, where women had disproportionately high representation. Administrative and clerical posts are among these, as we have seen. The Equal Employment Opportunity Commission was also successful in moving females into senior management, where females were scarce (Beasley & Gibbon, 1993).

A number of high-profile class action suits against such prestige newspapers as *The New York Times* (1972), *The Washington Post* (1974), and the *Detroit News* (1976) laid the groundwork for the implementation of equity concerns in the U.S. press 20 years earlier than action was taken in Canada. In the three newspaper cases, *The New York Times* response is most interesting because it embraced an affirmative action program, which specified that females be placed into one out of eight of the top corporate positions between 1978 and 1982. These included the publisher, all vice presidents, secretary, treasurer, and other directorships. Women were also to be placed into 25% of all top news and editorial department positions, including the posts of executive and managing editor, as well as what we have called the desk heads (metropolitan, foreign news, national news, sports, financial and the Washington bureau chief and *The New York Times Magazine* and the *Book Review*). In addition the 550 women working in *The New York Times* would share a back-pay award of $233,500 (Beasley & Gibbon, 1993). In *The Washington Post* case the EEOC concluded that females were not receiving promotions into higher paying positions on a similar basis with male employees and that they were discriminated in the hiring, assignment, and promotion processes because marital and family status played a role for them and not for the male candidates (Beasley & Gibbon 1993). Because these cases against the prestige press led to settlements, EEOC complaints and suits pursued throughout the following decades have been much more successful in pushing U.S. newspaper employers toward progress for women and minorities, than has been the case in Canada. Here, the Human Rights Commission lacks the supervisory resources to be an effective watchdog in the print domain and only one newspaper chain, owned by the Southam family, has consequently supported equity mandates. Even this initiative was, however, aborted when Conrad Black acquired their holdings in the 1990s, as Chapter 8 shows.

Although detailed gender surveys on the status of female personnel in the U.S. daily newspaper industry are lacking, there are some figures available from professional associations. In the newspaper industry, the U.S. Bureau of Labor Statistics confirms that total female employment in all types of newspapers increased substantially from 32% in 1975 to 40% in 1985, to near parity (46%) by 1995. These general increases however paint an overly optimistic picture, because they hide gendered differences in job categories, such as clerical and administrative, where 80% of all female workers were employed in the 1970s. Yet, 1997 figures from the American Association of Newspaper Editors, additionally demonstrate that equity initiatives also improved female access to positions in the news/editorial departments. Here there was a 15-percentage point increase between the mid-1970s and the mid-1990s: from 22% in 1971, to 34% in 1983 (Weaver & Wilhoit, 1991) to 37% in 1996 (ASNE, 1997). These increases indicate that the U.S. newspaper industry continued to grow during the last two decades, whereas there was a contraction in Canada. As in Canada, American female journalists as a group were, however, younger than their male colleagues and this fact affects both their promotional status and their mean salaries. As of the mid-1990s, females age 30 and under, reached parity (50%) in the editorial workforce, dropping to 37% in the 31- to 40-year age group and to about 34% of the older group (41 to 50 years). The fact that females are now half of the young news/editorial workforce and almost 40% of the older cadres suggest that access to the U.S. press has definitely improved for female staff.

Equity legislation has, however, not been nearly as effective in guaranteeing women and minorities equitable *promotion* opportunities in the U.S. newspaper industry. Between 1977 and 1986, women made only a 7.2% gain in directing editorships, moving from 5.2% to 12.4% and reached a mere 15% overall by the mid-1990s. Dorothy Jurney, a retired ASNE member, considers this a calamity for newspapers because they are "missing the richness of different voices, and [registering] a loss of readers [particularly females] . . . [and] thwarting females from fully realizing their careers" (Jurney, 1986b, p. 5). To evaluate promotional progress, I subdivided directing editorships into four hierarchical levels in Chapter 5 and showed (Table 5.2) that in contrast to Canada, female staff had a better chance of promotion in small circulation (less than 50,000) U.S. papers than in the other two groups. Comparisons with Canadian figures show that females had been promoted only to the two lowest levels of the management hierarchy: that of editorial chiefs (in the lifestyles sections) and managing editors, where they constituted a meagre 16% and 15%, respectively of these groups. The other three directing editorship positions in both middle-sized (50,000 to 100,000) and metropolitan newspapers were still firmly in the hands of the male hierarchy, with token female representations of 10% or less, except in the lowest rungs. These conditions mirror those in Europe as mentioned in Chapter 5, where the top rank of editor-in-chief is also virtually inaccessible. Only eight females were in this position at the beginning of the 1990s, among whom Katharine Graham of *The Washington Post* and Jane Amsterdam of *The New York Post* are most well known.

The reasons for these lesser promotional opportunities at U.S. versus Canadian newspapers are difficult to determine from the available evidence. However, Chapter 4 suggested that they may have something to do with the male managerial attitudes toward working females. The 1997 American Association of Newspaper Editors survey corroborates this hunch, by revealing heavily gendered perceptions about the promotional process on the part of female and male journalists. Although more females (62%) than males (47%) rated their chances of advancement good or excellent, they disagreed about the *grounds* on which this decision was based. Almost half (42%) of the women said it was based on office politics, whereas about one third (30%) believed it was based on merit. Among the males, these percentages were exactly reversed: 42% believed that promotion decisions were merit-based, whereas only 30% believed that they were based on politics. Even greater discrepancies were found concerning the treatment of people in the newsroom. Here, 43% of the females felt that males were treated better, whereas only 10% of males felt that way. Moreover, nearly one third (29%) of the female professionals were of the opinion that they had been treated unfairly, whereas only 10% of males were of this opinion. Consequently, almost two thirds (61%) of the males believed their paper had a strong commitment to gender diversity, whereas only about one third (37%) of females were of this opinion (ASNE, 1997). Together, these gender-based opinion differences reflect the two groups' polarized understandings of the newsroom power structures. Females, as a minority within this power structure, are much more aware of the implications of their underdog status than are the males who, as members of the majority, benefit from the existing biases.

What does all of this disparate evidence add up to and what has been learned about the efficacy of equity legislation and its impacts on female access and promotion within the press and broadcast industries? To begin with, it is important to emphasize that equity legislation grows out of different historical and legislative traditions in Canada, the United States, and the western European countries. Despite this, however, each of these countries interprets it as aiming toward what Sandra Burt (1986) calls "role equality," which means that its goal is to equalize the opportunities for females and males to compete for public roles. Only the Canadian and EC versions of equity legislation have so far moved to incorporate the aims of "role change," which means the inclusion of social laws that even the playing field between gendered professionals who want to combine work with family responsibilities.

The chapter also suggests that equity legislation is only effective if it is accompanied by agencies with the resources to supervise implementation. This is clearly demonstrated by the differing print and broadcast experiences in Canada and the United States. The former has a less effective watchdog, the Canadian Human Rights Commission, than its U.S. counterpart, the Equal Employment Opportunity Commission. We saw that Canada's commission lacks the human and investigative resources to supervise implementation in those media industries that are overwhelmingly privately owned, such as print. Because of these differences, the access of female journalists to the newspaper profession improved more in the United States than in Canada. Yet, there seems to be no direct link between the availability of a watchdog and promotional opportunities. In the United States, females have the best promotional chances in small circulation dailies, whereas in Canada, the opposite is true; females do better in the large metropolitan press.

Finally, the European Community evidence shows that to change organizational practices, equity initiatives have to be supported by top management. Egsmose's (2001) comparison of the public Radio Denmark and BBC networks indicated that the British "corporatist," top–down implementation approach is more effective, than Radio Denmark's bottom up approach. The reason for this is that a male–dominant power elite is difficult to persuade to yield influence without the involvement of top management. Among the organization-wide initiatives undertaken by the BBC was the printing of a corporate brochure explaining the equity policy. They also appointed an equity officer at the top management level to monitor and report progress to the board. The equity officer, in turn, was aided by a committee representing all units, which helps to set targets and to run information seminars. Finally, equity targets need to be set across all units and their implementation mandated and monitored in a specified time frame. Only a multilayered carrot-and-stick initiative will bear fruit in a work situation where an existing power elite must be encouraged to give up some of its accrued influence.

chapter **7**

EQUITY IN PORTRAYAL:
ITS IMPACT ON PROGRAMMING

THE FEMALE VIEWER AND HER DISCONTENTS

One of the important, yet overlooked phenomena in North America is the female audience's discontent with both the press and television programming. Even though reading is a favored leisure activity among women and they spend more time than men reading each week, it became abundantly clear by the early 1990s that female reader-viewers turned away from these two media as sources of information and pleasure. Comparative newspaper readership figures in Canada as well as in the United States demonstrate that readership has declined, although that of television viewership has increased. According to Christopher Dornan (1996), an expert on the Canadian newspaper industry, the most reliable indicator of a paper's status as a cultural form is total circulation. This number steadily slipped in Canada, from 5.8 million in 1989, to a mere 5.3 million in 1995. Dornan ascribes the circulation loss, despite the overall Canadian population growth, to what he calls the relentless contraction and downsizing of the industry in general. In this downsizing editorial employees have been less protected than their colleagues in production, and consequently the quality of the newspaper product has deteriorated (Dornan, 1996). Fewer reporters means less robust local coverage and the combination of hiring freezes and layoffs has increased workloads and demoralized the editorial staff. There has also been added competition from free weeklies, which unselfconsciously address a younger demographic. The upshot has been that newspaper readership has declined.

Most newspaper researchers have failed to notice an additional important reason for the readership losses, and that is gender. In the crucial sub-
group of the baby-boom generation (aged 25 to 50 years), which makes up
one third of the total adult population, male readership increased, whereas
that of females decreased. In Canada, the Royal Commission on
Newspapers (Kubas, 1980) found that although 69% of adults had consulted a newspaper in 1980, this figure dropped to the low 60s by 1994 (Dornan,
1996). Within this readership, males (73%) had an 8-point lead over females
(65%) in the 1980s, which increased to 10 points by the mid-1990s. The U.S.
data present a similar picture, with male readership increasing since 1986,
and females turning away from newspaper reading. In the United States, the
largest increase in the gender gap occurred between 1990 and 1992, particularly among women under 35 years of age. These young women were 7% to
9% more likely than their male counterparts, not to be newspaper readers.
This represents the largest gender gap in newspaper readership ever recorded. Overall, 65% of all males, but only 60% of females were newspaper
readers in the early 1990s in the United States (Miller, 1993). By the turn of
the century, this figure had further declined for both genders, with only 53%
of women reading a daily, as compared to 61% of men (NAA, 2001).
Demographic and employment statistics suggest that there are a variety of
reasons for this decline. Among them is the fact that baby-boomers (born
between 1946 and 1964) are in the busiest years of their lives. Moreover,
more than 50% of all females are presently full-time employed and thus bear
the traditional "double burden" of 84-hour work weeks. Of these, 40 hours
are devoted to paid labor and another 40-plus hours to family duties. No
wonder that females' spare time has shrunk to almost the vanishing point
and with it their newspaper reading and television viewing.

Yet, this is only part of the picture, according to Ellen Goodman,
columnist of the *Boston Globe*. She notes that women across the board are
more likely to feel that newspapers do not speak *to* them, or *about* them.
Tina Brown, editor of the *New Yorker Magazine* in the early 1990s, agrees
and argues that female readers object to the ways in which information is
presented in the press. In her 1991 talk to the American Newspaper
Association, she noted that "men talk about what happened and . . . (are)
obsessed with subtext, the meaning, the motive, the story behind the story."
As to the tone in which papers address female readers, Brown (1991) found
that, "women are turned off by news presented as unconnected, unassimi-
latable bits of information" rather than as "news you can use." According to
Brown, the same critique can be aimed at television (news), which tells only
what happened rather than *why* it happened.

Beyond lack of time for newspaper reading and their uninviting tone,
Susan Miller, president of news at Scripps Howard newspapers, mentions an
additional factor: North American newspaper content, which fails to

address female interests. A study by the Newspaper Advertising Bureau of what males and females "usually read" and "most like to read" discovered very little overlap between male and female content interests. At the top of the men's list were professional sports, international news, and local school sports. Topping the women's list were local community news, advice columns, and international news. The lowest topics on the women's list were business/financial news and local sports; lowest on the men's list were fashion and lifestyles, food pages, and letters to the editor. Yet, despite these findings, the resource distribution within editorial departments gives sports twice as much staffing and content, as it does features. Nineteen percent of all newsroom reporters are assigned to sports and another 7% to business, for a total of 26% of the staff, whereas family and lifestyle beats together had only 8% of these resources (Miller, 1993). No wonder female readers in the 1990s turned to other media like magazines and books, where their interests were better served and they were addressed as equals.

Even less is known about the discontents of female television viewers because broadcast analysts, despite competition from 24-hour cable news and computerized data banks, persist in believing that they know all they need to know about the female audience (Press, 1990). Yet, many of these pre-conceptions, which are grounded in outdated gender stereotypes, are products of traditional sampling methods, which treat female viewers as an undifferentiated group (Hay, Grossberg, & Wartella, 1996). As such, programmers on both sides of the Atlantic do not inquire into the female viewers' social conditions such as age, education, ethnicity, and employment status, which are extremely important determinants of audience preferences. Instead, bureaus of broadcast measurement start with the well-known gender stereotype that in a family setting, females watch the same TV programming as males. This leads them to the mistaken conclusion that parallel programming will not yield additional viewers in prime time. An additional mistaken conclusion arises from the fact that viewers are never asked to choose between the *total array* of programs, rather than just the top 10. Female viewers would make very different sets of choices in the former circumstance, whereas in the latter, their program preferences overlap 80% with those of the males in the sample. Broadcasters take this to mean that they can safely ignore female preferences (Kline & Murray, 1993).

A final mistaken conclusion arises from the gendered assumption that female program choices such as situation comedies, dramas, and variety shows are "fictional," whereas the male preferences for news, sports, and action-adventure signal a preference for "reality" content. Such a binary categorization is inadequate. It overlooks the fact that narrative style alone does not determine the degree of "reality" with which events and emotions are portrayed (Fiske, 1998). These portrayals depend as well on the acting skills of those impersonating the characters. The "neutral" reporting approach of

news anchors and sports reporters, for instance, are themselves narrative
styles. Both of these use an adversarial script, which views both politics and
sports as "games" that need to be won, rather than as an exercise in democratic expression or as a test of character (Robinson, 1998a, 2004). The narrative styles of situation comedies, in contrast, employ a more egalitarian
approach, which is grounded in family relationships. These types of programs are just as "real," but in a moral sense, in that they highlight the
importance of emotion in human relations and even out age and capacity
differences among family members.

Female viewers' discontent is further clouded by the gendered practices
of family viewing. What I am referring to here are remote control ownership and video use. The males in the family primarily operate both of these
technologies. Their mastery leads to the mistaken conclusion that females
will watch the programs chosen by males. Yet, in the North American
household of the 21st century, two television sets are the norm and the
practices of parallel viewing are wide-spread (Kline & Murray, 1993).
Beyond that, broadcast statistics obscure the fact that not all women use
television in the same way. There is a strong correlation between age and
gender, with women over 55 years viewing the most, and the baby-boom
generation spending the least time with television because of time constraints. In addition, as we know, education and lifestyle structure program
choices and suggest that certain soap operas like *Dallas* and *Murphy Brown*
are crossovers, watched by both genders, even though they are miss-classi-
fied as part of the female soap opera genre. A final televisual discontent is
the underrepresentation of females as subjects in both television news as
well as entertainment programming, except in daytime talk shows that are
gender stereotyped. No wonder that it is much more difficult for female
viewers on both sides of the Atlantic to find strong, authoritative and compelling characters with whom to identify (Commission, 1999; Jeffrey,
1995).

A cultural studies approach to television-viewing behavior indicates
that there is no simple and uniform reader–text relationship. Beyond that,
the family-viewing context and its technological dimensions, through
remote control ownership, zapping, and video registration capacities, suggests that the concept of the homogeneous viewer must also be abandoned.
Ien Ang (1991) concludes that media consumption consists of a complex set
of practices that cannot be adequately captured by Bureau of Broadcast
Measurement statistics alone, but requires ethnographic and participant
observation methods to determine the meaning viewers attach to their activity (Ang, 1991). Theme selection and presentation, language style and narra-
tivity, aesthetic and technical production values cannot be encompassed in
such binary categories as "fact" and "fiction." These program aspects are
developed in response to particular social situations and prevalent narrative

styles. This suggests that texts themselves reconstitute the cultural contexts in which they are created. The journalistic text is thus at one and the same time the result and the producer of culture.

CANADIAN CONTENT INITIATIVES

The regulatory responses to these female discontents are similar in North America and western Europe, although each of the participating countries has developed its own specific initiatives and monitoring structures. Overall, these link equity in portrayal initiatives (where these are mandated) to the participation of women in the broadcast and newspaper workplaces, making the questionable assumption that more females in the media will lead to a more balanced expression of female concerns in programming. In Canada, as seen at the beginning of Chapter 6, the framework for improving women's access to expression and decision making is anchored in three pieces of legislation, of which only one, the 1991 Broadcasting Act, mentions programming obliquely. The Canadian Charter of Rights and Freedoms (1982) bars discrimination on the basis of gender and ethnicity, and the Employment Equity Act (1986) requires the public broadcaster (CBC) and the majority of private broadcast and cable firms to improve the employment situation of four underrepresented groups, including women. Beyond that, the Broadcasting Act of 1991 states that the broadcast system should "through its programming and employment opportunities . . . serve the needs and interests and reflect the circumstances and aspirations of Canadian men, women and children, including equal rights." Under this act, the CRTC received the mandate to ensure that broadcasters and other licensees, including those with fewer than 100 employees, monitor equity concerns not only in the workplace, but also in portrayal (Jeffrey, 1995).

What this means in practice is that the CRTC, since the early 1980s, has sought public–private consensus for a framework for content supervision that does not infringe on freedom of speech. To develop equity criteria in programming, a task force was set up that submitted a 1982 report entitled *Images of Women in Canadian Broadcasting* (King, 1987). The report documented the lack of coverage of females and their concerns in both news and entertainment programming. Yet, differences in outlook between the industry, the public broadcasters (CBC and Radio Canada), and task force members drawn from viewer constituencies, hampered agreement on a definition of "sex-role stereotyping" or the goals of "more desirable portrayal." There was also reluctance on the part of the CRTC to become saddled with increased content supervisions for which financial and staff resources were lacking (Trimble, 1992). Despite these disagreements, the task force made 20 recommendations for improvement and couched its goals in gender-free language.

In 1984, after 2 years of self-regulation, a quantitative study of 600 hours of television programming indicated that hardly any change in female portrayal had occurred. The CRTC summarized this study in 1986 and directed the CBC and the private broadcast and cable associations to consult with women's groups and experts to refine their guidelines on sex-role portrayal. This initiative culminated in the *Adjusting the Image* conference of 1987, and the CRTC's decision that adherence to the revised industry guidelines would henceforth become a condition of license. The quantitative studies of 1987 and 1989 were compared by the CRTC in 1990 and it was found that fewer women than men appeared in almost every program category; that there was an overrepresentation of males aged 35 to 65; and that there were significant differences in the gender roles portrayed in ads, news, drama, and children's programming. These gender differences, furthermore, represented stereotypes, which in TV drama associate women with home and family activities and men with paid work. Overall, it appeared that 6 years after unbalanced content had been diagnosed, little had changed (Trimble, 1992).

Despite these findings, the CRTC and the private media industries were reluctant to embark on new content rules during the recessionary period of the late 1980s and early 1990s, when newspapers faced declining advertising revenues and the CBC faced budget cuts. The upshot was, as demonstrated in previous chapters, that Canada established an effective public–private workplace equity program, but decided to leave content monitoring to individual television stations and newspapers. The most extensive monitoring has occurred in the public-service English and French CBC networks, which developed their own code and complaint systems. In 1992, the corporation set up an Office for Equitable Employment and Programming and designated two persons to develop strategy and oversee implementation. They were the manager of employment equity and the director of equitable portrayal in programming, both of whom sat on the CBC's highest management forum, the President's Steering Committee (CBC Equity Newsletter, 1994). Their staff of nine people monitored progress and revised the CBC's "Guidelines on Sex-Role Portrayal," which recognize "that women and men are equal" and should be "represented and portrayed equitably in programs." The guidelines also note that programming must "reflect in a realistic manner the place that women and men have in contemporary Canadian society." The office was in operation until 1996, well after the CRTC announced that the corporation had met all its commitments (Jeffrey, 1995). After this point, the office was disbanded and its functions were moved to the relevant CBC departments.

At the same time, under pressure from the CRTC, Canadian private broadcasters banded together and formed the Broadcast Standards Council (BSC). The BSC practices self-regulation much like the Canadian Press Councils, through regional branches and has developed a sex-role stereotyping code, in consultation with women's groups. Although the BSC is committed to equity in broadcast employment, it has abandoned content monitoring and mandatory compliance (Trimble, 1992). The BSC complaint system puts the onus on the individual plaintiff to document infractions, which are then transmitted to the relevant station and adjudicated. The result is that only a small number of complaints were filed in the 1990s. Among these were an objection to a rape depiction; the killing of women and mutilation of their bodies in *Silence of the Lambs*, sexist and derogatory language vis-à-vis women, pornographic films and their objectification of women's bodies, the objectification of women in fashion shows, and various other forms of sexist content. Only rarely did the plaintiffs win, and the most spectacular successes were the expulsion of the woman-bashing Howard Stern show from Canadian radio and the reprimand of a Winnipeg station for its reporting of a nude female bicyclist (Kalckreuth-Tabbara, 2001). Interestingly, about half of the complaints were submitted by males, who objected to unequal treatment of their concerns on International Women's Day. This male utilization of the BSC follows a pattern observed in Europe as well, where inclusive criteria, which are supposed to ameliorate *systemic* discrimination patterns in the coverage of females and their concerns, are used to right *sporadic* coverage differences involving males. Within a male-stream society such a use of sex-role stereotyping criteria amounts to yet another form of "silencing."

As a result of these differential regulatory approaches to newspaper and broadcasting content, the only evidence whether sex-role portrayal codes have made a difference comes from the CBCs periodic program evaluations in the 1980s and 1990s. Its code addresses four concerns: Programming should (a) avoid the use of demeaning sexual stereotypes and sexist language, (b) reflect women and their interests in the reporting and discussion of current events, (c) recognize the full participation of women in Canadian society, and (d) seek women's opinions on the full range of public issues (Trimble, 1992). In carrying out the program content analyses, the Erin research firm notes that the principles of equality and social context are not easy to define or to measure (*Social Trends on CBC Prime Time Television, 1977–1992*). "Equality" can either be measured within the context of television programming (e.g., counting women and men in "given roles") and/or it can take into account demographic gender conditions in Canadian society and use these as a baseline for comparison. Both of these, the report concludes, were taken into account in the analysis of factual as well as fictional programming (Erin Research, 1993). The two program analyses of the

English (Erin, 1993) and the French Radio Canada (Caron & Ouellet, 1994) networks demonstrate that sex-role portrayal codes *do* make a difference, if they are *mandated* and if there is obligatory *monitoring*. Moreover, changes in female depiction never come about automatically, but depend on organizational as well as individual initiatives by program staff. These, as Chapter 6 demonstrated, can be fostered through organization-wide training and awareness sessions and the appointment of both females and males to selection and promotion committees.

Erin's 1987 to 1993 comparative content analysis of news and information programming is based on the activities of each person with a speaking role, and is thus able to associate gender with positions in the reporting hierarchy as well as the subject matter covered. The content analysis demonstrates that the horizontal segregation into lesser beats and the vertical segregation of female staff into less visible program positions are noticeable in all news programs. They also demonstrate that female reporters have breached the barrier in on-air reporting roles, by increasing their presence steadily since the 1980s. At that time, they were an infinitesimal 7% of on-air reporters, where by the late 1990s they have virtual parity in the presentation of English (46%), and near parity (40%) in the presentation of French news programs. This contrasts with a Canadian private broadcaster, where only 35% of the on-air reporters were female in 1992, up from 15% in 1989. The difficulty in breaking down the horizontal barriers is demonstrated by the fact that despite the increased *proportion* of female reporters, they are still covering the so-called "soft news" areas that frequently fail to make it into the evening newscast. On these prestigious programs, 65% of all stories continue to be filed by male personnel versus only 35% by females. Females also failed to move into the expert roles in significant numbers in the past 15 years, even though Toronto Women in Film and Television (TWIFT) prepared a female speaker directory that has been widely distributed. By the mid-1990s, the proportion of female experts in newscasts doubled from a tiny 7% to less than 15% in the CBC and about the same (14%) in the French Radio Canada network (Caron & Ouellet, 1994). The greatest increase in the visual presence of females in newscasts happened in the least prestigious role, namely that of women involved in newsworthy events, the so-called "people on the street" role. Here, they are questioned about their feelings rather than the "facts" of the situation, which is the domain of the "expert" role. Their participation rate, which used to be minimal, grew to 25% of all news appearances by the mid-1990s (Erin Research, 1993).

More difficult to assess are the portrayals of females in dramatic programming during prime time between 7 p.m. and 12 p.m. The Erin report used the same coding methods over six seasons (1987–1993) of dramatic programming, which yielded more than 40 roles and attributes. Again, for each person who had a speaking role, the coding system defined more than 50 characteristics and activities. These included appearance (age, manner of dress, etc.), participation in family and social roles, as well as work-related roles. Each character's participation in each role, covering 29 different drama series, was recorded in a database. In general, characters who had a larger part in the production, participate in a greater number of activities, and so contribute more information to the database (Erin Research, 1993). The 6-year comparison shows that despite seasonal changes in drama content (including movies and specials), the social reality of females and males portrayed remained remarkably stable between 1987 and 1993.

Table 7.1 compares the English and French CBC program schedules and shows that between 1987 and 1993, the percentage of female characters hardly budged, remaining between 39% in the English and 41% in the French public networks. This compares with the private CTV and Global figures, where female characters were reduced from 36% to 34% between 1987 and 1989, because monitoring and content equity were not supported by the private industry. The single study undertaken of a U.S. network confirms that even lower gender proportions (e.g., 29%) are found in private sector programming south of the border (Signorielli, 1989). All together, these comparisons suggest that situation comedies and soap operas (save for series like *Roseanne*, etc.) continued to purvey a very traditional social picture, which sharply distinguishes between the "private" world of women and the "public" world of men. It also maintains "ageism," the preference for younger over older female characters. In the fictional world of the 1980s, male characters were disproportionally middle-aged (35–65 years), whereas female characters were disproportionally under 30 years old. By 1993, these age dis-

TABLE 7.1 Characters in English and French Prime Time Drama (in percent females).

Year	CBC English[a] %	CBC French[b] %	Private Networks[c] %	Co- Productions %	Foreign Source %
1987	39	41	36	31	36
1989	40	38	34	37	34
1992	39	N/A	N/A	37	N/A
1993	39	41	N/A	42	N/A

[a]*Based on Erin (1993).*
[b]*Based on Caron (1994, p. 2, 10) (French Radio Canada).*
[c]*CTV, Global, and independent stations.*

crepancies began to narrow in both the English and the French dramatic programming and the majority of characters belonged to the baby-boom generation and were between 25 and 50 years old. Female age discrepancies did still exist in the sense that there was an overrepresentation of female characters in the younger 25- to 34-year group (23% females versus 16% males), and an overrepresentation of males in the 34- to 49-year group, where they outnumbered females by 10 percentage points (44% males to 34% females) (Erin Research, 1993).

In television drama, age and gender have traditionally been associated with authority, yet despite this finding, there has been a gradual reduction of male characters with paid jobs since the early 1980s, possibly under the impact of the recession. In 1987, 80% of all male characters had paid employment, whereas only about 63% of the females did. Six years later this had shrunk to 67% of the male and about 52% of the female characters. Despite this, the identifiable employment gap between female and male characters remained virtually unchanged, constituting 17% in 1987 and 15% in 1993. This indicates that power in the social world of drama was still identified with gender and occupation. A comparison of on-screen occupations demonstrates that not all occupations convey power, and equal representation of female and male characters exists only among powerless positions such as office/clerical workers, artists, students, and children. Increased power was wielded only by male characters in the professions, the military/police, and in trades and other occupational roles, where males predominated. To the extent that females were portrayed in these occupations, they tended to appear as the more junior characters, such as special detective, assisting doctor, or attending lawyer (Erin Reasearch, 1993). No one knows why overall professional identifications decreased in Canadian television dramas since the late 1980s.

Differences in the interpersonal relationships of television characters in the dramatic programming between 1987 and 1993 were also gender-related, just as they are in real life. Table 7.2 divides the characters' activities into three role clusters: interpersonal relations, family relations, and physical setting. On the personal level, there was typically more information on the marital status of female than male characters in both the English CBC and the French Radio Canada networks. Yet, here too, these identifications had diminished since 1987, when 41% of female characters, but only 21% of males had their marital status indicated (Erin, 1993). By 1993, these proportions had dropped to 30% of female and 17% of male characters in English drama and slightly lower figures (female 21% to male 16%) in the French dramatic series. Female characters in both networks also tended to be depicted as having more romantic partners than males 23% to 13% in English and 28% to 20% in French dramas. These two differences are significant at the $p = 0.05$ levels. Although one might have expected that more

Table 7.2 Adult Character Relationships in English and French Prime-Time Drama 1993 (in percent of characters portrayed in role)

| | English CBC[a] | | French CBC/Radio Cdn.[b] | |
| | Female Role | Male Role | Male Role | Female Role |
Role	N = 282	N = 478	N = 254	N = 372
1. Interpersonal relations				
Marital status unknown (F)	30[c]	17[c]	21	16
Romantic partner of opposite sex	23[c]	13[c]	28	20
In lovemaking scene	6	4	4	3
Has female friends	15[c]	5[c]	28[c]	15[c]
Has male friends	12	14	22	26
2. Family roles				
No information	54	71	73	82
Appears with family member	23	14	30[c]	16[c]
Interacts with children (under 18)	12	9	26	17
Performs household tasks	13	4	—	—
3. Physical setting				
Home, domestic	33	23	54[c]	38[c]
Paid work environment	45	55	29	32
Public space	29	26	37	34

[a]*Based on Erin Research (1993).*
[b]*Based on Caron and Ouillet (1994).*
[c]*Significance (p < 0.05)*

female roles would include a lovemaking scene than male roles, this is not borne out by the evidence. Interestingly, both genders were rarely portrayed in intimate settings, amounting to an infinitesimal 6% and 3% for female and male roles, in the English and French dramas. Beyond that, in the family domain, both networks represented the majority of characters without information about their family status. In the English CBC, 54% of all female and 71% of all male characters were unidentified, whereas these percentages were even higher in the French network, where 73% of all females and 82% of all males had no family identification. These findings might be related to Quebec's unique demographics, which show lower birth and marriage rates, than those in English Canada.

Despite this, Francophone female characters continued to appear more frequently than Anglophone female characters in family roles and in charge of children, a pattern that also remained virtually unchanged since 1987 (Erin, 1993). Table 7.2 shows that there were 30% female to 16% male characters in the French as compared to 23% female to 14% male characters portrayed in family roles in the English network. As to the physical setting, Table 7.2 shows that the location of French-language prime-time drama was also very different from that in the English service. In Quebec's téléromans, 54% of female roles are found in a domestic setting, whereas English situation comedies featured only 33% of female characters at home (Caron & Ouillet, 1994). Here, only the French CBC female–male role settings are significant at the $p = 0.05$ level. This discrepancy, which is certainly not due to actual social differences between Quebec and the rest of Canada, is best explained by the fact that French language sitcoms tended to have a working-class family focus, whereas the English soaps portrayed varied middle-class lifestyles. Consequently, more English than French dramas were staged in a work setting (45% female to 55% male characters) versus only 29% of female and 32% of males pictured at work in the téléromans. Interestingly, these differences were not reflected in the depiction of public space activities, where more French than English characters of both genders were found. The percentages here are French 37% females to 34% males versus English dramas' 29% female to 26% males. All together, these content analyses demonstrate that television programs are not *mirrors* of social reality, but *reconstructions* that take social reality as a point of departure.

According to German researcher Kalckreuth-Tabbara (2001), there are three things to learn from Canada's mixed public–private regulatory experiences in programming. First, she notes that it is impossible to design a single set of guidelines that will eliminate gender-role clichés once and for all. Since the civil and regulatory traditions of North American and European countries differ, each will have to devise its own codes and procedures. Furthermore, Canada's 30-year struggle for more equitable female representation would not have been possible without the involvement of those most implicated, namely various women's groups. Women's continued agitation has maintained the issue of sex-role stereotyping on the discussion agenda and raised public awareness of the connection between portrayals and viewers' understandings of the social world. Moreover, it appears that it is not as important to get the codes and guidelines "right," as it is to initiate a *process of review* that is flexible and can be adapted to changing circumstances. Canada's experience has furthermore shown that success depends on information exchange between all stake holders in the regulatory process, including public and private networks as well as viewer representatives (Kalckreuth-Tabbara, 2001).

Equity initiatives are much less clearly defined in the privately owned print sector than in broadcasting because they are based on voluntary compliance and are not systematically monitored by Canadian provincial bodies. Furthermore, equity legislation does not set goals or mention content criteria *explicitly*, assuming that there is a connection between the degree of female employment in the newsroom and more women-friendly newspaper content. This assumption, as is seen in the final section of this chapter, is highly problematic. It asserts that females as biological beings produce different content than males, which is patently false. There is no evidence that the individual differences in the application of news values are gender-based. It is much more probable that certain reporting *situations* do *trigger* gendered responses, but what exactly these situations are, is as yet not well understood. Comparisons in Chapters 5 and 6 demonstrated that equity legislation has increased the access of females to the U.S. journalistic profession at a faster rate than in Canada, although it has grown here as well. We furthermore saw that female managers had better promotion chances in Canada's smallest and largest metropolitan newspapers, which showed the largest circulation growth in the 1980s, but that pay equity was still out of reach. More important to remember is that under this "trickle-down" model, "equity in portrayal" is interpreted as the *personal* responsibility of certain staff members (e.g., that of females), rather than a *collective* one of the newsroom or the corporation as a whole, as in broadcasting. Among Canada's largest newspaper chains only the Southam Corporation established a Task Force on Equity in response to employee concerns, which reported in 1990 that females made up 32% of editorial employees, 5% of senior managers, and 85% of clerical workers. Numerous obstacles to female advancement were identified, but Southam's subsequent financial reversals, its take-over by Conrad Black, and the chain's ultimate sale to CanWest media conglomerate in 2000, pushed equity concerns on to the back burner where they remain (Frank, 1994).

Depite this relatively bleak picture, there is evidence that Canadian female journalists began organizing and that newspaper management became aware of female readership discontent through ongoing circulation losses. In 1990, females in the Canadian Association of Journalists organized their first "Women in Media" caucus, which has held annual conferences to sensitize colleagues to equity issues. By the 1992 Toronto conference entitled *Changing Face*, female professionals had gone beyond airing frustration and anger to trying to find ways of eliminating stereotypes and making news reflect women's concerns. Women at the conference also vowed not to marginalize, but to support their colleagues of color (Canadian Association of Journalists, 1993). Circulation slumps led to soul-searching, including market and product re-design studies on the part of the industry, which, according to the *Calgary Herald's* managing editor Gillian Steward, completely missed the mark. In all of these studies, readers' understanding that newspapers were an essential *community* service that must be published and administered in its own region, got lost in a conglomerate business culture, which increasingly focused on the bottomline, rather than the quality of the editorial content (Steward, 1996). The most drastic example of this misunderstanding is exemplified in the CanWest media conglomerate of Izzy Asper, as demonstrated in Chapter 4. In this climate, editorial departments that used to be the most important aspect of the business, lost their independence vis-à-vis the production and advertising departments. As a consequence, verisimilitude was reduced and the newspaper credo of service to the community was turned upside down. No wonder female readership has declined. Local reporting and people's organization of what may be called "grassroots democracy" has been virtually eliminated. Instead, to save money, newspaper conglomerates duplicate syndicated columns across their papers and focus on human interest stories, which further fragments the community focus. In this business culture, readers have been robbed of the public discussion forum about which they used to care (Steward, 1996).

Nevertheless, some changes have occurred in newspaper coverage and content. Yet, these cannot be automatically attributed to the increased female presence in the profession (Canadian Newspaper Guild, 1987). To regain female readership, a number of newspapers, including CanWest's *Montreal Gazette*, have re-introduced separate women's sections, either during the week or in their weekend editions. The *Gazette's Woman News* is a weekly section that features international news about women, profiles of community leaders, and a calendar of women's events. Despite the fact that it is difficult to find advertisers for the section according to the editor, readers feel that it has increased the value of the paper (Canadian Association of Journalists, 1993). Other changes have to do with narrative conventions, such as dropping the age, appearance, and marital status for female newsmakers, to match the more neutral conventions associated with males in public life.

In an annual survey of newspaper content called *A Good Day to be Female?*, MediaWatch (1992) concluded that use of sexist language has also declined but not disappeared completely, especially in the portrayal of female politicians (Robinson & Saint Jean, 1991). Beyond that, a study shows that references to women have increased to one quarter of all references in newspaper stories, which is well below an equitable one half. A 1994 Ryerson School of Journalism study of front-page stories in Toronto papers found that 33% of these stories were written by women, which represents their approximate status in the profession, as seen in Chapter 2 (Erin Research, 1993). However, just as in broadcasting, the segregation of females into less prominent news beats gave their stories less visibility. Overall, men tended to report on crime, economics, and government, whereas women covered accidents, education, and social issues, which were not as regularly featured on the front page. Despite these initiatives, the editorial division of the Canadian Daily Newspaper Association (CDNA) continued to misunderstand the importance of news about females to their shrinking readership. Although

78% of their 41 papers surveyed in 1994 had taken initiatives to cover a more diverse readership through content audits and community meetings, "Canadian publishers and editors do not appear to recognize either the opportunities or the urgency involved in improving the coverage and hiring of women, visible minorities and aboriginals" (Jeffrey, 1995, p. 16).

U.S. CONTENT INITIATIVES

What about content equity initiatives in the U.S. press and broadcasting? In the United States, even more than in Canada, equity in portrayal is viewed as a byproduct of equity in employment. The previous chapter demonstrated that Title VII of the Civil Rights Act (1964) and the Equal Opportunity Act of 1972 were strengthened by the Equal Employment Opportunity Commission (1973), which developed resources for enforcement. For broadcast outlets, Marc Fowler made gender-equity initiatives a precondition for license renewal in the 1970s and in print, the EEOC initiated a number of high-profile class-action suits at *The New York Times* and elsewhere. In this increasingly fractious climate the American Association of Newspaper Editors decided to set its own hiring goals, which would result in newsrooms reflecting the 30% gender and ethnic diversity of the U.S. population by the year 2000. As previously mentioned, the total female employment in the news/editorial departments grew from 22% in 1971 to 37% in 1995, although promotion chances to management positions increased much more slowly, from a mere 7% to 15%. In the same period, the participation rate of female television personnel tripled from 11% to 34%, as did female promotions to news directorships (from 8% to 20%). Yet, this proportion was not sufficient to increase female power over programming (Stone, 1995/2000b, p. 16). Black and Hispanic personnel did much worse in the same time frame, constituting only 19% of the broadcast workforce by 1993 and heading only 9% of television and 7% of radio news operations (Stone, 1994). Overall, Vernon Stone (1994) likened the progress in staff diversification in the U.S. media to a race between the broadcast "hare" and the newspaper tortoise from Aesop's fable. He points out that because newspapers did not have to worry about license renewals, they had no pressures to diversify their staffs to match the projected 30% minority composition of the U.S. population at the turn of the millennium. Consequently, daily newspaper newsrooms, which were 4% minority in 1978 when the ASNE set its goals, had increased its minority staff to a mere 11% by the early 1990s. At this pace, Stone estimates, it will take until 2050 for the newspaper tortoise to reach the millennium goal, whereas the broadcast hare is already more than two thirds of the way there (Stone, 1994).

Although it is well known that there is no one-to-one correspondence between newspaper employment figures and content innovation, Susan Miller (1993), who was vice president/news of Scripps Howard Newspapers in the early 1990s confirms that "opportunities have been squandered." She too ascribes this to the lack of incentives implied in the "trickle-down" approach to content change and proposes that editors of all sections be made accountable for losing women readers or for failing to lure them back. According to Miller, the falling number of female readers is *not* the result of ignorance, or conscious ill will . . . but (results from the fact) that journalists are saddled with outmoded and counterproductive philosophies, attitudes, practices and organizational schemes from which they judge the news" (p. 169). She points the finger at five problems, among them the 1970s prediction that baby-boomer women's and men's interests would converge, an outcome that I argued earlier is not borne out by contemporary readership studies. In addition, traditional journalistic definitions of the "news" are out of touch with present-day lifestyles and the needs of people (especially women) who are obsessed with a sense of "too little time." As a consequence, Miller argues, readers are focused on their own lives and concerns, and want "news that can be used." Moreover, traditional journalistic definitions of news stress confrontation and conflict, which turns female readers off. Women, according to her studies, prefer reporting approaches that give everyone a chance to express an opinion and that strive for a "win–win" consensus . . . which provides connections. Women want balanced local coverage, highlighting "good news"—community celebrations, the accomplishments of ordinary citizens, profiles of people who can serve as role models for themselves—and they want to read about problems that need attention. Miller believes that the abolition of the women's section in the 1970s was probably a mistake because it will be difficult to diffuse topics of interest to female readers throughout the paper, without additional resources to the features department (Miller, 1993).

Two other excuses by editors not to cater to women's reading interests are red herrings, she notes. The first excuse asserts that females "have no time to read" and the second that "the first amendment" prohibits papers from giving readers more relevant copy. Nowhere, Miller argues, does it say that journalists constitute a priesthood that has the right to dispense the "truth" as they see it (Miller, 1993). Overall, males in the profession believe that there has been more content change than has actually happened. This belief is equally prevalent in Canada and western Europe, as the final section of the chapter demonstrates. Yet, Miller knows from experience that females in management positions will not tell the boss what is wrong, unless there is clear evidence that changes will be welcomed and rewarded within the hierarchy. The Gannett chain is one of the few organizations that has introduced incentives and rewarded editors with extra staff, news holes, and promotions, based on how well the readership of their sections mirrors the demographic makeup of their communities. If more media companies used that yardstick, Miller believes, the readership gap ascribed to women would disappear.

EUROPEAN COMMISSION CONTENT INITIATIVES

In western Europe, the European Commission set up a Steering Committee for Equal Opportunities in Broadcasting in 1986, which sponsored both a workplace equity *Guide to Good Practice* in 1991 and an analysis, *Images of Women in the Media* in 1997. The latter surveyed existing program research in the EU. Both of these documents, like the legislation in Canada and the United States, make the assumption that there is a link between equitable employment of females in broadcast institutions and women's portrayal in programming. In contrast to North American legislation, however, the EC explicitly states that the link is "reciprocal." The *Guide* argues "effective equal opportunities policies in broadcasting should bring change not only in the composition of the workforce, but also in programme content. There is a two-way relationship here" (Guide, 1991, p. 6). To reduce sex-role stereotypes in broadcast programming, three initiatives were proposed that are similar to those suggested in North America. They are publishing guides of females with expert knowledge in current affairs (Belgium, Ireland, and Netherlands), increasing the number of female "experts" on news shows, and encouraging broadcasters to content analyze their programming (Netherlands, Belgium, and the United Kingdom).

In addition, the BBC developed a 5-point stereotype guide, which is so general that it cannot be compared to the CBC guidelines, which were discussed in the previous section. The BBC recommends "choosing programs which interest both sexes; knowing the demographic composition of the target audience; engaging both men and women as series consultants; seeking out women's perspectives; and planning to reflect the diverse roles of women and men at home and at work" (Guide, 1991, p. 7). The final two recommendations include providing prizes for the least stereotypical program (Swedish Prix Egalia; Commission's Prix NIKI) or its opposite, the most stereotypical program (Germany's Saure Gurke [sour cucumber prize]), and giving more access to the EC's independent producers, many of whom are female. As a result, the 1989 EC Directive on Television Broadcasting required all broadcasters to reserve at least 10% of their transmission time or programming budget for the work of independent producers (Guide, 1991b). The *Guide* notes, that "ensuring better representation of women in radio and television programs does not mean jeopardizing the broadcaster's

freedom. The initiatives outlined here are all intended to inspire and to stim-
ulate creativity, rather than to stifle or censor" (Guide, 1991, p. 5).

The Commission's Third Medium-Term Community Action
Programme (1991–1995) furthermore promised to "develop guidelines to
address the issue of representation of women in the media industry and their
portrayal by the media." The first step to accomplishing this vast task was
the *Images on Women* (Commission of the European Communities [CEC],
1999) report, which was designed to provide a baseline for future discussions. It found that in contrast to North America, interdisciplinary women's
studies were woefully neglected in Europe and that studies had been done in
only a small handful of countries. Among these are the Nordic countries, the
Netherlands, and the United Kingdom (Images, CEC, 1999). Surprisingly,
gender research was lacking in France, as well as in central and southern
Europe. The report ties this dearth of research to a lack of funding and to
the withdrawal of the United States and Great Britain from UNESCO in the
1980s, when, as mentioned earlier, developing countries pushed female
issues off the discussion agenda for 10 years (Mahoney, 1992). Furthermore,
comparative studies, which would allow sex-role changes to be measured
over time, as in the Canadian case, were also as yet nonexistent, making it
impossible to assess the influence of gender on themes, priorities, and repre-
sentational patterns throughout the EU (Images, CEC, 1999). Most importantly, the report also mentions that the European female audience had been
completely overlooked (Images, CEC, 1999). The Canadian experience
showed that this was a result of broadcaster hubris, which assumed (mistak-
enly) that they knew everything worth knowing about female readers/view-
ers. The adherence to this mistaken preconception has lost North American
newspapers and television stations their female baby-boom audience. These
viewers, as mentioned previously, constitute one third of the total audience
in the new millennium. Whether there are similar losses in the EC is as yet
unknown.

To ameliorate the extensive European research lacunae, the *Images*
report makes five "immediate" and six recommendations for "future"
action. These include the following:

1. The establishment of a European media monitoring group
   (EuroMedia Watch) to carry out regular, systematic monitoring of
   gender images in media content, similar to those undertaken by
   MediaWatch (Canada) founded in 1981, and Women, Men and
   Media (USA) founded in 1989.
2. A comparative study of the gender gap in women's access to new
   media such as the Internet.
3. Research to explore the role of the media in shaping perceptions of
   women in public life. Here, my own Canadian research has

demonstrated that very different coverage patterns pertain to female and male politicians (Robinson & Saint Jean, 1991).

4. Research to explore media access patterns for ethnic, new immigrant and minority groups of women, their uses of different media genres and their representation in the media.

5. Research to identify policy measures aimed at promoting conditions likely to increase the impact of female media content. This was addressed in the European Commission's strategy emphasis during the Second (1991-1995) and Third Action Programmes for Equal Opportunities (1996-2000) at the turn of the century. Unfortunately, there are as yet no published findings on the impact of these initiatives.

Future recommendations urge the creation of a database on European research into gender images and new media use modeled on the Nordicom system, to make the dispersed material more accessible. There is also a need for a European network for women on Internet, with a Website, newsgroups, and so on. Beyond that, longitudinal and comparative research on female media preferences need to be initiated to pinpoint female discontent with conventional program fare and compare it with North American findings. The targeting of female audiences through cable and satellite "narrowcasting" also requires evaluation to determine whether changes in broadcast regulations are necessary. Education and training in new media, as well as their use in education and distance learning are also lacking, as are the laborforce figures of those employed in these new, frequently private, media delivery systems (Images, CEC, 1999).

I know of only one European broadcaster, Sveriges Radio, that has come close to achieving employment equity (40% to 60%), to test the hypothesis that women's portrayal has improved with greater employment of female staff. Ulla Abrahamsson, chief of the Audience and Programme Research Department, comments that even under the best of circumstances it takes time to implement equity concerns in the media workplace and in representation. In Sveriges Radio there was an 8-year interval between International Women's Year (1975), the passage of the national equity act (1980), and its inclusion in the company's collective agreement in 1983 (Abrahamsson, 1990). The Swedish personnel equity policy has six goals, which echo many of the Canadian and EC concerns discussed in the previous section. Among these are "creating a positive attitude toward equality in the company; giving women and men equal opportunities for employment, training, promotion and development at work; working towards an even composition of women and men in different professional and working groups; enabling both genders to combine employment and parenthood; achieving equal pay . . . for jobs of equal value; and making training programs accessible to all" (Abrahamsson, 1986, p. 225). By 1990, after 15 years of initiatives, including many courses, seminars, and management feedback sessions, Abrahamsson reports that the first two goals had been achieved. Sveriges Radio had succeeded in creating a positive attitude toward equality in the company and was giving women and men equal employment and training opportunities. By the early 1990s, three goals were still outstanding. They were equal pay for work of equal value (to be achieved by 1993), equal numbers of men and women in technical and service occupations (to be achieved by 1995), and females in at least one third of all management positions (to be achieved by the middle of the 1990s; Abrahamsson, 1990). Unfortunately, information is lacking whether these goals have been achieved as of 2005.

It took even longer, about 10 years, to prepare guidelines against sex-role stereotyping in Sveriges Radio. Abrahamsson explains that the delay was partially caused by the need to reinterpret the "impartiality" rule in the Swedish Broadcasting Act. In Sweden, the act requires "that broadcasting shall be exercised impartially and factually" (to guarantee freedom of expression and information), but has the additional mandate to "assert the fundamental idea of the democratic constitution, together with the principles of the equality of all human beings and the liberty and dignity of the individual." Early formulations of equity in programming envisaged two goals: to give the same amount of attention to women and men and to describe women and men as human beings of equal value (Abrahamsson, 1986). Female personnel furthermore believed that women's issues should not be isolated into special program preserves, but integrated into the program schedule as a whole.

Content analyses of news/documentary and fictional programming showed that despite the nearly equitable (40%) female employment in Swedish broadcasting, which was 10 percentage points higher than the Norwegian, Danish, and United States, but similar to the Canadian situation (36%), the so-called "one-third rule" in programming has not yet been breached. On both sides of the Atlantic, female figures and voices constituted only between 27% to 33% of those shown and/or heard on television programs, as against 66% for males. In Sweden, furthermore, fictional as well as children's programming suffered from these gender disproportions, whereas the female presence in the prestigious news programs was even lower, at 20% of all characters (Abrahamsson, 1990). This indicates that despite the increase of female broadcasters, the traditional news and program values had hardly changed at all. Furthermore, females and their life experiences continued to be undervalued and bifurcated into traditional female and male reporting domains. Yet, despite this, Swedish males covered such topics as children, schools, education, environment and nutrition in TV programming, which supposedly offer opportunities for female expertise

(Abrahamsson, 1990). This suggests that the more prestigious television medium continues to be a male professional domain, whereas this has changed in Canada. Only regional and local Swedish programming has adapted its content and introduced the so-called "magazine format," where the public is invited to voice its own ideas.

Abrahamsson concludes that the equal representation of female and male perspectives in programming had not materialized and muses whether an equity in content requirement for license renewal might have speeded up the process (Abrahamsson, 1990). Because there has been no gender equity in content requirement promulgated anywhere in the world, this question has to remain open. What is clear, however, from the comparative evidence, is that the *assumption* that greater employment of females in the media professions will *automatically* lead to more equitable portrayal of women and their concerns is definitely mistaken. Although a better attitude toward equity in the workplace has been achieved in Scandinavian, British, and Canadian public-service institutions, the interpretive newsroom power structures, with their associated sexist news values, continue to exist and will require more than equity legislation to vanquish (Robinson & Saint Jean, 1995). As in the fight for greater workplace equity, concerned journalists of both genders must continue to agitate for change. This means that they will furthermore have to query why certain reporting domains are assigned on the basis of gender, rather than on terms of such neutral characteristics as competence, rotation, or preference. They must also continue to build lists of female experts and ethnic spokespersons, to enlarge the repertoire of voices through which the news discourse is constructed. Most importantly, as seen here, the whole editorial department, rather than the female minority, must be made responsible for progress in these domains.

IS THERE A GENDERED REPORTING STYLE?

What does this incomplete struggle for a more woman-friendly portrayal portend for the ongoing discussion, whether there is a gendered reporting style? Although the issue remains unresolved, the decades' long debate has yielded two analytic insights that may shed light on the complex philosophical and interpretive issues involved. The first, according to German feminist broadcaster Gisela Brackert (1992), concerns the duality of language, which complicates the detection and the description of its gendered uses. As a mediating instrument, language both describes (denotes) the world and indicates (connotes) the speaker's attitude toward the world. Consequently, what linguists call speech acts reflect gender differences in adjectival use, rhetorical features like exhortations, and the use of direct versus indirect formulations (Tannen, 1993). Yet, these language-use differences do not imply a difference in professional competence. Brackert (1992) notes that the query concerning "differences" places female practitioners into a classical double-bind. If the difference is denied, there is no compelling need for society to ensure that more women are involved in public opinion formation. Yet, if it is argued that women contribute something unique, owing to their different ways of perceiving things, and their different life conditions, they are quickly stereotyped and banished to the journalistic ghetto within the profession (Keil, 1993).

The second analytical difficulty derives from the way in which the question is posed by traditional media researchers like Weaver and Wilhoit (1986/1991, 1998b) and Weischenberg, Löffelholz, and Scholl (1994), who utilize what may be called a structural-systemic approach that downgrades the cultural and interpretive role of the profession. Structural theories conceptualize journalism in terms of social roles and power hierarchies that are useful for discovering the minority status of female personnel, as demonstrated in Chapters 2 and 3. Yet, they eliminate the concept of the acting "social subject," the fact that all journalists have to make choices as to how they are going to fulfill their professional obligations and under *what circumstances* gender might become a relevant factor. In addition, structural-systemic theories ignore the "informal" interpretive pressures, which are grounded in heterosexual workplace expectations for female media personnel. These expectations eradicate personal similarities such as a common minority experience, program goals, or topic preferences that might be shared across different personnel subgroups. This explains, among other things, why female journalists are more reluctant than males to seek promotion to high-profile management jobs, because they know that they will be cut off from their informal networks and treated as a powerless "tokens" (Keil, 2001; Lünenborg, 2001). Because of these drawbacks, I have argued that structural-systemic approaches have to be supplemented with a gender-focused cultural communication theory that enables me to discover and analyze under what *circumstances* gender plays a role in journalistic interpretations.

In order to move forward in the quest for understanding journalism as a collective activity, in which new narrative structures are developed and change occurs, it is important to locate the special circumstances that trigger such change. The global question about a supposedly "female journalism" is misleading. We need to find out instead, under what circumstances female and male journalists are willing to *step outside* their routine role understandings and rely on their own human understandings to accomplish their reporting tasks. Clearly, this will only happen rarely and in very particular conditions. Rephrasing the issue in this manner permits me to bring together varied interview evidence, which has queried Black, ethnic, full- and part-time female and male professionals in different countries and in different historical periods. This interview evidence seems, on the surface, to come to a contradictory set of conclusions. Both female and male respondents claim that: "No" gender is not relevant in doing their routine reporting job; "but" there are circumstances where gender *might* become salient in the choice of topics and in the framework or angle through which a situation or an event is explained. How to interpret these responses? I argued previously that the "no" response to the relevance of gender in doing one's reporting job merely signifies that females do not want to be assigned to the journalistic ghetto on the grounds that they are acting unprofessionally by not subscribing to the "neutrality" requirement. The "but" response indicates that there are circumstances when gender might become relevant. However, this is not a result of gender viewed as a *biological inevitability*, but because of the *ideological position* that so-called "feminist" practitioners might bring to their reporting work (Meyer, 1992).

Part of the problem with making sense out of this evidence lies in the fact that the different studies do not define what is meant by "feminism" or "female-friendly" approaches. They also fail to investigate the ways in which the professional power structure *modifies* the way in which female journalists use their female understandings in the practice of their profession. Lünenborg (1997), who studied female journalists in six European countries, is one of the only researchers to raise these questions. Her interviews revealed that there are three different ways of utilizing one's gender knowledge for professional purposes. She calls the first group "aware feminists," who have learned about the subordinate status of females in society. They utilize this knowledge only to explain equity initiatives in society, and not as a framework for action and interpretation in the journalistic profession. She calls the second group of mostly older female professionals "engaged feminists." These women constitute less than one quarter of her female interviewees and actively utilize their feminist understandings within the profession to explain societal gender biases in everyday life. The third group of mostly younger women are the "practicing feminists." Unfortunately, this is a somewhat misleading label. It is meant to indicate that this group of female journalists, who are the children of the baby-boomer generation, take the accomplishments of their countries' feminist movements for granted. They are aware of gender discrimination in the profession, but do not use this knowledge for interpretive purposes in the professional setting (Lünenborg, 1997).

The discovery of what might be called a tripartite pattern in the use of female understandings within the journalistic profession is tremendously useful, because it explains *why* there is a "no/but" response to the question concerning a gendered reporting style. Only one of the 3 groups, "engaged feminists" (Type 2), acknowledges that their ideological understandings might influence their professional practice. The other two groups deny this.

A return to the interview evidence gathered in Germany, Britain, and Scandinavia, applying the tripartite typology, makes the findings of these studies much more intelligible. Lünenborg, for instance, discovers that her German journalistic sample subscribes overwhelmingly to the Type 3, or "practicing feminists" outlook, which means that they are aware of gender discrimination on the structural level of the profession, but do not act on it on the personal reporting level (Lünenborg, 1997). The majority of Karen Ross' (2001) British samples are also Type 3 practitioners, subscribing to no gender criteria in their reporting work, but agreeing that females and males have different experiential backgrounds. Anita Werner's (1992) Swedish journalists, in contrast, belong to Type 1, those who are aware of equity issues in society, but do not believe that gender is relevant, except in special circumstances in pursuing one's work. All together, we find as expected, that only a small group of professionals consider themselves "engaged feminists," whereas the overwhelming majority (more than 75%) of all female journalists in western Europe and North America do not.

Marion Marzolf (1993) was one of the first U.S. researchers to explore the influence of gender in the media professions. In 1993, she interviewed the supervising editors of 52 of the 100 largest U.S. dailies (20 females and 32 males) to determine whether they thought that females had made a contribution to the profession and if so, what this might be. Of this group of editors, 94% was of the opinion that female contributions were primarily in what might be called the "social realm." A total of 88% thought that the newsroom environment had improved, with less cursing, off-color jokes, and sexual harassment, and that there was now more collaborative discussion and teamwork. The group furthermore opined (86%) that the range of topics covered had increased, adding such issues as sexual harassment, abortion, and more information on health, poverty, aids, parenting, social and educational issues. The supervising editors also believed that coverage was more people-oriented and thus responded to female readers' interest in "news that one can use." Only 50% of the editors, mainly males, believed that the use of females as news sources had increased, whereas only 12% thought that there were differences in writing style or language, a figure similar to Lünenborg's German findings (Marzolf, 1993).

To gain a more detailed picture of the impact of female professionals on the newsroom, I asked my Canadian proportional gender sample (see the appendix) whether females had made progress in the profession in the past 20 years? They were given nine options, which had been established by previous research. Table 7.3 indicates that there are indeed gendered variations in opinions. Both females (86%) and males (72%) agreed that women's important gains were in their growing number in the profession. Interestingly, a substantially higher proportion of male than female respondents believe that females have reduced disparities in salary (70% males to

TABLE 7.3 Progress Made by Canadian Female Journalists over the Past 20 Years 1995 (by gender and percent) ($N = 124$)

Areas	Females ($n = 49$) %	Males ($n = 75$) %	χ^2 Signif.
Increase in number of female journalists	86	72	0.073
Increase in females in management positions	18	26	n.s
Progress made on work schedule	31	53	0.013
Day-care facilities at work	3	5	n.s
Equal promotion opportunities	34	46	n.s
Disparities in salary range	60	70	n.s
Value of life experience	33	46	n.s
Importance given to women's topics	42	53	n.s
Autonomy in choice of topics and angles	56	53	n.s

Que: How would you evaluate the progress made by Canadian female journalists over the past 20 years? (Percentages derived from combining the 5- and 4-point responses on a 5-point scale. (5 very satisfactory, 1 totally unsatisfactory.) Based on gender sample found in the appendix.

60% females), promotional opportunities into management positions (26% males to 18% females), the value credited for life experience (46% males to 33% females), and the progress made on work schedules (58% males to 36% females). Overall, these findings corroborate that males believe that their female colleagues have made more progress in what may be called the *material* dimensions of the profession than has actually occurred. Chi-square significance tests indicate that only the first and third of these gendered differences in opinion are significant. This suggests that, as in Europe, the male majority interprets the one-third participation rate for Canadian female journalists as being closer to an equitable one half. Opinions vary more widely between the two groups on the three *nonmaterial* aspects of newsroom work. They include the importance given to women's topics, autonomy of topic choice and day-care facilities at work. None of these is significant, even though female staffers are more aware than their colleagues how difficult it is to place female topics on the news agenda. The generally higher percentages in the male column suggest that male professionals remain unaware of the costs of a female journalistic career, which must make a work–family choice that is not demanded of them. As previously mentioned, in our sample 81% of the males were married whereas 66% of females were not, because the double burden is virtually impossible to manage.

Not only are male professionals unaware of the costs of the so-called "double burden" of work–family accommodation, their majority status in the newsroom also impairs their judgment concerning the professional domains requiring further improvement. This is graphically illustrated in Table 7.4, which asks the proportionate gender sample: "Given the present situation of female professionals, to what extent would there be room for improvement in the following areas?" The evidence shows that gender is much more significant to these assessments than to those recorded in the previous table. Here six out of nine aspects are significant. The two strongest gender disparities, predictably, are found in progress made on work schedule ($p < 0.0001$), such as flex-time and a more normal 8-hour working day, as well as the value of life experience ($p = 0.0005$), in assignments and promotion, because females know that they are closely linked to ameliorating the effects of the "double burden." Other disparities pertain to equal promotional opportunities and disparities in salary range, both of which have significances ($p < 0.0001$), showing that female professionals continue to be aware of these discrepancies and do not share the male optimism demonstrated in the previous table. In three final areas needing

TABLE 7.4 Canadian Professional Domains in Need of Improvement 1995 (by gender, in percent) ($N = 124$)

Areas	Females ($n = 49$) %	Males ($n = 75$) %	χ^2 Signif.
Number of female journalists	44	28	n.s
Number of females holding management positions	87	69	0.09
Progress made on work schedule	56	10	<0.0001
Day-care facilities at work	87	75	n.s
Equal promotion opportunities	72	29	<0.0001
Disparities in salary range	36	8	<0.0001
Value of life experience	43	14	0.0005
Importance given to women's topics	37	19	0.03
Autonomy in choice of topics and angles	18	10	n.s

Que: Given the present situation of female professionals, to what extent would there be room for improvement in the following areas? (Percentages derived from combining the 5- and 4-point responses on a 5-point scale. 5 needs great improvement, 1 satisfactory). Based on gender sample found in the appendix.

improvement, the groups of female and male professionals are virtually agreed and the gender difference significances are therefore very weak. Included here are the importance given to women's topics (p = 0.03), number of females in management positions (p = 0.09). The previous section indicates that the EC public broadcasters are tackling similar concerns in their 5-year plans.

The fact that more women entered the media professions between 1975 and 1995 also had an influence on the ways in which content was handled and stories produced. To gain greater insight into how gender differences might manifest themselves, the Canadian proportional gender sample were asked: "Where would you say changes brought about by female journalists are most visible?" Marion Marzolf's (1993) study found four areas of difference, which I used as a starting point for my own inquiry, which is summarized in Table 7.5. They were, in order of importance, expansion of topics covered, newsroom environment, treatment of sources, and language and

TABLE 7.5 Changes Attributed to Females in the Canadian Profession 1995 (by gender in percent) (N = 124).

Changes	Females (n = 49) %	Males (n = 75) %	χ^2 Signif.
Higher degree of professionalism	38	14	.003
Wider range of topics covered	86	60	.003
Different angles of coverage	82	57	.004
Greater emphasis on ethics	29	9	.004
Increased range of experience	63	43	.05
Greater level of initiative	33	10	.002
Increased educational level	25	11	.061
Increased emphasis on cooperation by management	33	20	n.s
Increased competition	15	25	n.s
Improved newsroom climate	44	40	n.s
Improved treatment of sources	23	10	.07
Better language and writing style	11	7	n.s
Greater sensitivity toward sexism	64	70	n.s

Que: Were would you say changes brought about by females are most visible? (Percentages derived from combining the 5- and 4-point responses on a 5-point scale .5 very visible, 1 invisible). Based on gender sample found in the appendix.

writing style. The first two areas are easy to understand, whereas the last two are more ambiguous. Differences in treatment of sources are described as females having "greater awareness of sexist language, utilizing a female perspective, giving different types of play to female rape and victimization stories, and being more sensitive to stereotyping" (Marzolf, 1993, p. 8). As to differences in language and writing style, these are considered to result from what can be called differences in "framing." Marian Meyer (1992) defines *framing* as a "viewpoint from which an issue or topic is interpreted which leads to a coherent explanation and understanding." Meyer's own research found that gender differences in framing were either issue-specific, or job-specific (pp. 80, 87). For our purposes, this suggests that there are two kinds of *situations* in which gender becomes relevant in framing and interpretation. They are situations in which an ideological stance (Type 2 engaged feminism) is invoked, as for instance the coverage of a rape case. Or when the narrative conventions of a certain beat, such as the competitive win–lose framework of sport reporting, is so strong that a journalist cannot step out of her or his professional role conception to contravene it.

In trying to determine which changes brought about by females in the Canadian profession were most visible, female respondents turned out to be more aware on all aspects, than their male colleagues, except on *sensitivity to sexism*. This is indicated by the higher rankings to all response indicators listed in the female column of Table 7.5. Such a reaction is expected from a minority that is still fighting for equity in the workplace on both the material and the symbolic levels. However, the overall high ranks given by male respondents to the questions also confirm that the increased presence of women in the newsroom, as Chapter 4 suggests, has had an influence on the way work is done and is very slowly beginning to influence how professionalism is defined. This is indicated by the fact that Canadian female and male respondents agree that the three most visible changes are wider range of topics covered (86% females to 60% males), different angles of coverage (82% females to 57% males), and increased range of experience (63% females to 43% males). Although each of these aspects is significant, the quality of the gender difference is stronger in the first two aspects ($p = 0.003$, $p = 0.004$) than in the latter ($p = 0.05$). Comments from the proportional Canadian gender sample elaborate these gender differences. Female professionals understand "wider range of topics" as "covering issues that interest female readers," not only those of males. "Different angles" arise from female reporters' "tending to be more sensitive to minority views and representation, so that overall the reporting canvas becomes richer," whereas the "increased range of experience" is perceived by female staff as "being willing to elicit and incorporate the personal feelings of an interviewee and to relate the private to the public sphere of work and power." A male respondent, in contrast, interprets "sensitivity to sexism" as "women bringing different life experiences, sensitivity and world views to the job." For males, this seems to be the most important thing they have learned from female entry into the profession (64% females to 70% males).

In 2001, Jane Rhodes called for a new agenda in journalism studies saying "in the new millennium . . . the intellectual and political battle-ground must be shifted from access and employment, to the intransigent foundations of how news is made. . . . We need to know more about the epistemology of journalism and the sociology of the newsroom through the lens of feminist analysis" (p. 51). These are exactly the kinds of questions I have been addressing in this chapter. The opportunity to change news values toward a more equitable portrayal of women, the U.S. and European comparisons have shown, depend on four factors. The first is the level to which the female professional has risen in the editorial hierarchy. As Susanne Keil (2001) has shown, only those female managers who build a female network *across* organizational domains will be effective in breaking down the beat boundaries and in creating cooperative rather than competitive editorial teams. Marian Meyer (1992), furthermore, discovered that in addition to gender, certain beats carry implicit ideological stances. She documents that in certain midwest papers, the business and agricultural beats were inflected by a "free-trade" ideology that was not prevalent in other newsroom beats. The second important precondition for more equitable portrayal is that access to training and promotion must be supported by an equity program. Canadian newspapers are way behind broadcasters in instituting equity programs of any sort. As a consequence, I have argued, most daily newspapers have lost their important female baby-boomer readership base. The third important condition, according to Lünenborg (1997), are the journalistic role conceptions of the female staff themselves and the extent to which they define themselves as feminists. Female professionals can be divided into three ideological groups, each of which is *aware* of gendered inequalities in social and political life. However, there is only *one* of these groups that *acts on* this feminist understanding in their professional life: the engaged feminist professionals (Type 2) who comprise less than one fifth of all female journalists. Yet, it is these women who are willing to struggle against the malestream journalistic norms and wonder about what an "alternative journalism" might entail that takes female opinions seriously (Melin-Higgins, 2004; Melin-Higgins & Djerf-Pierre, 1998). The final factor in forging a more equitable portrayal of women grows out of the relationships that female staff foster with their viewers/readers and their use of females as experts and sources. MediaWatch in Canada and the Toronto Women in Film and Television (TWIFT) have supplied the press and broadcasters with lists of female experts in all domains and continue to host yearly conventions to assess the increase in female voices and issues covered in news programming. The previous sections have shown that female viewers/readers identify with journalists who are sensitive to their concerns and who interpret events in a more holistic and nonconfrontational manner.

Unfortunately, all of these initiatives continue to be "works in progress," rather than solid achievements at the beginning of the new millennium. For the present, the extensive evidence from the representative Canadian gender sample demonstrates that shared training and the continued minority, and therefore subordinate status, of Canada's female professionals, especially in the print media, colors not only workplace interactions, but also the ways in which they perceive the world around them. It also affects how the two professional groups negotiate their career and family roles. This validates Barbie Zelizer's (1993) claim that the newsroom interpretive culture is no longer homogeneous. The fact that many print and some television newsrooms are still far from egalitarian and that their operating values privilege males over females continues to result in qualitative differences along such indicators as working climate, discrimination, and sexual harassment. Overall, these patterns mirror those that exist in patriarchal society at large. Yet, this society is itself in the process of profound change, as globalization is taking its toll on the Canadian and U.S. economies and on public and private media enterprises. In this downsizing, female professionals might very well be disproportionately and unequally affected, as they have been in U.S. broadcasting after the abrogation of affirmative action initiatives in the Reagan era. In Canada, equity legislation continues to be on the books, but here too the requirements have been loosened and neither the CBC, nor the CRTC continues to collect and evaluate programming. Without such monitoring, the use of women's voices in future news and entertainment programming will surely remain at the magical one-third threshold, where it stands today. More depressingly, without further struggle by concerned female media groups like Media Watch and the U.S. National Organization of Women it might drop below the radar of public consciousness all together. This provides a special challenge for the youngest generation of female media professionals, who tend to believe that the feminist battles for professional equity have been won.

chapter *8*

GLOBALIZATION, GENDER, AND THE PUBLIC SPHERE

THE MEANING OF GLOBALIZATION AND CONVERGENCE

The gendered effects of globalization have not been researched in a systematic manner in either North America or Europe. What is offered here is therefore a tentative first sketch. In this sketch, I first elucidate key economic terms such as *globalization* and *convergence* as the political economists use them. More importantly, I trace the historical development of these processes, using the Canadian experience as a case study. Others will have to tackle the ways in which goods and services have become internationalized in the United States and in the European Union, to highlight how globalization and gender are intertwined. Two other social communication questions are closely associated with concerns about the effects of globalization. The first inquires into how the meaning of "public interest" has become redefined in the radically privatized media scape of the 21st century, whereas the second investigates how the "independent" news function, which is essential for democratic governance, has become undermined. What is at stake here is how entertainment conglomerates, which include television and newspaper chains, conceptualize their public service responsibilities and contemporary journalists interpret their "civic" reporting duties. Do these conceptualizations have anything in common with the "feminist" role conceptions, which were discussed in Chapter 7?

Globalization comprises a set of complex processes by which national economic systems are restructured into an integral whole. According to Byerly (2004b), globalization has engendered an international division of labor, quick transfers of capital through computerization, privatization of previously public services, and concentration of ownership in all major industries. In the communications industries, Robert Babe (1996b) notes, these restructurings are grounded in the notion of "convergence," which according to the Office of the European Community (OECD) Directorate of Science, Technology and Industry (DECD) has three dimensions: technical, functional, and corporate. Technical convergence means that increasingly a single mode of transmission, such as coaxial cable, simultaneously transmits diverse information: voice, text, data, sound, and image. Functional convergence, sometimes called "multimedia" points to new hybrid services that combine voice, data, text, and/or images, as in electronic encyclopaedias, whereas corporate convergence refers to mergers, amalgamations, and diversifications through which media organizations come to operate *across* previously distinct industry boundaries (Babe, 1996b, pp. 283-284). As a result, large news companies are today more or less inseparable from entertainment, educational, and other media enterprises. They have, since the 1980s, merged into six huge multinational conglomerates. Three of these: AOL Time Warner, Disney, and Viacom are headquartered in the United States. Two are in the European Community: Bertelsmann in Germany and Vivendi in France, while Murdock's News Corporation is located in Australia. United Nations data indicate that global communication industries generated profits of US $2 trillion in the decade between 1986 and 1996, more than doubling the $745 billion they had earned a decade before and had a profit margin that was triple the median industries' margin of 5.5% (Compaine & Gomery, 2000).

British sociologist Silvia Walby documents that in Western countries, globalization processes in the 20th century resulted in substantial "gender transformations" since the second feminist revolution in the 1960s. These changed gender relations can be described as moving women, who were largely confined to the domestic sphere throughout the early part of the century, into the public sphere. Increased female educational levels, greater labor-force participation, as well as economic globalization trends all contributed to this change. Yet, in the public sphere, women continue to face structural inequalities in the workplace, meaning segregation into unequal positions and into a limited number of job sectors (Walby, 1997). Walby cautions that change in patterns of inequality are complex and layered, rather than merely for the better or for the worse, because different groups of women are affected differently, depending on their age, ethnicity, education, and the sectors in which they work. As a result of this, all highly developed countries since the 1950s have witnessed a reduction of legislation restricting women's work, their ability to obtain abortions, and their capacity to sue for divorce in the face of unendurable marriages. Beyond that, Chapter 6 showed that since the 1950s, the introduction of equity legislation has wrought further changes. What this shows is that both convergence and polarization are occurring in the restructuring of gender relations. Convergence is evident in the cultural, media, and volunteer sectors, where women have gained substantial status. Chapter 3 comparisons showed that female journalists gained positions of authority in the Canadian cultural sectors of television and radio more rapidly, than in the daily press, whereas in the United States and Britain it was the print media that offered greater opportunities and smaller salary differentials between younger female and male staff.

The political and economic integration of the European Union has furthermore demonstrated that gender relations also have an impact on the national levels of economic performance because it is the nation–state that constructs the labor market through direct and indirect means. Direct regulations that set the appropriate terms and conditions of employment have mandated the elimination of legal differences between part- and full-time work, which affect health insurance and pensions, and fix statutory minimum wages and minimum rates of pay (Walby, 1997). Beyond that, the labor market is indirectly constructed through regulations concerning workplace conflict resolution, such as the right to organize in labor unions, regulations concerning picketing, and the formulation of industrial tribunals, which adjudicate health and other infringements. Despite these advances however, female workers on both sides of the Atlantic continue to be more likely to work part time, rather than full time. This is the case because under globalization and the outsourcing of data processing, for instance, these part-timers are no longer a reserve labor force, when male workers are unavailable. Instead, they have become a preferred option for employers in situations of economic restructuring, either up or down. According to Walby (1997), the workers so employed are not only cheaper, but are also flexible in terms of working hours, to suit peak demand.

The nation–state also affects working conditions through what may be called an economic performance philosophy that underlies its regulatory activities. Walby distinguishes between the "deregulation" and the "stakeholder" models. The former assumes that an economy thrives when competition is encouraged and barriers to free markets are removed. In the stakeholder model, on the other hand, a wide range of groups is seen as having a legitimate interest in the running of economic institutions, not only management and shareholders. Among these are workers, customers, the local community, and other affected groups. Walby (1997) calls this a "thick network" of representatives who are considered to be important for continued economic health. Since the 1980s, as seen earlier, the United States has followed primarily a deregulatory path in most economic sectors including the media, which is better described as re-regulation in favor of private industry. The EU, in contrast, through article 19 in the Treaty of Rome (1957), has continued to protect aspects of the welfare state. It enshrined equity for women way before this legislation was introduced into most of the European states and thus laid the foundation for the British Equal Pay Act (1970), the Sex Discrimination Act (1975), and the Equal Values Amendment (1994). Walby points out that all of these acts have strengthened the stakeholder regulatory model and counterbalanced British deregulatory initiatives under the Thacher regime.

In broadcasting, this deregulatory initiative coincided with competition from digital services, reductions in parliamentary subsidies, and losses of audience share to cable and satellite services in the early 1980s. As a result, Gillian Ursell (2000) discovered, in the 10 years between 1987 and 1996 the terrestrial broadcast network ITV shed 44% of its staff, whereas the British Broadcasting Corporation (BBC) lost about 33%. Simultaneously, the number of broadcast freelance workers rose from 39% of the labor force to 60%. BBC staffs, for their part, were subjected to the corporate strategy of "producers choice," which was intended to introduce competition into in-house production operations and which valued costing regimes higher than production values. Labor costs, at least in the commercial companies, were driven down, even on occasion halved, and earnings for around two thirds of all freelancers fell (Ursell, 2000). These falling salaries, however, are embedded in a welfare regime where Great Britain, like Canada, has socialized some forms of previously privatized domestic labor in its welfare state policies. These cover schooling, health, as well as child and other forms of public care, albeit at levels that do not satisfy women's demands. Such alliances between the labor movement and the social provision of health and child care, as well as maternity welfare schemes, are absent in the United States, where the labor movement was greatly weakened by the neo-conservative attitudes introduced by the Reagan administration in the 1980s (Byerly & Warren, 2003).

The conditions under which women are best able to use their skills fully in employment, as Chapters 3 and Chapter 5 indicated, are those where there are effective ways of reconciling working and family life. This reconciliation requires infrastructural support for female employment, such as systems of parental leave, care for children in affordable day care, and lifelong opportunities for learning and training, in addition to equal opportunity policies. Chapter 3 demonstrated that Canadian female journalists were largely unable to reconcile work with family life, because of the overly long North American journalistic working day. In Norway, this issue is addressed by statute, which restricts the working day to 7 hours in all occupations, for both males and females. Chapter 6 shows, additionally, that the 1970 Royal Commission on the Status of Women, chaired by Judge Abella, recommended that the role of "working mother" be incorporated into existing and future legislation, to improve women's opportunities in the public sphere. This review added an antidiscrimination clause to the Unemployment

Insurance Act (1972), led to the passage of the Canadian Human Rights Act in 1977 and fostered the National Employment Equity Act of 1986. The latter requires employers under federal jurisdiction, such as crown corporations like the CBC, banks, railroads, and airlines to adopt the principle of equal pay for work of equal value. Chapter 6 shows that these laws have been adopted by most of Canada's 10 provinces and territories, and that younger female journalists in metropolitan dailies have benefited more professionally than older female personnel in Canada's small and medium papers.

CANADA'S GENDERED EXPERIENCE WITH NEW TECHNOLOGIES

Two Canadian scholars have made a major contribution to our understanding of the complex interrelationships between gender and technological systems. They have begun to sketch not only the economic, but also the social dimensions of what may be called the information revolution of the 1980s. The first is Judy Wajcman (1991), who makes the important point that technology is more than hardware. It comprises, as well, a culture and a special set of knowledges about how to use the technological system. The culture of technology is gendered and excludes women in Anglo-Saxon countries by constructing technological competence as a crucial component of "maleness." Beyond this, feminist historical research indicates that technological innovations like the information highway, are not simply the product of rational technical imperatives, but become instituted, as seen here, as a result of political choices, which are in turn embedded into the very design and selection of the technology in question (Wajcman, 1991). How these choices are made depends primarily on who has the power and the resources to influence them. In the case of telecommunications convergence, there were at least three industry—telecoms, computer industry, online providers—and three regulatory players: the Canadian Radio Television Commission, Industry Canada, and External Affairs. Women were absent in the development of computer technology on which telecom development depends, because it originated as a war technology. This absence translated itself over time into a gender-based division of labor, in which females perform the lower paid subsidiary assembly of microchips jobs, as well as office services, such as data entry and data processing, for which "manual dexterity" are supposedly required. This traditional bifurcation of labor keeps women out of the higher status design and supervisory domains, and bars them from the new managerial jobs, such as system analysts, programmers and other information professionals, positions that are today overwhelmingly male-gendered in Canada as elsewhere (Wajcman, 1991).

Canadian theorist Heather Menzies has looked in greater detail at the social and female work implications of the information highway plan, which undergirds the new knowledge economy. This infrastructure of computers and coaxial cable networks has permitted work and economic activity to become digitalized, which means that tasks are redefined in terms that computers can program and control remotely. Menzies' surveys of Canadian labor force changes since the 1980s echo Walby's (1997) and Ursell's (2000) findings in Britain and indicate that the information highway plan has three deleterious consequences for peoples' livelihood, especially that of females. The first is the substitution of computers for people in all kinds of organizations such as banks, airlines, postal services, manufacturing, as well as broadcasting. The organizational "downsizing" furthermore eliminated whole strata of people, while investments in technology grew in size and complexity. The people-less efficiency growth in large bureaucracies is demonstrated in the Canadian federal public service, where in the first half of the 1990s, 45,000 public servants were laid off, while spending on information technology grew to $10.2 billion (Menzies, 1998). Similar figures are recorded in telephone companies and other networked industries, which extended their coaxial cable networks and downsized their personnel. A second, less well-documented by-product of increased uses of computerization, is that machine intelligence replaces human intelligence. This means that corporate control is moved to higher levels of management, where fewer females are employed. This development has hollowed out the middle levels of the administrative, sales, and service sectors of contemporary industries, which women had just begun to penetrate in the 1980s, and replaces them with system analysts, programmers, and other information professionals, most of whom are male.

Another deleterious effect of the information revolution is its polarization of the Canadian labor market, turning full-time jobs into part-time, shift and temporary jobs, associated with clerical work (Menzies, 1998). As already noted by Walby (1997), in Britain these positions are overwhelmingly held by females and often deprive them of social and pension rights. Because these jobs do not involve increased knowledge levels, but manual dexterity, they are undervalued and underpaid. Finally, once the wires are laid and the jobs restructured, the stage is set for a new local–global redistribution of jobs. The often part-time clerical workforce, made up mostly of women are "outsourced" to remote call centers or to their homes, which are turned into "virtual" work sites with even less pay. Beyond that, clerical work has been moved to less developed countries like Mexico and India, where women are paid one third of Canadian wages under the North American Free Trade Agreement (NAFTA). Menzies concludes that the new economy extends the scale of monopoly organization to its fullest, while ironically making it invisible through a new form of corporate organization. In this organizational setting, Canadian theorist George Grant (1962) warned in the 1960s, that people would be turned into servo-mechanisms, and the language of instrumental rationality, not the language of human reason, compassion, and community would gain the upper hand. The following history of telecom convergence demonstrates the extent to which Menzies' four gendered workforce changes resulting from globalization are manifested in the Canadian media and telecommunication sectors.

AN ASSESSMENT OF MEDIA AND TELECOMMUNICATIONS CONVERGENCE IN CANADA

Fifty years of Canadian development demonstrates that the regulatory regimes for the media and telecommunication sectors were initially based on a philosophy of media "divergence." As Wajcman (1991) suggests, this policy stance was not the result of purely technological concerns, but emerged from state regulatory interventions, which followed European postal precedents and viewed telecommunication carriers as natural monopolies. Between the end of World War II and the early 1990s, the regulatory rules of the telecommunications sector were consequently separated from those of online service providers, as well as from broadcasting and the press. Telecommunication carriers were regulated as public service utilities, online services were under the auspices of the Telecommunications Act of 1993, and broadcasting was supervised by the CRTC as a mixed public–private system, with national ownership requirements, universal access, and Canadian content rules (Winseck, 1998).

Only the Canadian press has, from the beginning, been governed purely by market forces and thus provides the clearest example of the social and political effects of "deregulated" concentration and monopoly ownership. Although the newspaper industry falls under the Competition Act (1985), which proscribes mergers that "prevent or lessen, or are likely to prevent or lessen, competition substantially," the act has not been enforced. Media researchers interpret this inaction as an outcome of the North American Free Trade Agreement (NAFTA), which has, since 1993, linked Canadian government outlooks to the U.S. deregulatory philosophy. Babe (1996a) notes that by the early 1990s, "corporate" convergence across previously distinct media industry boundaries was picking up steam. Where there had been more than a dozen newspaper chains in the 1980s, 10 years later only three chains remained and dominated 70% of Canada's daily newspaper circulation. The first chain with 38% of circulation, consisted of Southam Incorporated (17 dailies), Power Corporation's Gesca (4 papers), and Conrad Black's Hollinger Corp. (28 dailies). The Thompson Corp. chain (38 dailies) had another 21% of total circulation, whereas the Toronto Sun Publishing chain (11 papers) supplied 11% of national circulation. It is the ownership pattern of this last chain that is particularly interesting, because it provided the entry point for media cross-ownership in the 1990s, previously denied by regulations. The Toronto Sun Publishing chain, owned by McLean Hunter, is not only a magazine publisher, but also holds radio, television, and cable properties (Babe, 1996a).

The McLean Hunter changes suggest that Canada, like Great Britain, relaxed its cross-ownership rules in the early 1980s, resulting in full convergence between the press, various forms of broadcasting and telecommunications by the mid-1990s. The disastrous print and broadcast convergence began when Conrad Black's Hollinger Corp. bought the Southam chain of newspapers in 1997, and 3 years later sold it for about $3.1 billion to Can-West Global Communications Corp., owner of Global TV. When the tech market collapsed in 2000, Can-West did what Menzies (1996) predicted. It downsized its editorial personnel and increased the computer infrastructure to cut production costs (Dornan, 1996). The outcome resulted in increased concentration in Canada's print and broadcast sectors as demonstrated by Can-West's domination of more than 60% of Canada's daily newspaper circulation in the five major markets, to the detriment of opinion variety. As early as 1980, Tom Kent, head of the Royal Commission on Newspapers, called the trend: "a combination against the public interest which undoubtedly limits the role and scope of the information that reaches the public" (Chase, 2003, p. B7).

Convergence in the Canadian telecommunication sector has also moved toward consolidation, but at a different pace from that in the old media. Telecommunications convergence has passed through two quite distinct stages. In the first stage, between the 1970s and the 1990s, efforts were primarily directed at achieving change *within* telecommunications companies themselves, while respecting the government's "disassociation" stance between carriage and content. These companies were involved in what Babe has called technical convergence and the building of a single mode of transmission, such as a coaxial cable network for the distribution of multiple types of signals. The powers driving these first network changes were large business players such as the Canadian Banking Association, the Canadian Business Telecommunications Alliance, and the Information Technology Alliance of Canada. They sought competition, the ability to offer a broader range of telecommunication services at lower prices, and if possible, the removal of telecommunication companies from federal-provincial and from CRTC supervision. The second stage of telecom convergence, starting in the mid-1990s, aimed at convergence *across* media sectors, amounting to what Babe (1996b) has called corporate convergence. This change was driven by a different group of powerful players. Among them were telecommunication providers like Stentor (a consortium of telephone companies in the 10 provinces, among which Bell Canada is the largest), the computer industry, as well as the Canadian government.

As in the Canadian print industry, the government's switch in regulatory philosophy came not from national, but from economic considerations and the signing of the NAFTA treaty by the conservative Mulroney government in 1993. In this year, telecommunications alone already accounted for 3% ($15.6 billion) of Canadian gross domestic product, as compared to the much less spectacular 0.3% contribution made by broadcasting (Babe, 1996b). In the heat of the convergence mania, the Canadian government went so far as to make the unverified claim that national economic and cultural survival depended on the building of the so-called information highway. This integrated broadband communication network (IBN) was to be completed by 2005, primarily through telecom industry financing (Winseck, 1998).

The change in regulatory philosophy is evidenced by the fact that in 1995, the CRTC established three conditions under which the telecommunications companies could enter broadcasting. First, they lifted the ban on producing program content. In addition, the telecommunication companies could set up their own content production facilities without going through a separate affiliate. And finally, under the new policy, all carriers, including telephone companies, cable, satellite, wireless, and so on, would be regulated by the Telecommunications Act (1993) when providing telecommunication services and the Broadcasting Act (1991) when offering broadcast services. The result is convergence in facilities, but continued media separation in content regulation (Winseck, 1998). The vision of huge profits seemingly promised by the convergence blueprint is graphically illustrated by the activities of Bell Canada Enterprises (BCE), the largest player in the field. Between 1995 and 2000, it began to acquire various types of carriage and content assets, such as part-ownership of Express Vu, a new direct-to-home (DTH) satellite broadcast service, Teleglobe, a fiber optics carrier, as well as its own media content operation, consisting of the *Globe and Mail* newspaper and a private television network (CTV). Beyond that, BCE also invested in Emergis, an electronic commerce company, focusing on health care and financial services, and set up Bell Canada International (BCI), operating cell phone services in Latin America (Ebener, 2003).

The predicted pay-off of convergence in services did not however materialize. By 2003, Bell Canada Enterprises had changed its CEO and taken a write-off of $7.5 billion for Teleglobe, the largest loss ever recorded by a Canadian company. It had also jettisoned BCI, the Latin American cell phone provider, at a loss of $316 million. The reasons for the bursting of the telecommunications bubble are familiar: intense competition for long distance and data transmission, a weak Canadian economy, pricing pressures between competing providers, and as demonstrated previously, overly aggressive expansion plans that created huge debt loads. To return BCE to a firmer financial footing, Miachael Sabia, the new CEO, is simplifying the company by doing the usual shedding of an additional 1,700 personnel, plus 16 executives and by selling nonessential holdings, such as the directories business, for $3 billion (Goold, 2003). He is furthermore returning the company to its roots, buying back a 20% interest in Bell Canada from the San Antonio, Texas-based "Baby Bell" and "bundling" the company's businesses into three key areas: consumers, small- and medium-sized companies, and large enterprises, which together provide 82% of the company's operating profits (Ebener, 2003).

The predicted investment of the telecom industry in the information highway infrastructure has also not materialized, because of uncertain consumer demand for interactive services, such as video-on-demand or for other online services deliverable by a broadband network. In Canada, as in many other economically developed countries, a digital fiber network already connects most cities and provides the backbone for *intra-city* networks (Melody, 1996). With almost three quarters of Canadian homes subscribing to cable television, there is also an extensive broadband network connection to most homes. Yet, the cable companies lack the interactive networks stretching *across* cities, regions, or even the country and will be hard pressed to develop this capacity because of heavy debt burdens. Although computer terminals can serve as the interface between users and the network, it must be remembered that only about one third of Canadian homes have computers, and less than one quarter of these have Internet access. Furthermore, computer ownership remains the preserve of the affluent. All of this indicates that the problems of innovating the information highway (IBNs) are not technical, but economic, social, and cultural. Economically, there are huge costs involved in opening channels between people and the broadband network. Socially, research in Canada and Europe confirms that customers prefer to wait until broadband communication systems either mesh more closely with their needs, or are rendered cheap enough that participation does not entail high monthly costs. Culturally, Menzies (1998) points out, lifestyles changed drastically in the 1990s. Both females and males have to work longer hours for lower incomes and leisure time has therefore drastically declined, especially for working wives of the baby-boomer generation, as demonstrated in Chapter 7. All together, these developments make it impossible for families to devote more time to entertainment activities. Finally, contrary to the hyped expectations, the converged new services do not supersede, but have to compete with existing media. Among these are video rentals and film attendance. This leads Canadian technology researcher Dwayne Winseck (1998) to conclude that there will not be a substantial rise in consumer entertainment expenditures in the near future.

Given the lack of demand for, and the inelasticity of expenditures on communication/information services, Winseck wonders which regulatory model is most appropriate for Canada's telecommunication services in the new century. Under heavy pressure from the United States, Canada seems to be veering toward the "deregulation" model, even though there has been no thorough debate about the social implications of such a choice. This model, which is financed by advertising and service providers who collect personal buying information on their customers, is made easy by the relatively lax North American "privacy" laws. A second model, which Winseck calls the "luxury model," has already been implemented for certain kinds of "enhanced" services in Canada. It is based on higher monthly payments for the wealthy, among them information professionals, who congregate in the information "suburbs," while anaemic "free" services are available through public access in libraries and elsewhere. The third option would be a "universal ISDN" model that meets the demonstrable needs of business, professional, and residential users without the massive state/industry-led technology push that requires enormous subsidies to innovate the broadband information highway (Winseck, 1998).

Canadian researchers suggest that a more appropriate regulatory model for the 21st century is one that takes the public interest into account. It should be based on four considerations. The first is "appropriateness" for the services needed. They point out that the vast majority of new information services, even in the United States, can be accommodated on digital telephone lines and do not require a fiber optics information highway (Melody, 1996). ISDN is particularly suited for meeting commercial and individual needs for facsimile, data transmission, voice mail, electronic messaging, teleconferencing, and Internet services. Demand is high in all of these areas. Melody argues that with an ISDN-compatible network already in the ground and paid for by all Canadian users, it would be quite inexpensive to connect them to this network. The only remaining cost would be the terminal interface between the subscriber and the network, which in Canada would cost between $300 and $1,000 depending on the sophistication of the interface desired (Melody, 1996). Most Stentor phone companies in Canada already market ISDN as an enhanced "luxury" service, as do the United States and Great Britain. In Germany and France, in contrast, ISDN is considered part of the basic service and is priced as a regular phone line (Winseck, 1998).

Anthony Reddick of the Public Interest Advocacy Center suggests that another consideration of appropriateness is to call for competition in those services where the growth is greatest. This is primarily in Canadian Internet services, which were growing at 10% in 1995. "Free Nets" in public libraries and cyber-cafes attracted an additional 150,000 to 200,000 people to access the Internet, out of a total of 600,000 users then online (Reddick, 1995). The highway project, in contrast, where no growth is being recorded, is subsidized with $5 billion in government funds, only a small fraction of which was pinpointed for content production and for networking programs. German jurist Hoffman-Riem points out that the Canadian government is currently promoting irreconcilable goals: network competition as well as universal ISBNs. This cannot be achieved by competition regulations that ponder issues of efficiency, market power, and restraint of trade, rather than the diversity of speakers, the balance between speaker and listener rights, universal service, or factors that can distort the mediated communication experience (Hoffman-Riem, 1996). This warning echoes Grant's (1962) concern that the language of instrumental rationality is inadequate for arguing fair access for all to the information highway and must therefore be counterbalanced with a language of values.

A third consideration for determining whether the Canadian regulatory process has been appropriate takes other government agencies to task for interfering with the existing regulatory bodies. Since the mid-1990s, when telecommunications convergence *across* media sectors accelerated, the regulatory control of the CRTC has been circumvented, and the new media sectors have been shielded from public interference. The Canadian government should scale back and reallocate the current highway subsidies, promote the public sector through redirecting funds to the creation of a vibrant community media sector and support increased competition. Part of this can be achieved through liberalizing the Canadian ownership restrictions, which are in the process of being reduced from 80% to 66% in 2005. This does not imply that restrictions should be eliminated all together because cultural goals like protecting Canadian capabilities in content production vis-à-vis the global entertainment conglomerates need to remain in place. Canada also needs to keep the $100 million a year Canadian Television Fund (CTF) intact to support popular television productions, without which dozens of dramas, comedies, specials, and children's shows would not make it on the air (Adams & MacDonald, 2003).

Winseck (1998) concludes that the most important thing to do with respect to global telecommunication policy is to jettison the distinction between "basic" and "enhanced" services. This distinction no longer makes sense, as domestic monopolies are dismantled and the World Trade Organization (WTO) advocates competition in all telecommunication services. A better way to proceed is offered by the EC's "nonreserved category" of services. Its framework offers opportunities to reconcile competition with broader ideas of public service communication, and with redefinitions of cultural policy in the context of global electronic spaces. Not only would competition among media infrastructure (telephones) and service providers (cable) be allowed, but they would also enjoy editorial freedoms, as long as a certain portion of available bandwidth were set aside for online public media spaces. Moreover, it would still be possible to promote traditional cultural policy with respect to Canadian content, although this content requirement would be only one pillar in a more broadly defined public space (Winseck, 1998). In general, the rules of global trade need to be supplemented by normative regulations guaranteeing diversity of access and content to ensure a viable platform for the production of political opinion variety and popular sovereignty. The EU which has set goals of diversity, gender, and other aspects of media freedoms, offers a model for Canada to emulate in its regulatory approach.

THE DIMINUTION OF THE "PUBLIC SPHERE" UNDER CONVERGENCE

Concentration of broadcast and telecommunications media in both Canada and Great Britain, which have a mixed public–private system, has long raised questions about what constitutes popular sovereignty. How can the relationship between the media and democracy in late capitalist society, where a small number of media conglomerates subvert the notion of the public sphere through their use of commercial speech be defined? Juan Linz (1975) reminds us that the essence of democracy consists of the free formulation of political preferences, through the use of free association, information, and communication, for the purpose of competition between leaders to validate their claim to rule (p. 158). This definition highlights the rights of citizens to be informed in a democracy, so as to make proper choices about how to govern themselves.

Jürgen Habermas (1989) conceives of the public sphere where the citizen and the state come together as a neutral zone. In it, access to relevant information affecting the public good is widely available, discussion is free of domination by the state, and all those participating in the public debate, do so on an equal basis. The media's role in this process is to provide an arena for public debate and to reconstitute private citizens as a public body in the form of public opinion. But what happens if this public sphere, which used to be grounded in politics, has in late capitalism become supplanted by one grounded in commerce? James Carey (1995) argues that in such a setting the very definition of democracy has become undermined and the role of the media in politics becomes degraded. This has come about because competition between political parties with explicit programs has been supplanted by interest-group competition, which uses the state political parties as well as the press to control the distribution of economic goods. By definition, Carey argues, interest groups operate in the private sector *behind* the scenes, and their relationship to the public is essentially propagandistic and manipulative. Moreover, the struggle between interest groups turns the language of journalism into "public relations," that is, an instrument in the struggle for advantage, rather than a vehicle for truth (Carey, 1995). No wonder citizens denied a public arena in which to develop their civic competencies become either consumers of politics or escapists from it, because their civic competencies no longer have an outlet (Carey, 1995). These civic competencies refer to that dimension of each one of us that is responsible for, contributes to, and benefits from the cooperative endeavor of self-government (Goldmark, 2001).

The public interest can, therefore, not be redefined as "fair competition" *alone*, as convergence technocrats have argued, because market forces, without public service goals, do not automatically result in opinion variety, which citizens need for self-governance. As demonstrated in the Canadian case, convergence has resulted in a loss of diversity of both outlets and points of view, and enables single companies to control the distribution of information along a variety of channels. It furthermore entails the relaxation of ownership policies, and a concomitant increase in the relative importance of market forces. In the Canadian context, as we have seen, this has meant increased government interference in the regulation of the telecommunications sector and a softening of traditional public-service goals for media industries. Among these are the nation-building ethic, universality of telecommunications services, domestic ownership and control of media industries, Canadian content production requirements and a viable presence, if not predominance of noncommoditized communication (channels and voices) (Babe, 1996a).

Deregulation has also entailed the continued weakening of the public broadcasters and their nonmarket ethic of programming for all sectors of society. In both Canada and Great Britain, as we have seen, the license fee supported BBC and the federally financed CBC have had budgetary contractions for at least 10 years (Briggs, 2002). The Canadian CRTC has exacerbated this public sector emasculation by licensing some 30 pay and specialty TV channels, all but one of which (CBC's Newsworld) are in the private sector. In addition, ACCESS, the provincially owned educational broadcaster in Alberta, has been privatized, along with a radio station operated by the University of Alberta. Ontario's government, too, is thinking of privatizing its hugely successful educational channel, TV Ontario. As of 2005, the CBC with a budget of about $7 billion, captures only about 8% of the Canadian audience, whereas the BBC, with license fee-generated income of about $55 billion, attracts 38% of the British viewers (Simpson, 2003). Together, this diminution of public outlets, which represent a different point of view, has undermined opinion diversity in Canada and runs counter to the conduct of a sound democracy, which depends on the ability of the citizenry to make informed and wise decisions on matters of public concern.

Bill Moyers of the Public Broadcasting Service (PBS) makes a similar argument for the most highly concentrated U.S. media market, which has virtually eliminated the PBS. He notes that in the 1980s, there were 50 owners of America's major media outlets. As of 2003, there were 6. Two thirds of the newspaper markets were monopolies and more than half the radio audience was controlled by four corporations in 2003 (cited in Shister, 2003). The latest Federal Communications Commission ruling in June 2003 goes even further and seems to be dismantling the last barriers to U.S. carriage and content concentration. In television, it permits companies to own stations that reach 45% of the U.S. population, rather than the previous 35%. In local markets with five or more stations, a company can now own two, where previously it could have only one and in markets with 18 or more, a company can own three stations, while stipulating that only one of these can be among the top four in ratings. Cross-ownership of television with newspapers and radio stations is also permitted in markets with nine or more TV outlets, although in smaller markets, cross-ownership is prohibited (Carter & Routenberg, 2003). What this all adds up to is that the goals of information diversity, the life-blood of a healthy Canadian and U.S. democracy, have been severely curtailed and that it is time for regulators and the public to take note. A U.S. federal court of appeals did just that in June 2004. It repudiated the FCC's deregulation decision promulgated by chairman Michael Powell, son of Secretary of State Colin Powell. In a two to one decision, the judges threw out the rules that would have allowed greater ownership of television and radio stations in the same market. Although it pointed out that the FCC was within its rights to repeal a blanket prohibition on companies owning both a newspaper and a television station in the same city. It also reduced the size of the national audience that can be reached by a single TV owner to 39% from 45%, where the FCC had placed it (Sutel, 2004).

With such a predominance of commercial speech, how can the democratic information role of the 21st century media be rethought? James Curran (1992) suggests that the media's classically conceived single role needs to be enlarged into a tripartite agenda. The media's role to constitute the platform for public debate must be informed by a diversity of values and perspectives in both entertainment as well as in public affairs, so that all groups can decide how best to safeguard and advance their collective and individual welfare. Increased access by subordinate classes to ideas and arguments will enable them to explore how to change their situation and thus regain their feelings of political empowerment. Beyond that, the media system must act as an agency of representation in which alternative viewpoints receive attention and debate, rather than mere distribution. A public–private media set-up provides programming that gives a voice to different interpretive communities, organizations, and subcultures. In the Netherlands, the law demands that the broadcast space be apportioned according to party affiliation and parliamentary representation, whereas in Germany, opinion variety is guaranteed through representation on the broadcast councils, which oversee public-service programming. A third democratic media function is to assist in the realization of compromise between social groups with varying perspectives. Although national consensus will probably be more difficult to achieve in the increasingly multiethnic societies of Europe and North America, the centrifugal force can be mitigated through the introduction of new legal frameworks. These would lay down acceptable but minimal limits to freedom of expression. Among these might be restrictions on inciting racial hatred, distinctions between "commercial" and "political" speech, and the introduction of a number of fairness rules. Such rules would not only counterbalance the prevalence of economic propaganda, but also remind the journalistic profession that freedom of speech is not their personal domain, but extends to all citizens (Curran, 1992; McConnel & Becker, 2002).

MEDIA CONTENT AND POPULAR SOVEREIGNTY

The argument that media concentration and convergence lead to a narrowing of the notion of the "public interest" as traditionally defined is complex and multifaceted because it goes beyond the simple arithmetic of counting outlets. It entails, as well, a consideration of how the language and content of media productions have suffered. I approach this discussion from four different angles to document how the monetarization of news production is undermining content variety in Canada and why "public sovereignty" issues matter. The argument, first of all, entails a discussion of why the cultural industries market is different from automobile production and what this means for distribution strategies. Beyond that, we need to understand how shifts in journalistic practices impact on the *types* of media content that are produced. Canadian press researchers have described these strategies as "streamlining" and "homogenizing" newspaper content *across* chain papers to save money. And, finally, it is important to think about what the outcomes of streamlining will be for the Canadian citizen/viewer, for whom concentration means less content diversity and less resources for local reporting. All together, these transformations will indicate that the cultural realm's deepening commodification poses challenges concerning the conditions of access, funding, diversity, and quality of content, all of which are part of the popular sovereignty responsibilities of media owners in a democratic society.

The Canadian case study demonstrates that the so-called new media services, like video-on-demand and online publishing, have not been

snapped up by the public because they either do not respond to people's perceived needs or are priced too high. As a result, the industrialization and co-
modification of the so-called cultural industries market, as previously mentioned, is being driven not by new "immersive" media applications, but by
old media conglomerates, trying to save money after going on costly acquisition binges. Paschal Preston (2001), who has studied multimedia content,
concludes that the biggest success in the 1990s was in the use of the Internet
as a distribution system for games, using PC- based CD-ROM platforms.
Yet even here, less than 10% of all the CD-ROM content products published in the United States as well as in the EU during the 1990s have generated a profit. The only money-makers on both sides of the Atlantic are
pornography and certain types of e-commerce, selling such old media products as books and records, as well as airline tickets. The other success story
is Web broadcasting, which offers the promise of expanded news content-
related innovations for newspapers, broadcasting, and television. We must,
therefore, conclude that it is the mature media organizations that harness
their own core competencies to the new digital technologies and have, at the
beginning of the 21st century, positioned themselves to become the real mas-
ters of multimedia content markets.

The obvious question that needs answering is why there has been such
a disconnect between the promise and the performance of the new media in
the cultural content market. Preston (2001) suggests that this primarily has
to do with the economics of cultural content creation, which is very different from producing automobiles. Five of these differences are crucial.
Among them are the fact that media programming has very high first-copy
costs and very low costs for subsequent copies. This encourages media conglomerates to maximize circulation, sales, market share, and/or audience
reach for any specific book, newspaper, film, or TV production. In addition,
distribution plays a much more important role in ensuring the commercial
success of entertainment industries, than elsewhere, as the book *Harry
Potter and the Order of the Phoenix* demonstrates. What this means is that
cultural content companies do not merely have to own distribution channels, but much more importantly, they have to know how to promote and
recycle the company's total content portfolio. Furthermore, owners claim
that cultural productions are relatively "high risk" in the sense that only a
small proportion of stories, films, and so on, end up being profitable, compared to the situation in other industries where production risks are pre-
dictable and can be minimized. A fourth factor is that advertisers and their
agencies play a distinctive intervening role in the relationship between cultural product producers and their customers. These large agencies tend to
favor dealings with cross-media corporations that can most efficiently deliv-
er a particular mix of target audiences. A closely related point, which is strikingly demonstrated in the United States, is that a relatively large home mar-

ket helps ensure success on the international scene (Preston, 2001). All
Canadian cultural industries, including magazines, books, and films, as well
as broadcasting and video, have been on the receiving end of the three U.S.-
based global entertainment empires that undercut local production capacities by substantially reducing the export prices of their products. Canadian
regulators try to counterbalance this "dumping" tendency by Canadian
media ownership and content production rules, as well as by invoking the
Canadian Broadcasting Act's definition of "diversity of viewer interests," in
determining the placement of foreign-produced programming on cable
channels.

How has journalism as a profession been impacted by concentration?
Chapter 7 indicates that a number of Canada's small circulation newspaper
properties were abandoned with the usual displacement of personnel. Even
in the larger circulation metropolitan papers, however, where the greatest
readership increase has occurred since the 1980s, cross-ownership and concentration pressures have resulted in "downsizing" of editorial personnel
and what Heather Menzies (1998) calls "people-less" productivity growth.
More difficult to describe and insidious to discover are the effects of the current multimedia managers' "rationalization" mindsets and the ways in
which they mold the news product itself. David Bollier (2002) observes that:
"as conglomerates buy, sell and merge . . . many news corporations have
become small fiefdoms in large business enterprises. In the process, the culture of journalism has become folded into a larger universe of entertainment
media, managed by business executives who really do not understand or
even care about journalism as a professional calling or a democratic necessity" (p. 29). This situation creates a number of interrelated threats for news
production. Among these are the monetarization of the news product and
the restricted ways in which the news is imagined and crafted. What Bollier
(2002) is referring to here is the fact that editorial selection procedures are
being tilted toward the "marketability" of stories, rather than their long-
term sociopolitical relevance. Another threat to news production comes
from the fact that in Internet use no distinctions are made between news and
commentary, nor are accuracy and fairness, two important criteria of practice, observed (Bollier, 2002). Instead, fact and fiction, the personal and the
scientific are all intermingled, raising questions about how to evaluate the
truthfulness of press material published not only on Web sites, but also on
terrestrial broadcast channels whose public relations idiom subverts the
truth (Carey, 1995).

All of these issues of monetarization have surfaced in Canada's largest
multimedia company, the CanWest Global Communications Corporation,
which bought into the "convergence" hype in the mid-1990s and is now saddled with a large debt. We have already mentioned that CanWest, owned by
the Asper family of Winnipeg, went on a buying spree at the turn of the mil-

lennium. It added not only Conrad Black's chain of regional papers, but also television and radio stations in Australia, New Zealand and Ireland (EBIT-DA), to complement its six station Canadian (Global) network. As a result, in 2003 the company was $3.5 billion in debt and was forced to sell its Canadian regional papers for $255 million and its second Vancouver TV station (CKVU) for $63 million to cover carrying charges. Yet, these sales were insufficient to service the debt and CanWest also took journalistic initiatives to achieve editorial savings by trying to increase what Bollier (2002) calls the "marketability" of its stories across the chain. This was achieved by setting up an 18-person Canada News Desk at company headquarters in Winnipeg, "to identify the best national stories and make them available to the company's other papers." Although this is a laudable move for the production of the chain's "routine material," like TV listings, weather, sports, and business statistics, it raises broader editorial freedom concerns, if it is applied to other types of news production (Mills, 2003, p. 311).

Journalists have warned that the central news desk constitutes the first step in a broader strategy to reduce editorial staff and budgets at CanWest's individual papers, where money is needed to provide local coverage. Except for the *National Post* (Toronto), which has continued to lose $25 million per year since 2000, the conglomerate's other papers are generally very profitable, some producing profit margins of more than 30%, which is six times the margin in the manufacturing sector (Mills, 2003). Yet, these profits are insufficient to subsidize the company's other money-losing properties in the broadcast sector. The other fear results from the fact that CanWest's 40-person Ottawa news bureau, which covers the federal government and national politics, is slated to be supervised by the news desk in Winnipeg, where proximity to headquarters will create an irresistible temptation to meddle. This is evidenced by CanWest's controversial national editorial policy, instituted in 2001. It mandated that editors in the chain's top metropolitan dailies in Vancouver, Calgary, Ottawa, and Montreal run editorials on national issues written by the head office and not contradict these with local comment, as the sacked *Ottawa Citizen's* editor, Russell Mills did in his paper. The resulting journalistic outcry charging censorship of news selection and coverage led not only to the quiet abandonment of the policy, but also to the resignation of Murdoch Davis in 2003, who had developed the controversial policy (Damsell, 2003). Hopefully, the centralized news desk in Winnipeg will not be charged with second-guessing federal political coverage for the CanWest cross-media chain, even though it will centralize cultural coverage for all its papers.

So, how does content streamlining affect citizens' rights to opinion variety? To begin with, it must be remembered that newspapers play a central role in providing opinion variety because of their local focus in the immense and sparsely populated Canadian land mass. As such, they express the pluralism of the country, its various identities, perspectives, and values in greater detail than any other medium. Moreover, no media compete with newspapers in the number of journalists employed as seen in Chapter 2. Their pages and Internet sites provide the foundation for the production of the public discourse on issues of national interest across the realm. Unfortunately, globalization has treated cultures as exploitable resources, and has, in the process, redefined citizens with political rights, into "consumers," with nothing but commercial interests. Alison Beale (1999) notes that Canadian, British, and the EC state neo-corporatism seems to be preoccupied with securing an international place for their nationally based cultural industries, rather than with shielding institutions, such as publicly funded radio and television networks, from the forces of commerce (Beale, 1999). Yet, as seen in previous sections, the degree to which this has succeeded is different in the three countries, with Britain maintaining the most well-funded public-service broadcast network, Canada located in between, and the United States in the least favorable funding position, although some of these disadvantages are mitigated by the sheer size of its cultural industries and its audiences. How concentration is affecting information variety is the topic of a Senate Committee investigation into the state of "public sovereignty" in the Canadian media, which reported in 2004. This committee, which is chaired by Senator Joan Fraser, past editor of the *Montreal Gazette*, is revisiting the work of the 1980 Kent Commission on Newspapers, which advocated strict policing of the corporate dealings of media companies in the name of market diversity. The fact that it called for the break-up of cross-ownership in 1980 does not bode well for the current state of Canada's information variety.

A series of conclusions can be drawn from these findings. To begin with, my discussions of globalization and media cross-ownership have shown that these developments have more to do with economic than with technological factors. Moreover, Canada's mixed public–private media system, although not perfect, demonstrates, that state policies *do* matter in achieving public communication goals. This is because the multiplication of media channels and outlets do not automatically ensure diversity or plurality of content as the neo-conservatives claim. For this to happen, ethical standards and fairness rules have to be articulated and enforced, to set minimal limits to freedom of expression and distinguish between "commercial" and "political" speech. Finally, the technology-centred discourses about the inherent global scale of the Internet must also be challenged. The available evidence on Internet traffic in the developed world indicates that the majority of this traffic to and from sites turns out to be within national borders and not to locations outside. The one exception may be the Middle East states during the Iraq war, where Qatar's *El Jazeera* provided information not available in many of the autocratically ruled adjacent states.

GENDER AND THE "CIVIC JOURNALISM" MOVEMENT

Globalization and concentration of media production and distribution technologies have not only raised concerns about the "public" purpose of journalism in a democratic state, but also about the ways in which this purpose is performed by media professionals at the beginning of the new millennium. Benjamin Barber (1984) makes a useful distinction between what he calls *thin* and *public* journalism to describe these differences. Thin journalism, in terms of its democratic performance, is a journalism that is based on a representative logic of society in which legitimate authorities are featured as news makers and viewers/readers are distant stakeholders who cannot speak in their own voice (Barber, 1984). Furthermore, as James Carey (1995) so aptly argues, coverage that views politics as a struggle between interest groups turns the language of journalism into "public relations," that is, an instrument in the struggle for advantage rather than a vehicle for truth. The newspaper and broadcast content analyses in Chapter 7 document that over time, thin journalism has increased. It is a journalism in which females and ethnic minorities, as well as local political groups, have lost their voices both in the press and in broadcast news. Here, only the least prestigious "person-in-the-street" role has had an increase of female, ethnic, and other voices. The CanWest account has demonstrated that this loss of role and voice in newspaper coverage is related to the conglomerate's move to increase the "marketability" of its stories *across* the chain. The cutback of the local reporting resources gave rise to the increased coverage of "legitimate" authorities, to the detriment of local popular representatives and their concerns.

According to Glasser and Craft (1996), "public" journalism, in contrast, sets itself the task of promoting and improving public life, rather than just reporting on it. In doing so, public journalists pay particular attention to the everyday lives of citizens and treat their experiences as sources of valid information and knowledge. This information is often derived from discussion groups that are set up as *resources* for the newsroom or through other feedback mechanisms, like letters to the editor. In exchange, journalists make themselves available to citizens in three ways: by querying the accountability of those in power, by utilizing involved citizens and interest groups as information sources, and by providing citizens with a public platform for discussing relevant public issues. By 1997, the public journalism initiative in the United States had inspired more than 300 projects in different newspapers (Lambeth, Meyer, & Thorson, 1998; Rosen, 1996), as well as a few in Scandinavia (Heikkilä, 2000). The Scandinavian and U.S. experiments show that it is difficult for news personnel to give up their expert status because this is so closely related to the "neutral" stance, which is part of the "objective" reporting technique. This technique usually presents only

two official sides to any issue, leaving the voices of supposedly unrepresen-
tative interest groups, unreported. Yet, it is exactly these community groups
that, given a voice, safeguard the relevance of a newspaper's coverage in the
public's eye. Routine citizen consultation is additionally uncomfortable for
journalists to contemplate because it opens the news-making process itself
to public scrutiny and makes readers–viewers aware of reportorial short-
comings. Developing and liasing with citizen groups is also very labor inten-
sive and can only be maintained over time, if the whole newsroom supports
the experiment and substantial resources are made available (Heikkilä,
2000).

   Globalization as a threat to public journalism was also the focus of five
Communications and Society programs at the Aspen Institute in the years
between 1997 and 2002, which discussed the failure of conglomerates to
take their democratic public-service responsibilities seriously. Many of
these U.S. criticisms mirror the Canadian criticisms of CanWest's editorial
initiatives mentioned earlier. The conferences noted the erosion of U.S.
reader/viewer trust and their inability to determine the quality of the news,
both because of the abundance of sources of information and the fragmentation of the audience resulting from technological convergence (Goldmark,
2001). The Aspen conferees also targeted for concern the inadequacy of
local news production in the United States, resulting from the FCC's repeal
of the 5 minutes of news per hour requirement between elections, which
eliminated most local news production on Clear Channel's 1,200-station
network. Research during the 2000 election showed that these decisions led
to inadequate political coverage in the campaign in which George W. Bush
came to power. A study in the 50 largest markets showed that during that
campaign, four times as many political commercials as campaign stories
were aired, giving party-sponsored public relations messages the upper
hand over the balanced reporting that is needed for electoral information
(Goldmark, 2001). No wonder that the Republican political practices of
voter exclusion and voter misinformation in Florida could become so widespread. Hollywood writers and producers, as well as U.S. consumer advocates, furthermore decry the loss of affiliate autonomy in producing their
own programming to substitute for network shows. The Aspen participants
concluded that information variety in the United States had been eroded
and thus endangered the democratic functioning of the state (Carter &
Routenberg, 2003).

   Remedies were sought through the Civic Journalism movement, with its
call for the re-evaluation of the profession's core values. Bill Kovach, head
of the movement, concludes that in the fractured information environment,
the business that journalists have to be in is *meaning*, not news (Goldmark,
2001). What he is demanding is the age-old requirement for quality reporting, namely backgrounding and contextualizing of events, which Robert

Park and John Dewey demanded in the 1920s when newspapers were the dominant medium. To improve U.S. private broadcast news today, where news items are little more than headlines, the demand for backgrounding takes on new urgency. Proper backgrounding can be accomplished only by applying such journalistic maxims as accuracy in reporting, separation of fact from opinion, fairness of coverage, increased transparency about how news is produced, re-evaluating relevance, and being respectful of *how* people are covered (Goldmark, 2001). Robert MacNeil (1997) of the PBS, furthermore suggests that news producers need to listen to people's agendas, rather than that of the power brokers in deciding what news events are relevant and on giving public servants the benefit of the doubt. In a setting where more than half of the U.S. public no longer casts a vote, the media's gratuitous intrusions into the private lives of the highest office holders are partly to blame for voter apathy. He also advocated the creation of a press council, to adjudicate reader/viewer criticisms of coverage.

Canada, with a different set of political practices, including a parliamentary Question Period and different regulatory outlooks, has already instituted Press Councils in all provinces to deal with reader concerns and continues to regulate news requirements for both public and private stations. The Broadcasting Act also sets advertising limits per hour of programming and program diversity requirements to address the interests of different members of the public, including children and ethnic groups. All of these regulatory initiatives align the country's public/private broadcasting approach with that of Europe, rather than that of the United States. Canadian and European researchers are furthermore of the opinion that what is needed is a broadcast policy in which the public and private and the global and local sectors complement each other for the benefit of the citizen/viewer. In such a system, news coverage is less sensationalistic, distinctions between a politician's public and private persona continue to be respected, and a higher degree of voter engagement is maintained. Yet, exactly the opposite aim seems to have motivated the FCC's 2003 decisions to continue concentration among U.S. media conglomerates. Thank goodness this initiative was disallowed in a 2004 court challenge. The challenge did not, however, deny the possibility of what might be called tri-level mergers. These involve not only "technical" or single-mode transmission of different signals by coaxial cable, but also "functional" convergence, such as the production of hybrid services, all delivered under the umbrella of "corporate" amalgamations *across* previously distinct industry boundaries (Babe, 1996b). It is now possible to contemplate the mergers of the cable giant Comcast with the Walt Disney Company, owner of ABC as well as television stations, or the convergence of Viacom, owner of Paramount, CBS and MTV with Echostar (Kirkpatrick, 2003). Nowhere else in the world has such a level of broadcast concentration ever been allowed (LaMay, 2003).

Although the Aspen conference participants neglected to address the issue of gender in news production, the previous chapters demonstrated that the agendas of feminist journalists have a great deal in common with the aims of the Civic Journalism Movement. Researchers in Europe and North America have defined feminist journalism as being anchored in a preoccupation with giving women and minorities a voice in the public realm and the desire to contribute to social change. Five criteria differentiate this type of journalism. To begin with, it focuses on women and unrepresented groups and their place in the everyday world, rather than on the power holders. This speaks to the Civic Journalism Movement's call to re-evaluate the "relevance" criterion in terms of viewer/reader agendas, rather than the agendas of those who are in power. Margaret Lünenborg (1997) argues that such a search for more egalitarian news values involves a unique social agenda, which amounts to a "critical distancing" from the world made strange. Such distancing constitutes giving up the journalist's presumed "expert" position for a more egalitarian stance. Patrick Watson (1998), a former president of the CBC, calls this the "documentarist" approach. "Instead of taking the traditional television news posture, which asserts that because of superior resources and privileged positions, we know something that will be good for you to learn about . . . The documentarist, . . . says something more like: 'We've been on quite a trip, and we've seen some things we found so interesting that we'd like to share them with you'" (p. D18). As a result of its implicit egalitarianism, feminist journalism is person-oriented and makes "wholeness" not "singularity" of events its framework. This speaks to the Civic Journalism Movement's rethinking of the "fairness" requirement and to counterbalancing the commonly used adversarial stance with a more respectful attitude toward *how* people are covered (Goldmark, 2001).

Previous chapters have argued that the small group of Type 2 feminist journalists can lead the way in changing the descriptive power structure within their media organizations and show their colleagues how to create a more egalitarian narrative approach. This endeavour not only propels feminist journalism out of its "niche" or "ghetto" status, but it also provides a model for a wholly new descriptive regime that offers *all* journalists, not just female professionals, a vantage point from which "the everyday can be made problematic" (Lünenborg, 1992). Evidence from Canada and western Europe in Chapters 6 and 7 indicate that the opportunity to change news values toward a more equitable portrayal of women, ethnic minorities, and otherwise underrepresented groups depends on four factors. First is the level to which a female manager has risen in the editorial hierarchy of her institution. Canadian and German researchers found that the outcomes of networking for the purpose of mutual work benefits is enhanced by a person's managerial status, as well as her willingness to acknowledge the competence and authority of females *across* corporate levels in the media organization. Second, this organization, furthermore, must have an equity program in place, which facilitates the promotion of female and minority staff, through access and training initiatives. Experiences in Canada and the EC demonstrate that equity programs not only legitimate a more egalitarian perception of female contributions in the media workplace, but also and more importantly, began to add female and minority voices to broadcast programming and newspaper stories. To assess the efficacy of these initiatives, however, requires *ongoing vigilance* on the part of both the management and the staff.

A third and very important ingredient in changing news values has to do with a female journalist's professional role conception and the extent to which she defines herself as a "feminist." Lünenborg (1997) made the important discovery that the majority of her female journalists in the six European countries were aware of gender-based inequalities in their particular societies but did not act on these insights in their editorial work. Only one quarter of her interviewees actively utilized these understandings in their professional lives. My own investigation corroborates that only one fifth of the Canadian female editorial staff subscribes to what I have called a "feminist" professional role conception. Finally, there is the relationship that female staff foster with their readers/viewers and the extent to which they support organizations that agitate for gender equity in content through the use of female and minority expert lists and the utilization of these groups as news sources. These initiatives exist on both sides of the Atlantic and frequently involve media women with a feminist bent, cooperating with outside organizations to further a more egalitarian social and work agenda.

In conclusion, it is worth remembering that equity legislation comes in different formats, and that Canada's legislation is more effective because it is defined more broadly than elsewhere. In both North America and Europe, two major strategies have evolved. The first seeks to give female workers the same privileges as males via equal opportunity legislation, whereas the second seeks to offer justice by focusing on special treatment for females and accommodating their special needs. In the EU, the latter is undermined by the equal treatment conditions of the Treaty of Rome. As Chapter 6 indicated, this treaty does not permit preferential treatment of females in broadcast recruitment, even when it is done to rectify demonstrated gender imbalances in the technical and administrative domains. In Canada, such hiring preferences are legal under the Canadian Charter of Rights and Freedoms (1982), which permits both of the equity strategies. It is therefore considered the most advanced instrument in the world today, promising not only pay equity in the workplace, but also full citizenship rights for Canadian women. Section 15 (2) of the "affirmative action" clause potentially recognizes the necessity of different treatments to compensate for women's historical disadvantages in the media professions (MacKinnon, 1987). As a result of this legislation, as we have seen, the CBC/Radio Canada has diversified its on-air, as well as technical personnel in terms of gender, ethnic composition, and available expertise, way beyond that witnessed elsewhere. Although in Walby's (1997) terminology, equal treatment policies are part of the shift from a domestic to a public "gender regime," we have also demonstrated that the strategies for justice differ from country to country. The strategy for justice in the Canadian gender regime goes further than that in Britain or in the United States, in that it has laid the groundwork for what Sandra Burt (1988) calls "role change," rather than mere "role-equity" legislation. At the core of this legislation is the feminist argument that women should be allowed to remain different from men without being economically penalized for these differences.

APPENDIX

THE 1975 NEWSPAPER QUESTIONNAIRE

With the growth of the feminist movement in Canada and the United States, and female's increased labor-force participation since the 1970s, researchers began to focus on the position of women in various professions, including journalism. Unfortunately, only sketchy knowledge about the professional and working profile of female and male journalists existed in Canada in 1975. There were scattered submissions by the Canadian Women's Press Club (1963), and two pioneering studies conducted by Roger de la Garde (1972) and the CBC (1975) investigating the social and professional profile of Québec print journalists, and the distribution, status, and compensation of female and male broadcast personnel in the CBC.

Since William Bowman focused on the impact of gender on the U.S. media industry, I decided to use his 1974 U.S. study as a model for my inquiry. He was part of the 1971 national survey team of Johnstone, Slawski, and Bowman (1976) that produced one of the first studies of U.S. journalists. To keep the study manageable, I decided to focus on only one medium, Canadian daily newspapers, and to replicate Johnstone et al.'s studies as closely as possible, so that our findings would be comparable. I, too, followed a three-stage sampling plan to create a national sample of print journalists. The first task was to compile a list of Canadian daily newspapers from *Matthew's Media Directory* (1974). This list of newspapers involved no judgment on my part and provided contact information. Contrary to Johnstone et al. (1976), I did not have to use systematic random sampling because I covered the total universe of listed papers of which there were 114 at the time. The first stage involved verifying whether the listed papers were engaged in daily news production or not. This revealed that only 106 of the listed 114 dailies had independent newsrooms, with the rest co-producing under two different mastheads. These eight papers were counted only once in the final sample (Audley, 1983).

The second task was to obtain lists of all journalists working for these 106 papers. I did this in three steps: In June 1975 I sent a letter to all managing editors or their deputies explaining the study and requesting information on the number and gender of the full-time editorial personnel. In July, I sent a follow-up letter to all who had not responded and 4 weeks later followed up these letters with telephone calls. The third task was to set a time for a much more detailed telephone interview with the managing editor or his designate, to determine the number, distribution, organizational position, average salary, and beat covered by both female and male editorial staff within the organization. These extended interviews determined that the 1975 journalistic workforce in the Canadian daily press numbered 2,450, of which 79% (1,946) were male and only 21% (504) female.

THE ORGANIZATIONAL QUESTIONNAIRE (1995)

In the 1995 re-study, television stations were added to the daily newspaper survey. For comparability, the questionnaires used Canadian questions from my 1975 survey, as well as Weaver and Wilhoit's (1986/1991) U.S. journalistic inquiries. Once again, gender was used as a key variable to explain the professional and interpretive setting in which full-time female and male journalists do their work. Gender, it is assumed, is a structuring category of all social life and thus an important factor in understanding the types of social interaction and social sense-making that occur in the newsroom. The 1995 re-study used the same three-stage sampling plan as my 1975 and the Weaver and Wilhoit (1986/1991) studies. Again we used *Matthew's Media Directory* (1995) to determine the total number of newspapers and television outlets operating in English and French Canada. Again, all outlets were contacted by telephone to determine whether they were engaged in daily news production. For those newspapers or television stations with shared staff, only the central outlet was included in the final population. Of the 232 media outlets listed (114 papers and 118 TV stations), only 217 became part of the survey because the remaining 15 TV stations had either no newsrooms or were "regional" television transmission bureaus. In total, 114 dailies and 103 television newsrooms became part of the sample.

The second task was to obtain the lists of full-time editorial personnel working in each of the outlets and to identify the person responsible for news production. These lists indicated that the 114 dailies had a combined editorial workforce of 3,451, of which 27.9% (962) were female and 72.1% (2,489) were male. The 1995 Canadian television staff, in contrast, turned out to be much smaller, but contained proportionately more females. It numbered 1,305 of which 37.2% (486) were women and 62.8% (819) were men. Next, the responsible individual (typically a managing editor or news director) was contacted to arrange a telephone interview. Third, a copy of the questionnaire was sent to the respondent, which included a request to name a high-ranking female journalist within the organization. These female and male names were entered into a separate database, which provides the basis for the construction of the proportional gender sample and questionnaire discussed next. Finally, interviewers called each respondent to conduct the survey interview, which solicited detailed information on the total number of print and broadcast journalists, their social backgrounds, as well as education, work setting (position and subject area), average weekly remuneration, as well as career paths and job satisfaction. A pretest was conducted with information directors from four Quebec and Ontario weeklies. No major problems were encountered with the measuring instrument. In total, 217 questionnaires were sent out to dailies (114) and television stations (103) and 186 responses were received. Of these responses, 107 were from daily newspaper organizations and 79 were from television stations for a response rate of 94% and 76%, respectively

THE PROPORTIONAL GENDER SAMPLE
AND QUESTIONNAIRE (1995)

The proportional gender sample and questionnaire were constructed to provide a more detailed comparative study of gender differences in relation to professional values. It too utilized a three-stage sampling plan. To prepare the proportional representative sample of female and male journalists who would be queried in much greater detail about their professional experiences, we used the names of the high-ranking females and males elicited in the organizational questionnaire as a starting point. Where respondents' names were not available from this questionnaire, we used names randomly chosen from *Matthew's Media Directory*. The organizational questionnaire also provided the total number of both females and males working in any given Canadian print or television outlet. Together, this evidence permitted me to create a purposefully targeted proportionate representative sample of individual female and male print and television journalists, matched by age and position, as well as outlet size (small, medium, large) and the region in which they work (British Columbia, the Prairies, Ontario, Quebec, and the Maritimes).

For both the dailies and the television outlets, a separate 15-cell sampling grid was devised in which each cell received a numeric value depending on the exact numbers of staff employed in a particular outlet. Numerical values between 1 and 13 were used to indicate 13 different staff sizes, which were calculated on the basis of 50-person increments. This means that the numeric value of 1 stands for a staff of 1–49 people, all the way up to 13, which stands for a staff of 600–649 persons. The numeric values assigned to each cell determined the number of people and news outlets required for the sample. The proportionally targeted sample turned out to comprise 137 staff, of which 124 completed the extensive gender interview. Of these 83 (29 females and 54 males) were employed in daily newspapers and 41 (19 females and 22 males) in television newsrooms.

The 30-page proportional gender questionnaire used in the second phase of the 1995 research project was divided into five sections. The first section questioned respondents on demographic details (age, marital status, etc.). The second compared the professional conceptions, values, roles, and ethics of female and male personnel. The third section examined professional ideals, whereas the fourth elicited information on the working climate in the newspaper and television newsrooms. In the last section, respondents were asked to evaluate the progress female journalists had made since 1975. Of the 134 questionnaires sent out in three waves, 124 were returned for a response rate of 90%. The final sample of 124 people consisted of 49 females (30 in newspapers and 19 in television) and 75 males (50 in newspapers and 25 in television). All three data sets were coded and keypunched separately and analyzed using SPSS, a statistical analysis program. Statistical significances were determined by chi-square calculations.

BIBLIOGRAPHY

Abrahamsson, U. (1986). Strategies and results of the Equality of the Sexes programme in Swedish television. *Medie/Kultur, 4*, 220-237.

Abrahamsson, U. (1990). *Are we nearing the top of the hill? Notes from a decade of
working toward equality in Swedish broadcasting.* Paper presented at the 17th
conference of the International Association for Media and Communication
Research (IAMCR), Bled, Yugoslavia.

Adams, J., & MacDonald, G. (2003, May 7). CTF thrown funding life-line to popular programs. *The Globe and Mail*, p. B1.

Agocs, C. (1989). *Walking on the glass ceiling: Tokenism in senior management.*
Paper presented at the Canadian Sociology and Anthropology Association,
Quebec City, Quebec.

Agocs, C., Burr, C., & Sommerset, F. (1992). *Employment equity: Cooperative strategies for organizational change.* Toronto: Prentice-Hall.

Aldridge, M. (2001). Lost expectations? Woman journalists and the fall-out of the
Toronto newspaper war. *Media, Culture and Society, 23*(5), 607-624.

American Society of Newspaper Editors (ASNE). (1997). *The journalists.*
www.asne.org/kiosk/97 reports/journalists90s/journalists.html. Accessed
August 4, 2002.

Anderson, D. (1991). *The unfinished revolution: The status of women in twelve
countries.* Toronto: Doubleday.

Ang, I. (1991). *Desperately seeking the audience.* London/New York: Routledge.

Angerer, M. (1995). Frauen in der Audiovision [Women in audio-visual media].
Medien Journal, 19(2), 3-20.

Armstrong, P., & Armstrong, H. (1986). *The double ghetto: Canadian women and
their segregated work.* Toronto: McClelland & Stewart.

Armstrong, P., & Armstrong, H. (1990). *Theorizing women's work.* Toronto:
Garamond Press.

Arnette, E.C. (1987, March 6). Getting to the top more difficult. *The Globe and
Mail*, p. F1.

Audley, P. (1983). *Canada's cultural industries: Broadcasting, publishing, records and film.* Toronto: James Lorimer.

Babe, R. (1996a). Canada. In V. Macleod (Ed.), *Media ownership and control in the age of convergence* (pp. 23-46). London: International Institute of Communications.

Babe, R. (1996b). Convergence and the new technologies. In M. Dorland (Ed.), *The cultural industries in Canada,* (pp. 283-307). Toronto: James Lorimer.

Barber, B. (1984). *Strong democracy. Participatory politics for the new era.* Berkeley: University of California Press.

Barthes, R. (1977). *Image, music, text* (S. Heath, Ed.). Glasgow: Fontana.

Beale, A. (1999). From "Sophie's Choice" to consumer choice: Framing gender in cultural policy. *Media, Culture and Society, 21*(4), 435-458.

Beasley, M., & Gibbons, S. (1993). *Taking their place: A documentary history of women and journalism.* Washington, DC: The American University Press.

Becker, L. et al. (1987). *The training and hiring of journalists.* Norwood, NJ: Ablex.

Bennet, T. (1982). Media, reality, signification. In M. Gurevitch, J. Bennett, J. Curran, & J. Woollacott (Eds.), *Culture, society and media* (pp. 287-308). London: Methuen.

Berger, P., & Luckmann, T. (1966). *The social construction of reality.* Garden City, NY: Doubleday.

Berns, D. (1989, June 15). Stuck in the "same sex" ghetto. *Women, Men and Media-APME News,* pp. 41-45.

Bleier, R. (1987). A polemic on sex differences in research. In C. Garnham (Ed.), *The impact of feminist research in the academy* (pp. 111-130). Bloomington: Indiana University Press.

Bollier, D. (2002). *In search of the public interest in the new media environment.* Washington, DC: The Aspen Institute.

Blumer, H. (1969). *Symbolic interactionism: Perspective and method.* Englewood Cliffs, NJ: Prentice-Hall.

Bourdieu, P. (1977). *Outline of a theory of practice.* London: Cambridge University Press.

Bourdieu, P. (1991). *Language and symbolic power.* Cambridge: Polity Press.

Bowman, W. W. (1974). *Distaff journalists: Women, as a minority in the news media.* Unpublished doctoral thesis, Department of Sociology, University of Illinois, Chicago.

Brackert, G. (1992). Reflections on women and media. In G. J. Robinson & D. Sixt (Eds.), *women and power: Canadian and German experiences* (2nd ed., pp. 90-97). Montreal: McGill Studies in Communications & Goethe Institute.

Briggs, A. (2002). The public interest: An international perspective. In D. Bollier (Ed.), *In search of the public interest in the new media environment* (pp. 31-41). Washington, DC: The Aspen Institute.

Brown, T. (1991, June). Magazine editor urges tough, lively papers. *Press Time,* p. 3.

Brown, C., & Flatow, G. (1997). Targets, effects, and perpetrators of sexual harassment. *Journalism and Mass Communication Quarterly, 74*(1), 160-183.

Budd, B. (2003, November 18). Who can resist a ringing phone? *The Globe and Mail,* p. R3.

Bulkeley, C. (2004). Whose news? Progress and status of women in newspapers (mostly) and television news. In R. Rush, C. Oukrop, & P. Creedon (Eds.),

Seeking equity for women in journalism and mass communication education. A 30 year update (pp. 183-204). Mahwah, NJ: Erlbaum.

Burke, K. (1954) *Permanence and change: An anatomy of purpose.* Indianapolis, IN: Bobbs-Merrill.

Burks, K., & Stone, V. (1993). Career-related characteristics of male and female news directors. *Journalism Quarterly, 70*(3), 542-549.

Burt, S. (1986). Women's issues and the women's movement in Canada since 1970. In A. Cairns & C. Williams (Eds.), *The politics of gender, ethnicity and language in Canada* (pp. 111-170). Toronto: University of Toronto Press.

Burt, S. (1988). Legislators, women and public policy. In S. Burt, L. Code, & L. Lindsay (Eds.), *Changing patterns: Women in Canada* (pp. 129-156). Toronto: McClelland & Stewart.

Burt, S., Code, S. L., & Dorney, L. (Eds.). (1988b). *Changing patterns: Women in Canada.* Toronto: McClelland & Stewart.

Byerly, C. M. (1995). News consciousness and social participation: The role of Women's Feature Service in world news. In A. Valdivia (Ed.), *Feminism, multiculturalism and the media: Global perspectives* (pp. 105-122). Twin Oaks, CA: Sage.

Byerly, C. M. (1996). At the margins of center: Organized protest in the newsroom. *Critical Studies in Mass Communication, 13*(1), 1-23.

Byerly, C. M., & Warren, C. (1997). *Toward an examination of feminist intervention in newsmaking.* Paper presented to the Feminist Scholarship Interest Group, International Communication Association (ICA), Miami, FL.

Byerly, C. M. (2004a). Women and the concentration of media ownership. In R. Rush, C. Okrup, P. Creedon (Eds.), *Seeking equity for women in journalism and mass communication education. A thirty year update* (pp. 245-262). Mahwah, NJ: Erlbaum.

Byerly, C. M. (2004b). Feminist interventions in newsrooms. In K. Ross & C. Byerly (Eds.), *Women and media: International perspectives* (pp. 109-131). Oxford: Blackwell.

Canada, House of Commons Standing Committee on Communication and Culture. (1992). *Culture and communications: The ties that bind.* Ottawa: Minister of Supply and Services. Author.

Canadian Association of Journalists. (1993, January). *Changing face: Women in the media.* Ottawa: Carleton University.

Canadian Broadcasting Corp. (1975). *Women in the CBC.* Montreal: Author.

Canadian Broadcasting Corp. (1994) *Equity Newsletter, 1*(3).

Canadian Broadcasting Corp. (1994). CBC *Equity Newsletter, 2*(2).

Canadian Broadcasting Corp. (1997). CBC *Equity Newsletter, 5*(1).

Canadian Broadcasting Corp. (2000). CBC *Equity Newsletter, 7*(1).

Canadian Broadcasting Corp. (2001). CBC *Equity Newsletter, 8*(2).

CBC Annual Reports for 1995 and 2001.

Canadian Newspaper Guild. (1987, January/February). The guild and women's rights. *Content* (8-9).

Canadian Women's Press Club. (1963). Submission to the Royal Commission on the Status of Women. Ottawa: Author.

Caron, A., & Ouillet, M. (1994). *Représentation des groupes désignés dans la programmation de la SRC* [The representation of designated social groups in French language television]. Montreal: Sociéte Radio Canada.

Carey, J. W. (1988). *Communication as culture: Essays on media and society.* Boston, MA: Unwin Hyman.

Carey, J. W. (1995). The press, public opinion and public discourse. In T. Glasser & C. Solomon (Eds.), *Public opinion and the communication of consent* (pp. 373-402). New York: Guilford.

Carter, B., & Routenberg, J. (2003, June 3). Creative voices say television will suffer in new climate. *The Washington Post,* pp. C1, C9.

Catalyst. (1995). *Women in corporate leadership: Progress and prospects.* New York.

Chase, S. (2003, April 30). National strategy needed. Senate media probe told. *The Globe and Mail,* p. B7.

Cirksena, K. (1987). Politics and difference: Radical feminist epistemological premises for communication studies. *Journal of Communication Inquiry, 11*(1), 19-28.

Cirksena, K. (1996). Feminism after ferment: Ten years of gendered scholarship in communications. In D. Allen, R. Rush, & S. Kaufman (Eds.), *Women transforming communications: Global intersections.* (pp. 153-160). Thousand Oaks, CA: Sage.

Cirksena, K., & Cuklanz, L. (1992). Male is to female as___is to___: A guided tour of five feminist frameworks for communication studies. In L. F. Rakow (Ed.), *Women making meaning: New feminist directions in communication* (pp. 11-44). Norwood, NJ: Ablex.

Coates, M. L. (1986). *Employment equity issues, approaches and public policy framework.* Kingston: Industrial Relations Center, Queens University.

Commission of the European Communities. (1991). *Equal opportunities in European broadcasting: A guide to good practice.* Brussels: European Community.

Commission of the European Communities. (1999). *Images of women in the media: Report on existing research in the European Union.* Brussels: European Community.

Compaine, B., & Gomery, D. (2000). *Who owns the media? Competition and concentration in the mass media industry.* Mahwah, NJ: Erlbaum.

Crean, S. (1985). *Newsworthy: The lives of media women.* Toronto: Stoddard.

Creedon, P. (Ed.). (1993). *Women in mass communication* (2nd ed.). Newbury Park: CA: Sage.

Cuneo, C. (1990). *Pay equity: The labour-feminist challenge.* Toronto: Oxford University Press.

Curran, J. (1992). Mass media and democracy: A reappraisal. In J. Curran & M. Gurevich (Eds.), *Mass media and society* (pp. 82-117). London: Edward Arnold.

Damsell, K. (2001, Nov. 28). McQueen to retire as CTV president. *The Globe and Mail,* p. B15.

Damsell, K. (2003, May 17). News executive quits CanWest media chain. *The Globe and Mail,* p. A8.

De la Garde, R. (1972). *Pratique du journalisme au Québec.* Québec: Programme de journalisme de L'université Laval.

Demers, F. (1989). Journalistic ethics: The rise of the "good employee's model" a threat for professionalism? *Canadian Journal of Communication, 14*(2), 111-122.

Dorland, M. (Ed.). (1996). *The cultural industries in Canada: Problems, policies and prospects.* Toronto: Lorimer.

Dornan, C. (1996). Newspaper publishing. In M. Dorland (Ed.), *The cultural industries in Canada: Problems, policies and prospects* (pp. 60-92). Toronto: James Lorimer.

Ebener, D. (2003, May 8). BCE reorganizes Bell Canada for "competitive future." *The Globe and Mail*, pp. B1-3, B20.

Eichler, M. (1980). *The double standard: A feminist critique of feminist social science.* Guilford: Biddles, Ltd.

Egsmose, L. (2001). How do anti-discrimination policies work? Initiatives in older and younger television companies in Denmark and the UK. *Media, Culture and Society, 23*(2), 475-493.

Elliott, P. (1976). Media organisations and occupations: An overview. In *Mass communication and society reader* (pp. 101-129). London: Open University Reader.

Elshtain, J. B. (1982). Feminist discourse and its discontents: Language, power and meaning. In N. Keohane, M. Rosaldo, & B. Gelpi (Eds.), *Feminist theory: A critique of ideology* (pp. 127-146). Chicago: University of Chicago Press.

Epstein, C. F. (1988). *Deceptive distinctions: Sex, gender and the social order.* New Haven, CT & New York: Yale University Press & Russell Sage Foundation.

Epstein, C. F. (1992). Tinkerbells and pinups: The construction and reconstruction of gender. In M. Lamont & M. Fournier (Eds.), *Cultivating differences: Symbolic boundaries and the making of inequality* (pp. 232-256). Chicago: University of Chicago Press.

Erin Research. (1993). *Social trends on CBC prime time television 1977-1992.* Toronto, Ontario: Author.

European Commission, Steering Committee for Equal Opportunities in Broadcasting. (1992). *Recommendations for the promotion of equal opportunities, 1986-1991.* Brussels. Author.

European Commission. (1999). *Images of women in the media: Report of existing research in the European Union.* Luxembourg: Office of Official Publications.

Fishman, M. (1980). *Manufacturing the news.* Austin: University of Texas Press.

Fiske, J. (1998). *Television culture.* London: Methuen.

Flatow, G. (1994). Sexual harassment in Indiana daily newspapers. *Newspaper Research Journal, 15*, 32-45.

Foss, K. A., & Foss, S. (1989). Incorporating the feminist perspective in communication scholarship: A research commentary. In K. Carter & C. Spitzack (Eds.), *Doing research on women's communication: Perspectives on theory and method* (pp. 65-91). Norwood, NJ: Ablex.

Frank, T. (1994). *Canada's best employers of women.* Toronto: Frank Communications.

Frankel, M. (1999). Media madness and the revolution so far. In M. Frankel & D. Bollier (Eds.), *The Catto report of journalism and society* (pp. 1-17). Washington, DC: The Aspen Institute.

Franklin, S., Lurie, C., & Stacey, J. (1992). Feminism and cultural studies. In P. Scannell, P. Schlesinger, & C. Sparkes (Eds.), *Culture and power* (pp. 90-111). Newbury Park, CA: Sage.

Freedom Forum Media Studies Center. (1993). A field guide for women in media industries. *Media Studies Journal, 9*(1-2), 81-109.

Frye, M. (1983). Some reflections on separatism and power. In M. Frye (Ed.), *The politics of reality: Essays in feminist theory* (pp. 96-109). Trumansburg, NY: The Crossing Press.

Gallagher, M. (1984). *Employment and positive action for women in the television organizations of the EEC member states.* Brussels: Commission of the European Community.

Gallagher, M. (1986). Myth and reality in women's employment in broadcasting. Ten years of equal opportunity. *Medie/Kultur, 4,* 197-219.

Gallagher, M. (1995). *An unfinished story: Gender patterns in media employment.* Paris: Unesco.

Gannett Foundation. (1989). *Women, men and media.* Washington: Gannett Publishing.

Gans, H. J. (1979). *Deciding what's news: A study of CBS evening news, NBC nightly news, Newsweek and Time.* New York: Pantheon Books.

Gazette. (2001, November 10-16). Insistent disclosure. *TV Times,* p. 4.

Geertz, C. (1973). *The interpretation of cultures.* New York: Basic Books.

Gerson, J., & Peiss, K. (1985, April). Boundaries, negotiation and consciousness: Reconceptualising gender relations. *Social Problems, 32,* 317-331.

Glasser, T., & Craft, M. (1996). Public journalism and the prospects for press accountability. *Journal of Mass Media Ethics, 11*(3), 152-158.

Goffman, E. (1974). *An essay on the organization of experience.* New York: Harper & Row.

Goldmark, P. (2001). *Old values, new world: Harnessing the legacy of independent journalism for the future* (pp. 1-21). Washington, DC: The Aspen Institute.

Goold, D. (2003, May 7). Return to roots, new steadier earnings, lower risk for BCE. *The Globe and Mail,* p. B7.

Gorelik, S. (1991). Contradictions of feminist methodology. *Gender & Society, 5*(4), 459-477.

Gotell, L. (1990). The Canadian women's movement: Equity rights and the Charter. Ottawa: *Canadian Research Institute for the Advancement of Women (CRIAW), 16.*

Grant, G. (1962). A platitude. In *Technology and empire: Perspectives on North America* (pp. 137-143). Toronto: House of Anansi.

Grossberg, L., Nelson, C., & Treichler, P. (Eds.) (1992) *Cultural studies.* New York: Routledge.

Habermas, J. (1989). *The structural transformation of the public sphere.* Cambridge: Polity Press.

Hackett, R. (1991). *News and dissent: The press and the politics of peace in Canada.* Norwood, NJ: Ablex.

Hall, S. (1980) Encoding and decoding the television discourse. In S. D. Hall, A. Lowe, & P. Willis (Eds.), *Culture, media, language* (pp. 128-139). London: Hutchison.

Haraway, D. (1991). *Simians, cyborgs and women: The reinvention of nature.* New York: Routledge.

Hardin, H. (1974). *A nation unaware: The Canadian economic culture.* Vancouver: J. H. Douglas.

Harding, S. (1986). *The science question in feminism.* Ithaca, NY: Cornell University Press.

Harding, S. (1987). The instability of analytical categories of feminist theory. In S. Harding & J. F. O'Barr (Eds.), *Sex and scientific inquiry* (pp. 283-302). Chicago: University of Chicago Press.

Harper's Staff. (1997, December). Giving women the business: On winning, losing and leaving the corporate game. *Harper's Magazine*, pp. 47-58.

Hartley, J. (1996). *Popular reality: Journalism, modernity, popular culture.* London: Edward Arnold.

Hay, J., Grossberg, L., & Wartella, E. (Eds.). (1996). *The audience and its landscape.* New York: Westview Press.

Hekman, S. (1987). The feminization of epistemology: Gender and the social sciences. In M. Falco (Ed.), *Feminism and epistemology: Approaches to research in women and politics* (pp. 65-83). New York: Hayworth Press.

Heikkilä, H. (2000). How to make thin journalism strong? Experiences of a public journalism project in Finland. *Nordicom Review, 21*(2), 83-100.

Hemlinger, M. A. (2001). *Women in newspapers: How much progress has been made?* Evanston, IL: Media Management Center, Northwestern University.

Hoffman-Riem, W. (1996). New challenges for European multimedia policy. *European Journal of Communication, 11*(3), 327-346.

Human Resources Development. (1993). *Employment Equity Act.* Ottawa: Minister of Supply and Services, Canada.

Human Resources Development. (2001). *Women in the workplace* (4th ed.). Ottawa: Statistics Canada.

Ibarra, H. (1993, January). Personal networks of women and minorities in management: A conceptual framework. *Academy of Management Review*, pp. 56-87.

Jeffrey, L. (1995). *Progress in Canada toward women's equality and the media: Access to expression and decision-making 1980-1994.* Toronto: Offline Research.

Jeffrey, L. (1996). Private television and cable. In M. Dorland (Ed.), *The cultural industries in Canada: Problems, policies and prospects* (pp. 203-256). Toronto: James Lorimer.

Johnstone, W., Slawski, E., & Bowman, W. (1976). *The news people: A social portrait of American journalists and their work.* Urbana: University of Illinois Press.

Jones, B. (1997, December). Giving women the business. *Harper's Magazine Forum*, pp. 47-58.

Jurney, D. (1986b, November). Tenth annual survey reports women editors at 12.4 percent. *ASNE Bulletin*, pp. 5-9.

Kagan, J. (1986, October). Cracks in the glass ceiling: How women are really faring in corporate America. *Working Woman*, pp. 107-109.

Kalckreuth-Tabbara, A. (2001). Die Regulierung von Geschlechtsrollenklischees im kanadischen Rundfunk [The regulation of sex-role clichés in Canadian broadcasting]. *Medien & Kommunikationswissenschaft, 49*(4), 498-527.

Kaniss, P. (1991). *Making local news.* Chicago: University of Chicago Press.

Kanter, R. M. (1980). The impact of organization structure: Models and methods for change. In R. Ratner (Ed.), *Equal employment policy for women* (pp. 311-327). Philadelphia: Temple University Press.

Kanter, R. M. (1993). The impact of hierarchical structures on the work behavior of women and men. *Social Problems, 23*(3), 415-430.

Keil, S. (1993). Giebt es einen weiblichen Journalismus? [Is there a female journalism?] In R. Fröhlich (Ed.), *Der andere Blick: Aktuelles zur Massenkommunikation aus weiblicher Sicht* (pp. 37-54). Bochum: Universitätsverlag. Dr. Brockmeyer.

Keil, S. (2001). Einsame Spitze? Frauen in Führungspositionen im öffentlich-rechtlichen Rundfunk [Lonely top: Women in leadership positions in public broadcasting]. Münster: LitVerlag.

Kelly, R. M. (1988). *Comparable worth, pay equity and public policy.* New York: Greenwood Press.

Keohane, N. O., Rosaldo, M., & Gelpi, B. (1982). *Feminist theory: A critique of ideology.* Chicago: University of Chicago Press.

Kessler, S., & McKenna, W. (1978). *Gender: An ethno-methodological approach.* Chicago: University of Chicago Press.

King, L. (1987). *Broadcast policy for Canadian women.* Paper presented at "Adjusting the Image," National Conference on Broadcast Policy, Ottawa.

Kirkpatrick, D. (2003, June). New rules give big media chance to get even bigger. *The New York Times*, pp. C1, C9.

Klaus, E. (1998). *Kommunikationswissenschaftliche Geschlechterforschung: Zur Bedeutung der Frauen in den Massenmedien und im Journalismus* [Communicational gender studies: Women in journalism]. Opladen/Wiesbaden: Westdeutscher Verlag.

Klaus, E. (2000). Jenseits von Individuum und System: Journalismustheorien unter der Perspektive der Geschlechterforschung [Beyond individual and system: Journalism theories from the point of view of gender studies]. In M. Löffelholz (Ed.), *Theorien des Journalismus* (pp. 333-350). Wiesbaden: Westdeutscher Verlag.

Klein, M. (1986). *Frauensport in der Tagespresse: Eine Untersuchung zur sprachlichen und bildlichen Präsentation von Frauen in der Sportberichterstattung* [Women's sport in the press: Linguistic and pictorial styles in reporting]. Bochum: Universitätsverlag.

Kline, S., & Murray, C. (1993). *It matters who makes it: A review of research on women, audiences, and the media.* Burnaby: Mountain Media Lab.

Köcher, R. (1986, March). Bloodhounds or missionaries: Role definitions of German and British journalists. *European Journal of Communication, 1*(1), 43-64.

Kossan, P. (1992). Sexual harassment in the newsroom and on the job. *APME News, 195*, 1-11.

Kubas, L. (1980). *Newspapers and their readers* (Vol. 1). Royal Commission on Newspapers (Kent). Ottawa: Research Publications.

Lafky, S. (1993). The progress of women and people of color in the U.S. journalistic workforce: A long slow journey. In P. Creedon (Ed.), *Women in mass communication* (2nd ed., pp. 87-103). Newbury Park: Sage.

LaMay, C. (2003). *Democratic enterprise: Sustaining media and civil society.* Washington: The Aspen Institute.

Lambeth, E., Meyer, P., & Thorson, E. (Eds.). (1998). *Assessing public journalism.* Columbia: The University of Missouri Press.

Lamont, M., & Fournier, M. (1992). *Cultivating differences: Symbolic boundaries and the making of inequality* (pp. 232-256). Chicago: University of Chicago Press.

Lee, M. D. (1992). *Women's involvement in professional careers and family life: Theme and variations* (Working Papers Series #NC 92-7005). London, Ontario: Western Business School, University of Western Ontario.

Linz, J. (1975). Totalitarian and authoritarian regimes. *Handbook of Political Science,* (Vol. 3). Reading, MA: Addison-Westley.

Löfgren-Nilsson, M. (1994, July). *Journalism, gender and newsroom working climate.* Paper presented at the International Association for Media and Communication Research (IAMCR), Seoul, Korea.

Lubin, J. (1971). *Discrimination against women in the newsroom.* Unpublished master's thesis, Stanford University, Stanford, CA.

Lünenborg, M. (1992). Feministischer Journalismus [Feminist journalism]. In R. Fröhlich (Ed.), *Der andere Blick: Aktuelles zur Massenkommunikation aus weiblicher Sicht* (pp. 207-220). Bochum: Brockmeier.

Lünenborg, M. (1997). *Journalistinnen in Europa: Eine international vergleichende Analyse zum gendering im sozialen System Journalismus* [Female journalists in Europe: An international comparison on gendering in journalism]. Opladen: Westdeutscher Verlag.

Lünenborg, M. (2001). Geschlecht als Analysenperspektive in der Journalismusforschung: Potenziale und Defizite [Gender as a perspective in journalism research: Potentials and deficits]. In E. Klaus, J. Rösser, & U. Wischermann (Eds.), *Kommunikationswissenschaft und Gender Studies* (pp. 124-143). Wiesbaden: Westdeutscher Verlag.

MacKinnon, C. (1987, September). Opinion on the Meech Lake accord. *Women's Legal Education and Action Fund.*

MacNeil. R. (1997). *Market journalism: New highs and lows.* Washington, DC: The Aspen Institute.

Mahoney, E. (1992). Women, equality and media: An appraisal for the 1990s. *Intercom, XV*(1), 80-97.

Mallick, H. (2000, February). Women don't matter. *Report on Business Magazine,* pp. 36-39.

Marzolf, M. T. (1993, August). *Women making a difference in the newsroom.* Paper prepared for the Commission on the Status of Women, AEJMC, Kansas City, MO.

Matthew's Media Directory, (1974, 1995).

McCombs, M., & Shaw, D. (1972). The agenda-setting function of mass media. *Public Opinion Quarterly, 36,* 176-187.

McConnel, P., & Becker, L. (2002). *The role of media in democratization.* Paper presented at the International Association for Media and Communication Research (IAMCR), Barcelona, Spain.

Mead, G. H. (1962). *Mind, self and society.* Chicago: University of Chicago Press. (Original work published 1934)

Melin-Higgins, M. (2002). *Opportunities and problems in feminist methodology.* Paper presented at the International Association for Media and Communication Research (IAMCR). Barcelona, Spain.

Melin-Higgins, M. (2004). Coping with journalism: Gendered newsroom cultures. In M. de Bruin & K. Ross (Eds.), *Gender and newsroom cultures: Identities at work* (pp. 195-220). Cresskill, NJ: Hampton Press.

Melin-Higgins, M., & Djerf-Pierre, M. (1998). *Networking in newsrooms: Journalists and gender cultures.* Paper presented at the International Association for Media and Communication Research (IAMCR), Glasgow.

Melody, W. (1996). Toward a framework for designing information society policies. *Telecommunications Policy, 20*(4), 243-259.

Menzies, H. (1998). *Whose brave new world? The information highway and the new economy.* Toronto: Between the Lines.

Meyer, M. (1992). Reporters and beats: The making of oppositional news. *Critical Studies in Mass Communication, 9*(1), 75-90.

Miller, S. (1993). Opportunity squandered—Newspapers and women's news. *Media Studies Journal, 7*(1-2), 167-182.

Mills, R. (2003, January 22). CanWest plan a threat to local independence. *The Globe and Mail*, p. B11.

Mintzberg, H. (1975). The manager's job: Folklore and fact. *Harvard Business, 53*(4), 49-61.

Morgan, N. (1988). *The equality game: Women in the federal public service (1908-1987).* Ottawa: Advisory Council for the Status of Women.

Morley, D. (1980). *The nationwide audience.* London: The British Film Institute.

Newspaper Association of America. (2001). *Facts about newspapers.* Vienna, VA: Author.

Ogan, C. (1983). *Life at the top for men and women newspaper managers: A five year update of their characteristics* (A Report for the Center for New Communications). Bloomington: Indiana University.

O'Leary, V., & Hansen, R.D. (1985). Sex as an attributional factor. In T. Sonderegger (Ed.), *The Nebraska Symposium on Motivation* (Vol. 32). Lincoln: University of Nebraska Press.

O'Leary, V., & Ickovics, J. (1992). Cracking the glass ceiling: Overcoming isolation and alienation. In U. Sekaran & F. Leang (Eds.), *Womanpower: Managing in times of demographic turbulence* (pp. 7-30). Newbury Park, CA: Sage.

Pandian, H. (1999). Engendering communication policy: Key issues in the international women-and-media arena and obstacles to forging and enforcing policy. *Media, Culture and Society, 21*(4), 459-480.

Papper, B., & Gerhard, M. (2001). Up from the ranks: Grooming women and minorities for management. *Communicator*, 1-3.

Paris, R. (1991). Ähnlichkeiten mit Lebenden sind zufällig. Oder: solidarische Beutezüge. Zur Theorie der Seilschaft [Comments on a theory of male bonding]. *Frankfurter Rundschau, 294*, 17.

Péricard, A. (1995). Études féministes et interculturalité. In *Communication et interculturalité en Afrique de l'ouest francophone.* Unpublished doctoral thesis, Graduate Program in Communications, McGill University, Montreal.

Pleck, J. (1984). The work–family role system. In P. Voydanoff (Ed.), *Work and family: Changing roles of men and women* (pp. 8-19). Palo Alto: University of California Press.

Press, A. (1990). Class, gender and the female viewer. In M. E. Brown (Ed.), *Television and women's culture: The politics of the popular* (pp. 158-182). London: Sage.

Preston, P. (2001). *Reshaping communications.* Thousand Oaks, CA: Sage.

Pritchard, D., & Sauvageau, F. (1999). *Les journalistes Canadiens: Un portrait de fin de siècle* [Canadian journalists at the turn of the century]. Saint Nicolas: Les Presses de l'Université Laval.

Raboy, M. (1983). *Libérer la communication. Médias et mouvements sociaux au Québec, 1960-1980* [Liberate communication practices: The media and social movements in Quebec]. Montréal: Nouvelle Optique.

Raboy, M. (1996). Public television. In M. Dorland (Ed.), *The cultural industries in Canada: Problems, policies and prospects* (pp. 178-202). Toronto: James Lorimer.

Rakow, L. F. (1986). Gender research in mass communication. *Journal of Communication, 36*(4), 11-26.

Rakow, L. F. (Ed.). (1992). *Women making meaning: New feminist directions in communications.* New York: Routledge & Kegan Paul.

Reddick, A. (1995). *Sharing the road: Convergence and the Canadian information highway.* Ottawa: Public Interest Advocacy Center.

Reskin, B., & Hartmann, H. (1986). *Women's work and men's work: Sex segregation in the job.* Washington DC: National Academy Press.

Rhodes, J. (2001). Journalism in the new millennium: What's a feminist to do? *Feminist Media Studies, 1*(1), 49-53.

Robinson, G. J. (1975). The politics of information and culture during Canada's October Crisis. In. G. J. Robinson & D. Theall (Eds.), *Studies in Canadian communications* (pp. 141-162). Montreal: McGill University.

Robinson, G. J. (1977). The future of women in the Canadian media. *McGill Journal of Education, XII*(1), 123-133.

Robinson, G. J. (1981). *Female print journalists in Canada and the United States: A professional profile and comparison* (Working Papers in Communications). Montreal: McGill University.

Robinson, G. J. (1987). Visuelle Präsentationsformen von Fernsehnachrichten: Ein Vergleich zwischen Frankophonen und Anglophonen Programmen in Canada [Visual presentation forms in Canadian TV news programs.] In M. Grewe-Partsch & J. Gröbel (Eds.), *Mensch und Medien: Festschrift in Honor of Hertha Sturm* (pp. 58-78). Munich: K. Saur.

Robinson, G. J. (1992). Women in the media in Canada: A progress report. In H. Holmes & D. Taras (Eds.), *Media power and policy in Canada* (pp. 260-270). Toronto: Harcourt Brace Jovanovich, Canada.

Robinson, G. J. (1998a). *Constructing the referendum on Quebec television: French and English media voices.* Toronto: University of Toronto Press.

Robinson, G. J. (1998b). Monopolies of knowledge in Canadian communication studies: The case of feminist approaches. *Canadian Journal of Communication, 23*(1), 65-72.

Robinson, G. J. (2000b). Remembering our past: Reconstructing the field of Canadian communication studies. *Canadian Journal of Communication, 25*(1), 105-126.

Robinson, G. J. (2001). Medienforschung aus Sicht der Sozialwissenschaften unter Berücksichtigung der Geschlechterforschung [German media research using gender studies]. In U. Hasebrink & C. Matzen (Eds.), *Forschungstand Öffentliche Kommunikation* (pp. 145-154). Baden-Baden: Nomos.

Robinson, G. J. (forthcoming). Theorizing the impact of gender in Canadian journalism. In R. Fröhlich & S. Lafky (Eds.), *Gender, culture and journalism: A
study of industrialized nations.* Cresskill, NJ: Hampton Press.
Robinson, G. J., & Hildebrandt, K. (1993). Germany: The end of public service
broadcasting as we know it? In R. Avery (Ed.) *Public service broadcasting in a
multi-channel environment* (pp. 53-74). New York: Longman.
Robinson, G. J., & Saint Jean, A. (1991). Women politicians and their media coverage: A generational analysis. In C. Megyvery (Ed.), *Women in Canadian politics:
Toward equity* (pp. 127-164). Toronto: Dundee Press.
Robinson, G. J., & Saint Jean, A. (1995). From Flora to Kim: Thirty years of repre-
sentation of Canadian women politicians. In H. Holmes & D. Taras (Eds.),
Seeing ourselves: Media power and policy in Canada (2nd ed., pp. 23-36).
Toronto: Harcourt Brace.
Robinson, G. J., & Saint-Jean, A. (1997). *Women's participation in the Canadian
news media: Progress since the 1970s.* Summary Report of Findings. Montreal:
McGill University & Sherbrooke: Université de Sherbrooke.
Robinson, G. J., & Saint-Jean, A. (1998). Canadian women journalists: The "other
half" of the equation. In D. Weaver (Ed.), *The global journalist* (pp. 349-370).
Cresskill, NJ: Hampton Press.
Rosaldo, M. (1982) Introduction. In N. Keohane, M. Rosaldo, & B. Gelpi (Eds.),
Feminist theory: A critique of ideology, (pp. vii-xii). Chicago: University of
Chicago Press.
Rosen, J. (1996). *Getting the connections right: Public journalism and the troubles of
the press.* New York: 20th Century Fund.
Ross, K. (2000). *Sexing the news: Gender politics and newsroom culture.* Paper pre-
sented at the International Association for Media and Communication
Research, Singapore.
Ross, K. (2001). Women at work: Journalism as en-gendered practice. *Journalism
Studies, 2*(4), 531-544.
Saint-Jean, A. (1998). Journalistic ethics and referendum coverage in Montreal. In G.
J. Robinson, *Constructing the Quebec referendum: French and English media
voices.* (pp. 37-51). Toronto: University of Toronto Press.
Saint-Jean, A. (2002). *Éthique de l'information: Fondements et pratiques au Québec
dequis 1960* [Information ethics: Foundations and practices in Quebec].
Montréal: Les Presses de l'Université de Montréal.
Saunders, D. (1998, December). Screen queens. *The Globe and Mail,* pp. C1, C5.
Schudson, M. (1992). The sociology of news production revisited. In J. Curran
& M. Gurevitch (Eds.), *Mass media and society* (pp 141-160). London:
Arnold.
Shephard, A. (1993). High anxiety: The call for diversity in the newsroom has white
men running scared. *American Journalism Review, 15*(9), 19-24.
Signorelli, N. (1989). Television and conceptions about sex roles: Maintaining the
status quo. *Sex Roles, 21*(5/6), 341-360.
Simpson, J. (2003, May 31). Television's cultural colony. *The Globe and Mail,* p.
A13.
Shister, N. (Ed.). (2003). *Media convergence, diversity and democracy.* Washington,
DC: The Aspen Institute.

Smith, C., Fredin, E., & Nardone, C. (1993). The nature of sex discrimination in local television news shops. In P. Creedon (Ed.), *Women in mass communication* (2nd ed., pp. 172-182). Newbury Park, CA: Sage.

Stevens, G. (1985). Discrimination in the newsroom: Title VII and the journalist. *Journalism Monographs, 24*.

Steward, G. (1996). The decline of the daily newspaper. In H. Holmes & D. Taras (Eds.), *Seeing ourselves: Media power and policy in Canada.* (2nd ed., pp. 273-284). Toronto: Harcourt Brace Canada.

Stone, V. (1987). Trends in the status of minorities and women in broadcast news. *Journalism Quarterly, 64*(2), 288-293.

Stone, V. (1990). Two decades of changes in local news operations. *Television Quarterly, 25*(1), 41-48.

Stone, V. (1991, May). Minority share of work force grows for third year. *RTND Communicator,* pp. 20-22.

Stone, V. (1992, January). Women and men as news directors. *RTND Communicator,* pp. 143-144.

Stone, V. (1994, August). Status quo. *Communicator,* pp. 16-18.

Stone, V. (1997). Women break glass ceiling in tv news. www.missouri.edu/~jours/tvers.html.

Stone, V. (2000a). Gender gaps and factors in television news salaries. www.missouri.edu/~jours/tvers/html.

Stone, V. (2000b). Minorities and women in television news. www.missouri.edu/~jours/tvers.html. (Original work published 1995)

Stone, V. (2000c). Television news people. www.missouri.edu/~jours/tvers.html.

Stone, V. (2001). Race, gender and tv news careers. www.missouri.edu/~jours/tvers/html.

Stone, V., & Forte Duhe, S. (1992, September). Half of female news directors surveyed report harassment. *St. Louis Journalism Review,* pp. 1-4.

Sutel, S. (2004, June 25). Court chucks FCC ownership rules. *The Globe and Mail,* p. B9.

Tannen, D. (1993). The relativity of linguistic stratification: Rethinking power and solidarity in gender and dominance. In D. Tannen (Ed.), *Gender and communicational interaction* (pp. 165-188). New York: Oxford.

Trimble, L. (1992). Coming soon to a station near you? The CRTC policy on sex-role stereotyping. In H. Holmes & D. Taras (Eds.), *Seeing ourselves: Media power and policy in Canada* (pp. 135-155). Toronto: Harcourt Brace Jovanovich Canada.

Tunstall, J. (1996). *Newspaper power: The new national press in Britain.* New York: Oxford University Press.

Tuchman, G. (1978). *Making news.* New York: The Free Press.

United States Senate. (1992). *Women and the workplace: The glass ceiling.* Washington, DC: U.S. Government Printing Office.

Ursell, G. (2000). Television production: Issues of exploitation, commodification and subjectivity in UK television labour markets. *Media, Culture, Society, 22*(6), 805-825.

van Zoonen, E. A. (1992). The women's movement and the media: constructing a public identity. *European Journal of Communication, 7*, 453-476.

van Zoonen, E. A. (1994). *Feminist media studies.* London: Sage.

Wajczman, J. (1991). *Feminism confronts technology.* University Park: Pennsylvania State University Press.

Walby, S. (1997). *Gender transformations.* London: Routledge.

Walsh-Childers, K., Chance, J., & Herzog, K. (1996). Sexual harassment of women journalists. *Journalism and Mass Communication Quarterly, 73*(3), 559-581.

Watson, P. (1998, October 17). The journalist as story teller. *The Globe and Mail,* pp. D18-19.

Weaver, D., & Wilhoit, C. (1986/1991) *The American journalist: A portrait of U.S. news people and their work* (1st & 2nd ed.). Bloomington: Indiana University Press.

Weaver, D., & Wilhoit, C. (1998b). Journalists in the United States. In D. Weaver (Ed.), *The global journalist: News people around the world* (pp. 395-414). Cresskill, NJ: Hampton Press.

Weaver, D. (Ed.). (1998a). *The global journalist: News people around the world.* Cresskill, N.J: Hampton Press.

Webster, J. (1996). *Shaping women's work: Gender, employment and information technology.* London: Longman.

Weischenberg, S., Löffelholz, M., & Scholl, A. (1993) Journalismus in Deutschland: Design und erste Befunde [Journalism in Germany: First findings]. *Media Perspektiven, 23*(1), 21-33.

Weischenberg, S., Löffelholz, M., & Scholl, A. (1994). *Frauen im Journalismus* [Women in journalism]. Stuttgart: IG Medien, Fachgruppe Journalismus

Werner, A. (1992). *Women and men as producers and receivers of discussion programs on television.* Paper presented at the International Association for Media and Communication Research (IAMCR), Sao Paulo, Brazil.

Wilenski, H. (1964). The professionalization of everyone? *American Journal of Sociology, 70*(2), 137-158.

Williams, R. (1981). *Culture.* Glasgow: Fontana.

Winseck, D. (1998). *Reconvergence: A political economy of telecommunications in Canada.* Cresskill, NJ: Hampton Press.

Wolfe, F. (1972). *Television programming for news and current affairs.* London: Prager.

Wolfe, L. (1989, January). Women's share of directing editor jobs increased slightly in 1988. *ASNE Bulletin,* pp. 10-14.

Zelizer, B. (1993). Journalists as interpretive communities. *Critical Studies in Mass Communication, 10*(3), 219-237.

AUTHOR INDEX

SUBJECT INDEX

A

audience
  baby boomer generation defined, 160
  broadcast & press content preferences female & male compared, 161
  cultural approach theory, 162
  dearth of females TV programming, 164, 167-168
  in press reports, 160-161
  definition program categories, 166-167
  discontent, 159, 160, 161, 162, 171
  equity in portrayal legislation in Canadian broadcasting & print, 163-164, 170, 171, 176, 180
  program monitoring in CBC & private networks, 164, 165, 167-170
  readership Canada & U.S. compared, 159-160
  sex-role stereotyping codes & CBC guidelines compared, 164-165

B

Britain (United Kingdom), 4, 75-76, 78-79, 144, 146-147, 150, 157, 176, 182
British Broadcasting Corporation (BBC), 150, 192, 201-202, 208, 214

British economic performance philosophies, 175, 191
  equity in programming initiatives, 149, 175
  implementation strategies compared, 149-150, 175
  legislation promoting equity, British, 147-147, 190
    Equal Pay Act (1970), 192
    Equal Values Amendment (1994), 192
    Sex Discrimination Act (175), 192
Broadcast organizations Canada, 53
  access for females & minorities, 55, 61
  beats, 58-59
  concentration, 189
  equity legislation & it's effectiveness, 151, 153, 157-158
    Broadcasting Act (1991), 141
    Canadian Broadcast Standards Council (CBSC), 142
  job categories (TV), 57-58
  market size definition, 55
  ownership, 53
  regional distribution, Canada, 53-54, 153
  salary discrepancies, female, 60, 61, 62

Printed in the United States
43884LVS00005B/225

9 781572 736139